The Complete Book of
Modern Entertaining

General manager Christine Whiston
Editorial director Susan Tomnay
Creative director Hieu Chi Nguyen
Designer Caryl Wiggins
Senior editor Stephanie Kistner
Food director Pamela Clark
Introduction Kylie Boyd
Additional text Alexandra Somerville
Director of sales Brian Cearnes
Marketing manager Bridget Cody
Business analyst Rebecca Varela
Operations manager David Scotto
Production manager Victoria Jefferys
International rights enquiries
Laura Bamford lbamford@acpuk.com

ACP Books are published by
ACP Magazines a division of
PBL Media Pty Limited
Group publisher, Women's lifestyle
Pat Ingram
Director of sales, Women's lifestyle
Lynette Phillips
**Commercial manager, Women's
lifestyle** Seymour Cohen
Marketing director, Women's lifestyle
Matthew Dominello
**Public relations manager,
Women's lifestyle** Hannah Deveraux
**Creative director, Events,
Women's lifestyle** Luke Bonnano
Research Director, Women's lifestyle
Justin Stone
PBL Media, Chief Executive officer
Ian Law

The publishers would like to thank the
following for props used in photography:
Bodum; Dandi; Maxwell & Williams;
Nordic Designs; Papaya; Shimmy;
Waterford Wedgwood.

Produced by ACP Books, Sydney.
Published by ACP Books, a division of ACP Magazines Ltd.
54 Park St, Sydney NSW Australia 2000. GPO Box 4088, Sydney, NSW 2001.
Phone +61 2 9282 8618 Fax +61 2 9267 9438
acpbooks@acpmagazines.com.au www.acpbooks.com.au
Printed in China.

Australia Distributed by Network Services, GPO Box 4088, Sydney, NSW 2001.
Phone +61 2 9282 8777 Fax +61 2 9264 3278
networkweb@networkservicescompany.com.au
United Kingdom Distributed by Australian Consolidated Press (UK),
10 Scirocco Close, Moulton Park Office Village, Northampton, NN3 6AP.
Phone +44 1604 642 200 Fax +44 1604 642 300 books@acpuk.com www.acpuk.com
Canada Distributed by Publishers Group Canada,
Order Desk & Customer Service, 9050 Shaughnessy Street, Vancouver, BC V6P 6E5.
Phone (800) 663 5714 Fax (800) 565 3770 service@raincoast.com
New Zealand Distributed by Southern Publishers Group, 21 Newton Road,
Newton Auckland. Phone +64 9 360 0692 Fax +64 9 360 0695 hub@spg.co.nz
South Africa Distributed by PSD Promotions, 30 Diesel Road Isando, Gauteng Johannesburg.
PO Box 1175, Isando 1600, Gauteng Johannesburg.
Phone +27 11 392 6065/6/7 Fax +27 11 392 6079/80 orders@psdprom.co.za

Title: The complete book of modern entertaining:
the Australian women's weekly/food director Pamela Clark
Publisher: Sydney: ACP Books, 2008.
ISBN: 978-1-903777-69-5
Notes: Includes index.
Subjects: Cookery; Entertaining.
Other authors/contributors: Clark, Pamela.
Also titled: Australian women's weekly.
Dewey number: 641.5
© ACP Magazines Ltd 2008
ABN 18 053 273 546
This publication is copyright. No part of it may be reproduced or transmitted in
any form without the written permission of the publishers.

To order books, phone 136 116 (within Australia).
Send recipe enquiries to: askpamela@acpmagazines.com.au

Chapter opener photography
Photographer John Paul Urizar
Stylist Sarah DeNardi

Photographers Alan Benson, Steve Brown, Luke Burgess, Chris Chen, Joshua Dasey, Ben Dearnley,
Joe Filshie, Louise Lister, Andre Martin, Rob Palmer, Prue Ruscoe, Brett Stevens, Tim Robinson, Rob
Taylor, John Paul Urizar, Ian Wallace, Dean Wilmot, Andrew Young, Gorta Yuuki, Stuart Scott, Tanya Zouev
Stylists Wendy Berecry, Julz Beresford, Hannah Blackmore, Janelle Bloom, Margot Braddon, Kate
Brown, Kirsty Cassidy, Marie-Helene Clauzon, Sarah DeNardi, Yael Grinham Jane Hann, Trish Heagerty,
Amber Kellar, Opel Khan, Anna Last, Michaela Le Compte, Vicki Liley, David Morgan, Kate Murdoch,
Michelle Noerianto, Justine Osborne, Sarah O'Brien, Louise Pickford, Christine Rooke, Stephanie Souvlis

THE AUSTRALIAN
Women's Weekly

The Complete Book of
Modern Entertaining

54 sensational modern menus

acp
books

contents

Entertaining today is different from the way it used to be. More people are working, leaving less time to cook, and there are more convenience foods available as each year passes. So unless it is a very special occasion, you won't be making everything from scratch. Buying pre-packaged salads, pre-prepared dips and barbecue chickens eases the burden of being a host and gives you more time to enjoy yourself.

Make a party memorable by incorporating personal touches into the planning. These can be as simple as your choice of music, making your own bread or chocolate, or using an interesting dinner set.

The menu

Menus today can be the traditional three courses, or a degustation menu, made up of many small courses (tricky and time-consuming to pull off at home, but it can be done if you restrict yourself to four or five simple courses) or one main course and a bought starter and dessert. There are no rules — it's about making what's appropriate for the occasion.

Wine and food matching

We'd have to devote a whole chapter to this subject to do it justice. However, there are a few general rules that hosts can follow if they are trying to match wine to their food. The best basic rule for wine and food matching is 'red with red and white with white'.

However, light red wines are delicious with chicken or veal so once again it comes down to personal taste. If you're asking your guests to bring a bottle of wine, let them know what's on the menu.

Music

Music can instantly change the mood of your party and you should spend time choosing what to play. Leave out a selection of CDs so that guests can choose their own songs, or use an MP3 player or computer to store all your music. These options tend to be more portable and have the ability to play numerous tracks so you are not restricted to a 13 track CD. The 'shuffle' and 'continuous play' buttons can also make selection easier.

For a large-scale party, a DJ or a band could be looked into – you can leave the technical and equipment worries up to them. Otherwise, hire large speakers so that the music can be heard by everyone.

The table

Set the table first. If you have your table set, but are running behind with the food, no-one will suspect everything isn't going to plan.

Use a tablecloth and cloth napkins, sparkling glassware and a low vase of flowers — not too highly perfumed. The simpler the table decorations the more effective they will be.

introduction

Beware of food restrictions

The worst thing you can do at a party is to leave one person feeling singled out. Whether they are diabetic, on a weight-loss diet, lactose-intolerant, allergic to nuts or eggs, vegetarian or have any other special food requirement, be aware in advance and your guests will appreciate that you've kept them in mind when preparing the meal. Avoid having a 'normal' meal and one 'special' meal for a guest on a restrictive diet. Unless quite a number of allergies are stated and there is no choice, it is best to cook a meal that all can enjoy and that doesn't leave one guest feeling they are a burden on the host. Soups and stir-fries work well in this situation, but look in specialty cookbooks for recipes that cater to people on restrictive diets.

How to throw a last-minute party

Organising a dinner or party with hardly any notice calls for swift commando action. Raid your local deli of its stuffed vine leaves, roasted vegetables, baked ricotta, prosciutto — anything that's high in quality. It won't be cheap, but it will make a wonderful antipasto platter. Other excellent, but expensive, last-minute party foods are a whole fillet of beef (sear first, then roast on high heat) or a whole salmon. For a much cheaper option, make lots and lots of pizzas using bought pizza bases and a whole range of good-quality toppings.

How to entertain on a budget

Not every dinner needs to be extravagant. In fact, sometimes the classic and simple dishes such as Shepherd's Pie or a barbecue are bigger hits than formal dinners. Create 'organised chaos' on your table with patterns and colours — don't worry if things don't match. Borrow items from your friends or family — sometimes an old water jug or biscuit tin will be more interesting, not to mention cheaper, as the centrepiece than a bouquet of flowers.

When planning a meal, look for ingredients in season — it's when they're at their best and cheapest. Try adding a twist to well-known recipes — for example, if you are making a quiche perhaps add shiitake or porcini mushrooms. If you still think you're going to blow the budget, ask everyone to bring a plate of food — let them know a food theme to stick to, otherwise you may get a mish-mash of dishes that don't complement each other.

Think smart

Why not gather some friends around for a breakfast or dinner party in support of a charity? Everyone should bring a donation to support a cause such as breast cancer, animal abuse or disadvantaged children.

Try to think 'green' when planning your party supplies and cleaning. Although disposable plates can keep cleaning up to a minimum, if there are no more than three washing-up loads, use china plates and the dishwasher. If you are using disposable plates, choose paper over plastic.

When cleaning, think of environmentally-friendly cleaning products such as vinegar and bicarbonate of soda. Remember to also be water-wise — don't use the tap more than you have to while cleaning up, and only turn on the dishwasher when it is full.

Themes and decorations

A theme can go a long way to spice up a party, and even though it may require a bit more planning, the right theme can make a party a lot more fun.

Cocktail party The cocktail party has made a big comeback. With the glamour and carefree attitude a cocktail party brings, it is a fun idea for a birthday or to vary the dinner party routine.

One thing to remember is to state a dress code when inviting guests so people don't come over- or under-dressed.

When buying alcohol, plan for about four drinks per person. But plan only two to three types of cocktails to ensure you only have to buy a few varieties of liquor. Don't forget to include some beer and soft drink for those who are not too keen on wine or spirits. If this sounds a little daunting or expensive, remember you can always delegate each guest or group to bring a bottle of alcohol or a mixer. Remember who is bringing what, otherwise you may end up with six bottles of one thing and none of another.

Cocktail parties tend to have a set time frame, or 'cocktail hour'. It depends on whether you are planning a cocktail party around a dinner. If you are simply serving cocktails with appetisers, a suggested time frame is 6:30 to 8:30pm.

Decorate keeping in mind the retro feel of a cocktail party — dig up those old decanters you received as a gift, and borrow or hire a full set of cocktail glasses, swizzlers and a shaker. For the music, play a selection of Frank Sinatra, Peggy Lee, up-tempo big band tunes, swing music and other retro classics. For a more modern feel, play some pop favourites. Classical music or soft jazz will kill the party atmosphere.

Wine tastings Wine tastings are becoming quite popular as events in their own right or as an introduction to a dinner party. Structure tastings around wines from a certain area or genre, for example, Italian wines or chardonnays. Cover the labels so your guests are not swayed by opinion of the vineyard or the label design.

Some wineries even offer wine tastings as sort of a modern 'Tupperware party', where the host will invite a representative of the winery who will bring bottles from their range, set up a wine tasting table and give you the option of buying.

Casino party A casino party can be a fun way to play with a theme and a great idea for a large party as it gets everyone in a festive mood and provides endless conversation starters.

If you are a bit uncomfortable about winning money off a distant relative or neighbour, you could play with chips that are not given any monetary value, or donate the winnings to a charity.

Music can be anything from upbeat background music to pop music. Shiny and sparkly decorations work well in this situation.

Have enough chips, dice and cards for guests, and a large-enough flat surface on which to play. You could also provide how-to sheets for those who are not well-practised on the finer points of blackjack and other card games. And, the possibilities are endless if you want to go all the way — party 'poker machines', wheels to play games of chance and professional card dealers are all available for hire. Most party supply shops will have the number of a supplier.

Carnival Both kids and adults will enjoy this theme. Best done in summer, the carnival atmosphere can be achieved by decorating your home or backyard with fairy lights and coloured flags. Continue the theme with your food and provide hot dogs and sausage rolls. Depending on your budget, you could hire a bouncy castle, candy floss machine, or clairvoyant, all of which you can find in your local directory; they are cheaper than you may think. If you include treats such as a lucky dip, for both adults and children, and play loud pop music, just like at a real carnival, you will have a great party atmosphere that guests are sure to enjoy.

Kids' parties

The ultimate kids' party has colour, music, games, sweets and, of course, the cake. Below are a few ideas for you to choose from when planning your next kids' party.

Halloween What child won't love a party based on ghouls, goblins and monsters. Make it fun with 'scary' games, and a scavenger hunt for sweets. Decorations are straightforward for this one — as many skeletons, witches and vampires as you can fit in your home. Kids will freak out over cotton wool spider webs, plastic skeletons and carved pumpkins.

Movie party Let the kids dress up as their favourite movie character, whether it is Superman, Cinderella or Dracula. Put on a few DVDs, base games and decorations around glamour — lay out a red carpet and hand out disposable cameras so the kids can have fun playing a 'celebrity'.

The clean up

Always the hardest part of the party, the clean up can be a daunting task, even for the most organised planner. Besides delegating chores you can always hire a cleaner to lift the burden. Cleaners charge by the hour. If you are not at your own home and are at a holiday location or at a hall, enquire in advance whether a cleaning fee is included. If you are cleaning up yourself, or getting others involved, use the following guide to make life easier:

The night of Put glasses, plates, bowls and cutlery in the sink or the dishwasher. Push chairs back to where they were originally and if you see any stains deal with them straight away. Get a large garbage bag and throw all loose rubbish away.

The morning after Vacuum and mop if need be, clean table tops and finally approach the kitchen.

You are invited to

Breakfast with Friends

Dress down and prepare to stay a while...

Healthy

pineapple, orange and
passionfruit frappé
—
bran and cranberry muesli
—
spinach omelette
—
spiced plums with yogurt

Kickstart the weekend with a dose of fruity sunshine.

pineapple, orange and passionfruit frappé

preparation time 10 minutes
makes 1.5 litres (6 cups)

½ cup (125ml) passionfruit pulp
1 medium pineapple (1.25kg), chopped coarsely
¾ cup (180ml) orange juice
1 teaspoon finely grated orange rind
2 cups crushed ice

1 Strain passionfruit pulp through sieve into small bowl; reserve seeds and liquid.
2 Blend or process pineapple, orange juice and reserved passionfruit liquid, in batches, until smooth.
3 Add rind and ice; pulse until combined. Stir in seeds.
nutritional count per 250ml 0.2g total fat (0g saturated fat); 284kJ (68 cal); 11.6g carbohydrate; 1.8g protein; 5g fibre

bran and cranberry muesli

preparation time 10 minutes
serves 4

2 cups (180g) rolled oats
1½ cup (110g) All-Bran
½ cup (70g) dried cranberries
1⅓ cup (320ml) skimmed milk
150g fresh blueberries

1 Combine oats, bran and cranberries in small bowl to make muesli mixture.
2 Place ⅓ cup muesli in each bowl; top with milk and berries. Store remaining muesli in an airtight container.
nutritional count per serving 1.7g total fat (0.4g saturated fat); 606kJ (145 cal); 24g carbohydrate; 6g protein; 4.5g fibre

Dr Bircher-Benner introduced his famous muesli to the patients at his clinic in Zurich, Switzerland in the early 20th century. Since then it's become the favourite breakfast dish for millions of people around the world.

spinach omelette

preparation time 10 minutes
cooking time 10 minutes
serves 4

2 eggs
8 egg whites
4 spring onions, chopped finely
cooking-oil spray
60g baby spinach leaves
¼ cup coarsely chopped fresh mint
4 slices rye bread, toasted
2 tablespoons low-fat ricotta cheese

1 Whisk eggs, egg whites and onion in small jug.
2 Spray small frying pan with cooking oil; heat pan. Pour half of the egg mixture into pan; cook, tilting pan, until mixture is almost set. Sprinkle half of the spinach and mint over half the omelette; fold omelette over to enclose filling, then cut in half. Repeat with remaining egg mixture, spinach and mint.
3 Spread toast with cheese; serve with omelette.
nutritional count per serving 5.7g total fat (1.6g saturated fat); 878kJ (210 cal); 21.2g carbohydrate; 16.3g protein; 4g fibre

spiced plums with yogurt

preparation time 10 minutes
cooking time 10 minutes (plus cooling time)
serves 4

1 litre (4 cups) water
½ cup (125ml) orange juice
⅓ cup (75g) caster sugar
5cm strip orange rind
2 star anise
4 cloves
1 teaspoon mixed spice
1 cinnamon stick
1 vanilla pod, split lengthways
8 red plums (900g), unpeeled
1⅓ cups (375g) plain yogurt

1 Place the water, juice, sugar, rind and spices in medium frying pan. Scrape vanilla seeds into pan then add pod; cook mixture, stirring, until sugar dissolves.
2 Add plums to pan; poach, uncovered, over low heat 10 minutes or until just tender. Using slotted spoon, place two plums in each of four serving dishes; reserve 2 tablespoons of the poaching liquid. Cool plums 20 minutes.
3 Combine yogurt and reserved poaching liquid in small bowl; serve with plums.
nutritional count per serving 3.4g total fat (2.1g saturated fat); 906kJ (217 cal); 39.1g carbohydrate; 5.7g protein; 4.1g fibre

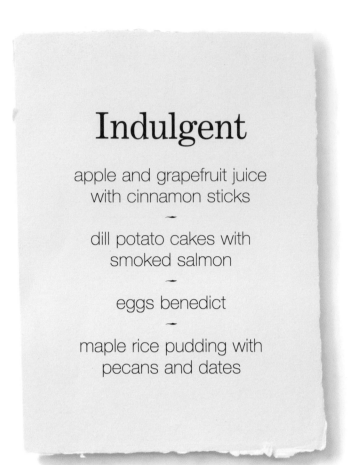

Indulgent

apple and grapefruit juice
with cinnamon sticks

-

dill potato cakes with
smoked salmon

-

eggs benedict

-

maple rice pudding with
pecans and dates

Indulge your epicurean side for a special occasion.

apple and grapefruit juice with cinnamon sticks

preparation time 5 minutes (plus refrigeration time)
cooking time 5 minutes
makes 2 litres (8 cups)

1 litre (4 cups) apple juice
4 cinnamon sticks, halved lengthways
1 litre (4 cups) grapefruit juice

1 Combine apple juice and cinnamon in medium saucepan; bring to the boil. Remove from heat; cool to room temperature. Transfer to large jug, cover; refrigerate 3 hours or overnight.
2 Add grapefruit juice to apple juice mixture; stir to combine.
3 Serve juice with cinnamon stick.
nutritional count per 250ml 0.1g total fat (0g saturated fat); 355kJ (85 cal); 20.1g carbohydrate; 0.6g protein; 0g fibre

dill potato cakes with smoked salmon

preparation time 20 minutes
cooking time 30 minutes
makes 16

1kg potatoes, chopped coarsely
¼ cup (60ml) olive oil
2 medium brown onions (300g), chopped finely
¼ cup finely chopped fresh dill
⅓ cup (80g) soured cream
½ cup (75g) plain flour
50g butter
⅔ cup (160g) soured cream, extra
200g sliced smoked salmon
16 fresh dill sprigs

1 Boil, steam or microwave potato until tender; drain. Mash potato in large bowl until smooth. Cool 10 minutes.
2 Meanwhile, heat 1 tablespoon of the oil in medium frying pan; cook onion, stirring, until soft.
3 Add onion to potato with chopped dill and soured cream; stir to combine. Using hands, shape ¼-cups of the potato mixture into patty-shaped cakes; coat in flour, shake off excess.
4 Heat half of the butter and 1 tablespoon of the remaining oil in large frying pan; cook half of the potato cakes until browned lightly both sides. Repeat with remaining butter, remaining oil and remaining cakes.
5 Divide extra soured cream and salmon among potato cakes; top with dill sprigs.
nutritional count per cake 12.6g total fat (6.2g saturated fat); 757kJ (181 cal); 11.7g carbohydrate; 5.3g protein; 1.3g fibre

"All happiness depends on a leisurely breakfast."

John Gunther, American author

eggs benedict

preparation time 30 minutes
cooking time 25 minutes
serves 8

1 teaspoon salt
1 tablespoon white vinegar
16 eggs
1 loaf ciabatta (440g), cut into 16 slices
300g wafer-thin ham
¼ cup finely chopped fresh chives

HOLLANDAISE
1½ tablespoons white vinegar
1 tablespoon lemon juice
½ teaspoon peppercorns
2 egg yolks
150g butter, melted

1 Make hollandaise.
2 Half-fill a large shallow frying pan with water; bring to the boil. Break 1 egg into cup then slide into pan. Working quickly, repeat process with 3 more eggs. When all 4 eggs are in pan, return water to the boil. Cover pan, turn off heat; stand about 4 minutes or until a light film of egg white sets over each yolk. Using a slotted spoon, remove eggs one at a time from pan; place spoon on absorbent-paper-lined saucer to blot up poaching liquid. Repeat process with remaining eggs.
3 To serve, toast bread, top with ham, poached eggs, hollandaise and chives.
HOLLANDAISE
Bring vinegar, juice and peppercorns to the boil in small saucepan; simmer until reduced by half. Strain; cool. Combine yolks and vinegar mixture in small bowl set over a small saucepan of simmering water. Whisk until mixture thickens and becomes pale in colour. Remove from heat; gradually whisk in melted butter in thin steady stream until mixture is thick.
nutritional count per serving 29.4g total fat (14.3g saturated fat); 1960kJ (469 cal); 25.2g carbohydrate; 25.5g protein; 1.7g fibre

maple rice pudding with pecans and dates

preparation time 10 minutes
cooking time 40 minutes
serves 8

1½ litres (6 cups) milk
2 cups (500ml) double cream
⅔ cup (160ml) maple syrup
¼ teaspoon ground cinnamon
⅔ cup (130g) medium-grain white rice
½ cup (85g) coarsely chopped pitted dates
½ cup (70g) toasted pecans, chopped coarsely

1 Combine milk, cream, syrup and cinnamon in large saucepan; bring to the boil, stirring occasionally.
2 Gradually stir in rice; cook, uncovered, over low heat, stirring occasionally, about 40 minutes or until rice is tender.
3 Serve rice pudding with combined dates and nuts; drizzle with a little more maple syrup, if desired.
nutritional count per serving 41.1g total fat (23.3g saturated fat); 2420kJ (579 cal); 45.4g carbohydrate; 9.6g protein; 1.4g fibre

French

chocolate hazelnut croissants

—

gruyère, leek and bacon tart

—

crêpes with strawberries
and cream

—

vanilla café au lait

No one does a decadent breakfast quite like the French.

chocolate hazelnut croissants

preparation time 15 minutes
cooking time 15 minutes
makes 8

2 sheets ready-rolled puff pastry
⅓ cup (110g) chocolate hazelnut spread
30g dark chocolate, grated finely
25g butter, melted
1 tablespoon icing sugar

1 Preheat oven to 220°C/200°C fan-assisted. Grease two oven trays.
2 Cut pastry sheets diagonally to make four triangles. Spread chocolate spread over triangles, leaving a 1cm border; sprinkle each evenly with chocolate.
3 Roll triangles, starting at one wide end; place 3cm apart on trays with the tips tucked under and the ends slightly curved in to form crescent shape. Brush croissants with melted butter.
4 Bake croissants about 12 minutes or until browned lightly and cooked through. Serve warm or at room temperature, dusted with icing sugar.
nutritional count per croissant 17.7g total fat (4.8g saturated fat); 1166kJ (279 cal); 26.4g carbohydrate; 3.4g protein; 0.9g fibre

gruyère, leek and bacon tart

preparation time 30 minutes
cooking time 1 hour
serves 8

50g butter
2 medium leeks (700g), sliced thinly
2 rindless bacon rashers (130g), chopped finely
2 sheets ready-rolled puff pastry
2 eggs
½ cup (125ml) double cream
1 teaspoon fresh thyme leaves
½ cup (60g) finely grated gruyère cheese

1 Preheat oven to 220°C/200°C fan-assisted. Oil 24cm-round loose-based flan tin; place tin on oven tray.
2 Melt butter in medium frying pan; cook leek, stirring occasionally, about 15 minutes or until soft. Remove from pan. Cook bacon in same pan, stirring, until crisp; drain on absorbent paper.
3 Meanwhile, place one pastry sheet in flan tin; overlap with second sheet to form cross shape, trim away overlapping pastry. Prick pastry base with fork, cover with baking parchment; fill with dried beans or uncooked rice. Bake 20 minutes. Remove paper and beans; cool pastry case.
4 Reduce oven to 200°C/180°C fan-assisted.
5 Whisk eggs, cream and thyme in small bowl.
6 Spread leek into pastry case; top with bacon. Pour in egg mixture; sprinkle with cheese. Bake about 20 minutes or until filling sets. Cool 10 minutes before serving.
nutritional count per serving 26.1g total fat (15.1g saturated fat); 1463kJ (350 cal); 17.6g carbohydrate; 10.8g protein; 2.1g fibre
TIP Tart can be made the day before; reheat, covered with foil, in 160°C/140°C fan-assisted oven for 15 minutes before serving.

crêpes with strawberries and cream

preparation 10 minutes (plus standing time)
cooking time 15 minutes
serves 8

¾ cup (110g) plain flour
1 tablespoon caster sugar
pinch salt
2 eggs
1¾ cups (430ml) milk
50g butter, melted
300g strawberries, quartered
300ml whipping cream, whipped

1 Combine flour, sugar and salt in large bowl. Whisk in eggs and ¾ cup (180ml) of the milk until smooth. Gradually whisk in remaining milk. Cover; stand 1 hour.
2 Heat a 20cm crêpe pan (or frying pan); brush with a little of the butter. Pour about 2 tablespoons of the batter into pan, tilting pan so batter coats the base evenly. Cook, loosening edge with a spatula until crêpe is browned lightly underneath. Turn crêpe and cook until browned on other side. Transfer crêpe to a plate or ovenproof dish; cover to keep warm. Repeat with remaining butter and batter to make 16 in total; stack crêpes on a plate.
3 Fold crêpes into quarters; serve topped with strawberries and cream. Drizzle with maple syrup, if desired.
nutritional count per serving 22.7g total fat (14.4g saturated fat); 1246kJ (298 cal); 17g carbohydrate; 6.4g protein; 1.3g fibre

vanilla café au lait

preparation time 5 minutes
cooking time 5 minutes
serves 8

1 cup (90g) coarsely ground coffee beans
2 litres (8 cups) milk
2 teaspoons vanilla extract

1 Stir ingredients in large saucepan over low heat until heated through, but not boiling.
2 Pour through fine strainer into heatproof serving glasses.
nutritional count per serving 9.8g total fat (6.5g saturated fat); 715kJ (171 cal); 12.1g carbohydrate; 8.5g protein; 0.1g fibre

You are invited to a

Cocktail Party

Turn down the lights, turn up the music...

Oriental

lychee caipiroska

–

green mango salad on
betel leaves

–

prawn laksa shots

–

spicy teriyaki tuna

–

duck in crisp wonton cups

Get your guests talking with a hint of the exotic.

lychee caipiroska

preparation time 5 minutes
serves 1

2 fresh lychees (50g)
2 teaspoons caster sugar
45ml vodka
2 teaspoons lime juice
½ cup crushed ice

1 Using muddler (or pestle and mortar), crush lychees
with sugar in cocktail shaker. Add vodka, juice and ice;
shake vigorously.
2 Pour into 180ml old-fashioned glass.
nutritional count per serving 0.1g total fat (0g saturated fat);
656kJ (157 cal); 15.3g carbohydrate; 0.5g protein; 0.5g fibre
TIP When making several serves, make up to three
quantities of recipe in cocktail shaker at a time.

green mango salad on betel leaves

preparation time 25 minutes
makes 24

3cm piece fresh ginger (15g), grated
2 tablespoons rice vinegar
1 tablespoon groundnut oil
2 teaspoons mirin
2 teaspoons soy sauce
½ small green mango (150g), grated coarsely
2 spring onions, sliced thinly
1 fresh long red chilli, sliced thinly
½ cup (40g) beansprouts
½ cup loosely packed fresh coriander leaves
50g mangetout, trimmed, sliced thinly
1 cup (80g) shredded wombok (Chinese cabbage)
24 large betel leaves

1 Combine ginger, vinegar, oil, mirin and sauce in medium bowl. Add mango, onion, chilli, beansprouts, coriander, mangetout and wombok; toss gently to combine.
2 Place one level tablespoon of the mango mixture on each leaf.
nutritional count per leaf 0.8g total fat (0.1g saturated fat); 50kJ (12 cal); 0.8g carbohydrate; 0.3g protein; 0.3g fibre

prawn laksa shots

preparation time 10 minutes
cooking time 15 minutes
makes 24

24 cooked small prawns (600g)
2 teaspoons groundnut oil
¼ cup (75g) laksa paste
1 clove garlic, crushed
1 fresh kaffir lime leaf, sliced thinly
½ teaspoon ground turmeric
1 spring onion, sliced thinly
140ml can coconut milk
1½ cups (375ml) water
2 tablespoons lime juice
3 teaspoons fish sauce
24 fresh small coriander leaves

1 Shell and devein prawns, leaving tails intact; reserve prawn heads.
2 Heat oil in medium saucepan; cook paste, garlic, lime leaf, turmeric, onion and prawn heads, stirring, until fragrant. Add coconut milk and the water; bring to the boil. Reduce heat; simmer, covered, 10 minutes.
3 Strain laksa through sieve into large jug; discard solids. Stir juice and sauce into laksa.
4 Divide laksa among shot glasses, place 1 prawn over rim of each glass; top each with coriander leaf. Serve warm.
nutritional count per shot 1.7g total fat (1.1g saturated fat); 130kJ (31 cal); 0.3g carbohydrate; 2.8g protein; 0.2g fibre

spicy teriyaki tuna

preparation time 30 minutes (plus refrigeration time)
cooking time 15 minutes
makes 24

¾ cup (180ml) japanese soy sauce
2 tablespoons honey
¼ cup (60ml) mirin
1 tablespoon wasabi paste
1 teaspoon sesame oil
300g sashimi tuna steak
2 tablespoons thinly sliced drained pickled ginger

1 Combine sauce, honey, mirin, wasabi and oil in medium bowl; reserve ½ cup of marinade in small jug. Place tuna in bowl with remaining marinade; turn tuna to coat in marinade. Cover; refrigerate 3 hours or overnight.
2 Cook drained tuna in heated oiled medium frying pan until browned both sides and cooked as desired (do not overcook as tuna has a tendency to dry out).
3 Cut tuna into 24 similar-sized pieces (about 2cm each).
4 Place chinese spoons on serving platter. Place one piece of tuna on each spoon; top with 1 teaspoon of the reserved marinade and a little ginger.
nutritional count per spoon 0.9g total fat (0.3g saturated fat); 138kJ (33 cal); 2.2g carbohydrate; 3.6g protein; 0.1g fibre

duck in crisp wonton cups

preparation time 20 minutes
cooking time 20 minutes (plus cooling time)
makes 24

24 wonton wrappers
cooking-oil spray
1 chinese barbecued duck
1 tablespoon hoisin sauce
1 tablespoon soy sauce
2 tablespoons coarsely chopped fresh coriander
2 spring onions, chopped coarsely
2 spring onions, extra, sliced thinly

1 Preheat oven to 180°C/160°C fan-assisted. Oil two 12-hole mini (1½-tablespoons/30ml) muffin tins.
2 Press wonton wrappers into tin holes to form a cup shape; spray lightly with oil. Bake about 8 minutes until browned lightly. Remove from muffin tins, cool.
3 Remove flesh and skin from duck, slice thinly; discard fat. Place duck on oven tray, cover with foil; heat in oven about 10 minutes.
4 Combine duck with sauces, coriander and chopped onions in medium bowl.
5 Spoon duck mixture into wonton cups; top with sliced onions.
nutritional count per cup 13.5g total fat (3.9g saturated fat); 732kJ (175 cal); 3.6g carbohydrate; 10g protein; 0.3g fibre
TIPS Wonton cups can be made a day ahead; store in an airtight container. The filling can be prepared several hours ahead. Assemble close to serving.
Chinese barbecued duck is available from Asian grocery stores.

Black Tie

apple cranberry cosmopolitan

~

camembert with pear compote
on pumpernickel

~

sesame-crusted tuna with
wasabi mayo

~

gazpacho with oysters

~

chicken and port pâté on
polenta crisps

A formal occasion requires perfect presentation.

apple cranberry cosmopolitan

preparation time 5 minutes
serves 1

1 cup ice cubes
45ml vodka
30ml Cointreau
2 teaspoons cranberry juice
1 tablespoon apple juice
2cm strip apple peel

1 Combine ice cubes, vodka, Cointreau and combined juices in cocktail shaker; shake vigorously.
2 Strain into chilled 230ml glass. Garnish with apple peel.
nutritional count per serving 0.1g total fat (0g saturated fat); 832kJ (199 cal); 15.5g carbohydrate; 0.1g protein; 0g fibre
TIP When making several serves, make up to three quantities of recipe in cocktail shaker at a time.

camembert with pear compote on pumpernickel

preparation time 20 minutes (plus cooling time)
cooking time 10 minutes
makes 24

½ cup (75g) dried pears, chopped finely
2 tablespoons dried cranberries, chopped finely
1 cinnamon stick
1 tablespoon caster sugar
¼ cup (60ml) water
200g whole camembert cheese
24 cocktail pumpernickel rounds (250g)
1 tablespoon roasted pistachios, chopped finely

1 Combine pear, cranberries, cinnamon, sugar and the water in small saucepan; bring to the boil. Reduce heat; simmer, uncovered, 10 minutes. Cool to room temperature. Discard cinnamon.
2 Cut cheese into 24 wedges.
3 Place pumpernickel rounds on serving platter; top each round with a wedge of cheese, ½ teaspoon of the compote then a sprinkle of nuts.
nutritional count per piece 2.6g total fat (1.5g saturated fat); 268kJ (64 cal); 8.1g carbohydrate; 2.4g protein; 1.3g fibre
TIP If you can't find cocktail pumpernickel rounds, buy sliced pumpernickel and cut out rounds with a pastry cutter.

sesame-crusted tuna with wasabi mayo

preparation time 20 minutes
cooking time 5 minutes
makes 24

300g sashimi tuna steak
1 tablespoon white sesame seeds
1 tablespoon black sesame seeds
1 tablespoon sesame oil
2 tablespoons mayonnaise
1 teaspoon wasabi paste

1 Coat both sides of tuna with combined seeds.
2 Heat oil in medium frying pan; cook tuna until browned both sides and cooked as desired (do not overcook as tuna has a tendency to dry out).
3 Cut tuna into 24 similar-sized pieces (about 2cm each).
4 Serve tuna topped with combined mayonnaise and wasabi; skewer with toothpicks.
nutritional count per piece 2.5g total fat (0.5g saturated fat); 155kJ (37 cal); 0.3g carbohydrate; 3.4g protein; 0.1g fibre

45

gazpacho with oysters

preparation time 15 minutes (plus refrigeration time)
makes 24

2 medium plum tomatoes (150g), chopped coarsely
1 small red pepper (150g), chopped coarsely
¼ cucumber (65g), chopped coarsely
½ small red onion (50g), chopped coarsely
1 clove garlic, crushed
2 tablespoons olive oil
1 tablespoon white wine vinegar
1 cup (250ml) tomato juice
3 drops Tabasco sauce
½ teaspoon white sugar
2 tablespoons water
24 oysters, on the half shell

1 Blend or process tomato, pepper, cucumber, onion, garlic, oil, vinegar, juice, sauce, sugar and the water until mixture is smooth. Push gazpacho through sieve into large jug; discard solids.
2 Cover jug; refrigerate gazpacho for 2 hours.
3 Remove oysters from shells; discard shells. Divide gazpacho among shot glasses; add 1 oyster to each.
nutritional count per shot 1.8g total fat (0.3g saturated fat); 113kJ (27 cal); 1.2g carbohydrate; 1.5g protein; 0.3g fibre

chicken and port pâté on polenta crisps

preparation time 30 minutes (plus refrigeration time)
cooking time 20 minutes
makes 48

50g butter, softened
300g chicken livers, trimmed
2 shallots (50g), chopped finely
1 clove garlic, crushed
2 tablespoons port
½ cup (100g) drained pitted sour cherries
48 fresh chervil sprigs

POLENTA CRISPS
1 cup (250ml) water
2 cups (500ml) chicken stock
¾ cup (125g) polenta
30g butter
vegetable oil, for deep-frying

1 Make polenta crisps.
2 Meanwhile, heat half of the butter in medium frying pan; cook livers, in batches, until just browned.
3 Cook shallots and garlic in same pan, stirring, until shallots soften. Add port; cook, uncovered, until almost all of the liquid has evaporated.
4 Blend or process livers with shallot mixture until smooth. Push mixture through sieve; discard solids.
5 Blend or process pâté mixture with remaining butter until smooth. Transfer to small bowl, cover; refrigerate 2 hours.
6 Serve pâté on polenta crisps, each topped with a cherry and sprig of chervil.
POLENTA CRISPS
Oil 8cm x 25cm cake tin. Combine the water and stock in medium saucepan, bring to the boil; gradually add polenta, stirring constantly. Reduce heat; simmer, stirring, about 10 minutes or until polenta thickens. Stir in butter then spread polenta into tin; cool 10 minutes. Cover; refrigerate about 2 hours or until firm. Trim edges; cut in half lengthways, then slice into 1cm pieces. Heat oil in wok; deep-fry polenta, in batches, until browned. Drain on absorbent paper.
nutritional count per piece 2.5g total fat (1.1g saturated fat); 159kJ (38 cal); 2.3g carbohydrate; 1.5g protein; 0.1g fibre

Summer

mango bellini
—
oysters with two dressings
—
mini lamb and mint skewers
—
asparagus and prosciutto frittata
—
raspberry and lemon
mascarpone parfaits

Food to complement the hues of a summer sunset.

mango bellini

preparation time 5 minutes
serves 1

¼ cup (60ml) mango nectar
15ml mango liqueur
1 teaspoon lime juice
½ cup (125ml) chilled brut champagne

1 Place nectar, liqueur and juice in chilled 230ml
champagne flute; stir to combine.
2 Top with champagne.
nutritional count per serving 0.1g total fat (0g saturated fat);
765kJ (183 cal); 17.2g carbohydrate; 0.6g protein; 0g fibre
TIP When making several serves, make up to three
quantities of recipe in cocktail shaker at a time.

oysters with two dressings

preparation time 10 minutes
makes 24

24 fresh oysters in half shell
RED WINE VINEGAR DRESSING
1½ teaspoons finely chopped shallots
1 tablespoon red wine vinegar
1 teaspoon extra virgin olive oil
SPICY LIME DRESSING
1½ tablespoons fresh lime juice
½ teaspoon piri piri sauce
1 teaspoon chopped fresh coriander

RED WINE VINEGAR DRESSING
Combine shallot, vinegar, oil, and pepper in small bowl.
Spoon mixture over 12 oysters.
nutritional count per oyster 1g total fat (0.3g saturated fat);
92kJ (22 cal); 0.2g carbohydrate; 3.1g protein; 0g fibre

SPICY LIME DRESSING
Combine lime juice, sauce and coriander in small bowl.
Spoon mixture over 12 oysters.
nutritional count per oyster 0.6g total fat (0.2g saturated fat);
79kJ (19 cal); 0.3g carbohydratc; 3.1g protein; 0g fibre

For the ultimate in oyster eating, shuck fresh oysters yourself and take care to preserve the precious oyster liquor found within. The oyster liquor provides the fresh, salty flavour of the sea that so exquisitely complements the tender texture of the flesh.

mini lamb and mint skewers

preparation time 20 minutes (plus refrigeration time)
cooking time 10 minutes
makes 24

¼ cup (60ml) olive oil
2 tablespoons lemon juice
2 cloves garlic, crushed
1 tablespoon sumac
1 teaspoon ground allspice
500g lamb fillet, diced into 3cm pieces
¼ cup (70g) greek-style plain yogurt
¾ cup firmly packed fresh mint leaves
1 spring onion, chopped coarsely
24 fresh mint leaves, extra

1   Combine oil, juice, garlic, spices and lamb in medium bowl. Cover; refrigerate 3 hours or overnight.
2   Blend or process 1 tablespoon of the yogurt with mint and onion. Combine in small bowl with remaining yogurt.
3   Cook drained lamb, in batches, on heated oiled grill plate (or grill or barbecue) until cooked as desired. Cover; stand 5 minutes.
4   Skewer 1 mint leaf then 1 piece of the lamb on each toothpick; serve with minted yogurt.
nutritional count per skewer 4.4g total fat (1.3g saturated fat); 247kJ (59 cal); 0.4g carbohydrate; 4.6g protein; 0.2g fibre

asparagus and prosciutto frittata

preparation time 25 minutes
cooking time 20 minutes
makes 48

170g asparagus (choose thin spears)
6 eggs, beaten lightly
½ cup (125ml) double cream
¼ cup (20g) coarsely grated parmesan cheese
3 slices prosciutto (45g)
½ cup (75g) drained semi-dried tomatoes,
    chopped finely

1   Preheat oven to 200°C/180°C fan-assisted. Oil 19cm x 29cm baking tin; line base and sides with baking parchment.
2   Boil, steam or microwave asparagus until just tender; drain. Rinse under cold water; drain.
3   Whisk eggs, cream and cheese in medium bowl until combined.
4   Place asparagus, in single layer, alternating tips and bases, in tin; pour egg mixture over asparagus.
5   Bake frittata, uncovered, about 20 minutes or until firm. Stand 10 minutes in tin.
6   Meanwhile, cut each slice of prosciutto into 16 squares. Cook prosciutto in medium non-stick frying pan, stirring occasionally, until crisp.
7   Cut frittata into 48 pieces; top each with 1 piece of the prosciutto and ½ teaspoon of the tomato.
nutritional count per piece 2.1g total fat (1.1g saturated fat); 113kJ (27 cal); 0.7g carbohydrate; 1.5g protein; 0.3g fibre

raspberry and lemon mascarpone parfaits

preparation time 20 minutes (plus refrigeration time)
makes 24

85g packet raspberry jelly crystals
1 cup (250ml) boiling water
¾ cup (180ml) cold water
2 tablespoons Cointreau
250g mascarpone cheese
300ml whipping cream
½ cup (80g) icing sugar
1 tablespoon lemon juice
240g fresh raspberries

1 Place jelly crystals in jug; add boiling water. Stir to dissolve; add cold water and liqueur. Pour into 24 small glasses; place glasses on tray, refrigerate until set.
2 Meanwhile, whisk mascarpone in medium bowl until thickened slightly.
3 Beat cream, sifted icing sugar and juice in small bowl with an electric mixer until soft peaks form. Fold cream mixture into mascarpone. Top jelly with lemon mascarpone mixture. Cover; refrigerate.
4 Top with raspberries before serving.
nutritional count per parfait 10.7g total fat (7g saturated fat); 564kJ (135 cal); 8.4g carbohydrate; 0.8g protein; 0.5g fibre

Mascarpone is a fresh, smooth, unripened triple-cream cheese from Italy's Lombardy region. It is most often used in sweet recipes, such as this decadent raspberry parfait.

You are invited to a
Barbecue

Everyone relax, this is simple entertaining...

Greek

grilled haloumi

–

feta and olive dip with
garlic toast

–

greek salad

–

greek roast lamb with skordalia
and lemon-scented potatoes

Embrace the easy style of the Mediterranean.

grilled haloumi

preparation time 5 minutes
cooking time 5 minutes
serves 6

400g haloumi cheese, sliced
150g drained pickled green chillies
1 lemon, cut into wedges
¾ cup (75g) kalamata olives
¾ cup (60g) green olives

1 Cook cheese on a heated oiled barbecue flat plate,
in batches, until browned lightly.
2 Arrange cheese on serving platter with chillies and
lemon wedges; serve immediately with olives and, if desired,
pitta bread.
nutritional count per serving 11.7g total fat (7.4g saturated
fat); 803kJ (192 cal); 6.6g carbohydrate; 14.6g protein;
1.2g fibre

feta and olive dip with garlic toast

preparation time 10 minutes
cooking time 5 minutes
serves 6

½ cup (60g) pitted green olives
200g soft feta cheese
1 clove garlic
200g plain yogurt
1 loaf ciabatta (440g)
2 tablespoons olive oil
2 cloves garlic, extra, crushed

1 Blend or process ⅓ cup of the olives with cheese, garlic and yogurt until smooth. Chop remaining olives finely; stir into dip.
2 Preheat grill.
3 Cut ciabatta into 18 slices. Combine oil and extra garlic in small bowl; brush slices with oil mixture. Place slices under hot grill until browned both sides.
4 Halve slices diagonally; serve with dip.
nutritional count per serving 17.9g total fat (7.1g saturated fat); 1668kJ (399 cal); 43.3g carbohydrate; 14.3g protein; 3.1g fibre

greek salad

preparation time 15 minutes
serves 6

4 medium plum tomatoes (300g), sliced thinly
1 cucumber (260g), chopped coarsely
1 small red onion (100g), sliced thinly
½ cup (75g) pitted kalamata olives
150g feta cheese, chopped coarsely
2 tablespoons olive oil
2 tablespoons lemon juice
2 teaspoons fresh oregano leaves

1 Combine tomato, cucumber, onion, olives and cheese in large bowl.
2 Combine remaining ingredients in screw-top jar; shake well. Drizzle dressing over salad.
nutritional count per serving 12.2g total fat (4.7g saturated fat); 656kJ (157 cal); 6g carbohydrate; 5.5g protein; 1.6g fibre

greek roast lamb with skordalia and lemon-scented potatoes

preparation time 40 minutes (plus refrigeration time)
cooking time 3 hours 20 minutes
serves 6

2.5kg leg lof amb
3 cloves garlic, crushed
⅔ cup (160ml) lemon juice
¼ cup (60ml) olive oil
2 tablespoons fresh oregano leaves
2 teaspoons fresh lemon thyme leaves
6 large potatoes (1.8kg), diced into 3cm pieces
2 tablespoons olive oil, extra
1 tablespoon finely grated lemon rind
2 tablespoons lemon juice
1 teaspoon fresh lemon thyme leaves, extra

SKORDALIA
1 large potato (300g), quartered
3 cloves garlic, quartered
1 tablespoon lemon juice
1 tablespoon white wine vinegar
2 tablespoons water
⅓ cup (80ml) olive oil
2 tablespoons warm water

1   Combine lamb with garlic, juice, oil, oregano and thyme in large bowl. Cover; refrigerate 3 hours or overnight.
2   Place lamb in large disposable aluminium baking dish; cook, in covered barbecue, over low heat, about 3 hours or until cooked as desired.
3   Meanwhile, make skordalia.
4   Toss potato in large bowl with combined remaining ingredients; place, in another disposable baking dish. Cook potato in covered barbecue for last 30 minutes of lamb cooking time.
5   Remove lamb from barbecue; cover to keep warm.
6   Increase barbecue temperature to high. Remove potatoes from dish; cook, uncovered, on flat plate, turning occasionally, about 20 minutes or until crisp and tender. Serve potatoes and lamb with skordalia; sprinkle with extra fresh lemon thyme leaves, if desired.
SKORDALIA
Boil, steam or microwave potato until tender; drain. Push potato through food mill or fine sieve into large bowl; cool 10 minutes. Place garlic, juice, vinegar and the water in bowl with potato; stir until well combined. Place potato mixture in blender; with motor operating, gradually add oil in a thin, steady stream, blending only until skordalia thickens (do not overmix). Stir in the warm water.
nutritional count per serving 34.5g total fat (7g saturated fat); 3327kJ (796 cal); 40.3g carbohydrate; 77.9g protein; 5.4g fibre

Sausage Sizzle

sausages with white bean
and parsley salad

—

caramelised red onions

—

spicy tomato chutney

—

coleslaw

—

sliced tomato, basil and
red onion salad

An unbeatable crowd-pleaser with all the trimmings.

sausages with white bean and parsley salad

preparation time 10 minutes
cooking time 20 minutes
serves 6

12 Italian pork sausages
6 medium plum tomatoes (450g), deseeded, chopped
1 small red onion (100g), sliced thinly
1 clove garlic, crushed
⅓ cup (80ml) red wine vinegar
½ cup (125ml) extra virgin olive oil
½ cup coarsely chopped fresh flat-leaf parsley
½ cup loosely packed fresh basil leaves
2 x 400g cans cannellini beans, drained, rinsed

1 Cook sausages on heated oiled barbecue about
15 minutes or until cooked through. Cover to keep warm.
2 Meanwhile, combine tomato, onion, garlic, vinegar, oil,
herbs and beans in medium bowl; toss gently to combine.
3 Serve sausages with bean mixture.
*nutritional count per serving 61.3g total fat (19.6g saturated
fat); 3143kJ (752 cal); 18g carbohydrate; 29.1g protein;
9.7g fibre*

caramelised red onions

preparation time 15 minutes
cooking time 40 minutes
makes 1½ cups

50g butter
4 medium red onions (680g), sliced thinly
1 tablespoon brown sugar
⅓ cup (80ml) dry red wine
1 tablespoon balsamic vinegar

1 Melt butter on heated barbecue flat plate; cook onion, over low heat, tossing occasionally, about 20 minutes.
2 Add sugar; cook, tossing gently, about 5 minutes or until onion has caramelised. Add wine and vinegar; cook until liquid evaporates.
nutritional count per tablespoon 2.3g total fat (1.5g saturated fat); 159kJ (38 cal); 2.8g carbohydrate; 0.6g protein; 0.5g fibre

spicy tomato chutney

preparation time 15 minutes
cooking time 1 hour
makes 2 cups

4 large tomatoes (880g), peeled, chopped coarsely
1 medium brown onion (150g), chopped coarsely
½ cup (110g) firmly packed brown sugar
1 cup (250ml) white wine vinegar
1 tablespoon ground ginger
1 medium green apple (150g), chopped coarsely
½ cup (85g) raisins
1 teaspoon dried chilli flakes
1 teaspoon cracked black pepper
2 tablespoons tomato paste

1 Combine ingredients in large saucepan; bring to the boil, stirring. Reduce heat; simmer, uncovered, stirring occasionally, about 1 hour or until chutney thickens.
nutritional count per tablespoon 0g total fat (0g saturated fat); 13kJ (3 cal); 0.3g carbohydrate; 0.2g protein; 0.2g fibre

coleslaw

preparation time 10 minutes
serves 6

1 small cabbage (1.2kg)
2 medium carrots (240g), grated coarsely
6 spring onions, sliced thinly
½ cup (150g) mayonnaise
2 tablespoons lemon juice

1 Using sharp knife, remove core from cabbage; shred cabbage finely.
2 Place cabbage, carrot and onion in large bowl with combined mayonnaise and juice; toss gently to combine.
nutritional count per serving 8.3g total fat (1g saturated fat); 648kJ (155 cal); 12.5g carbohydrate; 3.7g protein; 8.3g fibre

sliced tomato, basil and red onion salad

preparation time 15 minutes
serves 6

6 large plum tomatoes (540g), sliced thinly
1 medium red onion (170g), sliced thinly
¼ cup small fresh basil leaves
¼ teaspoon cracked black pepper
1 teaspoon caster sugar
1 tablespoon balsamic vinegar
1 tablespoon extra virgin olive oil

1 Alternate layers of tomato, onion and basil on serving plate; sprinkle with pepper and sugar.
2 Drizzle salad with vinegar and oil.
nutritional count per serving 3.2g total fat (0.4g saturated fat); 226kJ (54 cal); 4.3g carbohydrate; 1.3g protein; 1.7g fibre

Italian

marinated mini bocconcini
with prosciutto

—

pizza trio

—

fontina, pancetta and
sage chicken

—

char-grilled mediterranean
vegetables with
fresh oregano dressing

Italian food utilises a barbecue's versatility.

marinated mini bocconcini with prosciutto

preparation time 20 minutes (plus standing time)
makes 20

200g baby bocconcini (mini mozzarella) cheese
1 clove garlic, crushed
1 fresh long green chilli, deseeded, chopped finely
2 tablespoons olive oil
5 slices thin prosciutto (75g)
1 cup firmly packed fresh basil leaves

1 Combine bocconcini, garlic, chilli, and oil in medium bowl. Stand 30 minutes. Drain bocconcini; reserve marinade.
2 Halve prosciutto slices crossways, then halve lengthways.
3 Wrap a piece of prosciutto and a basil leaf around each bocconcini; secure with a toothpick.
4 Serve bocconcini drizzled with reserved marinade.
nutritional count per piece 3.6g total fat (1.3g saturated fat); 176kJ (42 cal); 0.1g carbohydrate; 2.4g protein; 0.1g fibre

pizza trio

preparation time 40 minutes (plus standing time)
cooking time 10 minutes
makes 3 thin pizzas (6 slices per pizza)

2 teaspoons (7g) dried yeast
½ teaspoon caster sugar
¾ cup (180ml) warm water
2 cups (300g) plain flour
1 teaspoon salt
2 tablespoons olive oil
3 teaspoons olive oil, extra

ANCHOVY OLIVE TOPPING
2 teaspoons olive oil
⅓ cup (80ml) bottled tomato sauce
7 anchovy fillets, halved
¼ cup (30g) black olives, pitted, halved
12 fresh basil leaves

PANCETTA TOPPING
2 teaspoons olive oil
⅓ cup (80ml) bottled tomato sauce
2 cloves garlic, sliced thinly
½ cup (40g) shaved parmesan cheese
6 thin slices chilli pancetta

SPICY SAUSAGE TOPPING
2 teaspoons olive oil
⅓ cup (80ml) bottled tomato sauce
175g cooked spicy italian sausages
1 long red thai chilli, sliced thinly
¼ cup (30g) olives, pitted, halved
100g mozzarella cheese, sliced
2 tablespoons fresh oregano leaves

1 Combine yeast, sugar and the water in small bowl; cover, stand in warm place about 10 minutes or until frothy. Sift flour and salt into large bowl, stir in yeast mixture and oil; mix to a soft dough. Bring dough together with your hands and add a little extra water, if needed, until ingredients are combined.
2 Knead dough on floured surface 10 minutes or until smooth and elastic. Place dough in oiled large bowl; cover, stand in warm place about 1 hour or until doubled in size.
3 Meanwhile, preheat covered barbecue.
4 Punch dough down with fist; knead on floured surface until smooth. Divide dough into three portions.
5 Roll each portion on a wooden or marble board to about a 16cm x 40cm rectangle.
6 Layer two pieces of aluminium foil large enough to fit one rectangle of dough. Brush foil with 1 teaspoon of the extra oil. Place one portion of dough on top; repeat with extra foil and remaining oil and dough.
7 Turn off burners underneath middle grill plate, leaving outer burners on to cook by indirect heat. Place dough on foil on grill plate, cover barbecue, cook about 4 minutes or until underneath is browned.
8 Carefully remove pizza bases from barbecue, close cover. Turn pizza bases over on foil, brush cooked side with oil, then spread with tomato sauce; top with selected ingredients for each topping except the fresh herbs. Return pizzas to barbecue on foil; cover barbecue, cook about 5 minutes or until well browned underneath and crisp. Sprinkle pizzas with the herbs.

anchovy olive topping (6 slices)
nutritional count per slice 5.1g total fat (0.8g saturated fat); 506kJ (121 cal); 14.7g carbohydrate; 3.4g protein; 1.1g fibre
pancetta topping (6 slices)
nutritional count per slice 7.9g total fat (2.5g saturated fat); 644kJ (154 cal); 13.7g carbohydrate; 6.3g protein; 1.2g fibre
spicy sausage topping (6 slices)
nutritional count per slice 16g total fat (5.5g saturated fat); 1045kJ (250 cal); 15.5g carbohydrate; 10.7g protein; 1.2g fibre

From top to bottom: Anchovy and olive pizza, Pancetta pizza, and Spicy sausage pizza.

fontina, pancetta and sage chicken

preparation time 15 minutes
cooking time 20 minutes
serves 6

6 x 180g chicken breast fillets
6 thin slices fontina cheese (150g)
6 slices pancetta (90g)
2 tablespoons coarsely chopped fresh sage
2 tablespoons olive oil
2 cloves garlic, crushed
20 whole sage leaves

1 Slit a pocket in one side of each fillet but do not cut all the way through. Divide cheese, pancetta and chopped sage among pockets; secure with toothpicks. Brush chicken with combined oil and garlic.
2 Cook chicken, both sides, on heated oiled grill plate, about 20 minutes or until cooked. Remove toothpicks before serving.
3 Cook whole sage leaves on same oiled grill plate until golden brown. Serve chicken topped with sage leaves.
nutritional count per serving 19.8g total fat (7.5g saturated fat); 1597kJ (382 cal); 0.2g carbohydrate; 50.1g protein; 0.2g fibre

char-grilled mediterranean vegetables with fresh oregano dressing

preparation time 20 minutes
cooking time 35 minutes
serves 6

1 medium red pepper (200g)
1 medium yellow pepper (200g)
1 large red onion (300g), halved, cut into wedges
1 small sweet potato (250g), sliced thinly lengthways
2 baby aubergines (120g), sliced thinly lengthways
2 medium courgettes (240g), halved lengthways
340g jar artichoke hearts, drained, halved
100g pitted kalamata olives
1 small radicchio (150g), trimmed, leaves separated

FRESH OREGANO DRESSING
¼ cup (60ml) olive oil
2 tablespoons red wine vinegar
2 tablespoons lemon juice
2 cloves garlic, crushed
1 tablespoon finely chopped fresh oregano

1 Quarter peppers, remove and discard seeds and membranes; cut peppers into thick strips.
2 Place ingredients for fresh oregano dressing in screw-top jar; shake well.
3 Cook peppers, in batches, on heated oiled grill plate until browned and tender. Cook onion, sweet potato, aubergines, courgettes and artichoke, in batches, on same grill plate until browned.
4 Place chargrilled vegetables, olives and dressing in large bowl; toss gently to combine. Serve with radicchio.
nutritional count per serving 9.9g total fat (1.3g saturated fat); 736kJ (176 cal); 15.2g carbohydrate; 4.3g protein; 5.1g fibre

Seafood

seafood antipasto
—
lobster tails with lime butter
and pineapple mint salsa
—
beetroot, asparagus
and feta salad
—
sweet lime mangoes

Skip the sausages and reel in a feast fit for a king.

seafood antipasto

preparation time 25 minutes (plus refrigeration time)
cooking time 20 minutes
serves 4

12 uncooked large king prawns (840g)
8 sardine fillets (360g)
8 whole cleaned baby octopus (720g)
2 cloves garlic, crushed
2 tablespoons olive oil
440g loaf ciabatta, sliced thickly
170g asparagus, halved lengthways
200g mini plum tomatoes
1 cup (150g) pitted kalamata olives
250g haloumi cheese, sliced lengthways into 8 pieces
GARLIC CHILLI DRESSING
4 cloves garlic, crushed
1 tablespoon finely grated lime rind
¼ cup (60ml) lime juice
2 fresh small red thai chillies, chopped finely

1 Shell and devein prawns, leaving heads and tails intact. Combine prawns in large bowl with sardines, octopus, half the garlic and half the oil. Cover; refrigerate 3 hours or overnight.
2 Combine remaining garlic and oil in small bowl; brush bread slices, both sides, with garlic oil. Toast bread, both sides, on heated oiled flat plate.
3 Place ingredients for garlic chilli dressing in screw-top jar; shake well.
4 Cook asparagus, tomatoes, olives and cheese, in batches, on flat plate, until asparagus is tender.
5 Cook seafood, in batches, on same flat plate until cooked as desired; drizzle with dressing. Serve with vegetables and cheese.
nutritional count per serving 51.1g total fat (15.4g saturated fat); 4840kJ (1158 cal); 63.2g carbohydrate; 108g protein; 6.2g fibre

lobster tails with lime butter and pineapple mint salsa

preparation time 20 minutes
cooking time 10 minutes
serves 4

100g butter
1 teaspoon finely grated lime rind
1 fresh small red thai chilli, chopped finely
2cm piece fresh ginger (10g), grated
4 uncooked small lobster tails in shells (660g)

PINEAPPLE MINT SALSA
1 small pineapple (900g), chopped coarsely
2 tablespoons lime juice
½ cup finely chopped fresh mint
1 fresh long red chilli, chopped finely

1 Combine ingredients for pineapple mint salsa in medium bowl.
2 Melt butter in small saucepan; cook rind, chilli and ginger, stirring, 2 minutes.
3 Using scissors, cut soft shell from underneath lobster tails to expose meat; cut lobster tails in half lengthways. Brush with butter mixture; cook, in batches, on heated oiled grill plate until cooked through.
4 Serve lobster with salsa.
nutritional count per serving 21.9g total fat (13.8g saturated fat); 1538kJ (368 cal); 10.1g carbohydrate; 31.1g protein; 3.1g fibre

"A truly destitute man is not one without riches, but the poor wretch who has never partaken of lobster."
Anonymous

beetroot, asparagus and feta salad

preparation time 10 minutes
cooking time 5 minutes
serves 4

170g asparagus, halved
½ cup loosely packed fresh mint leaves, torn
½ x 450g can beetroot wedges, drained
100g feta cheese, crumbled
¼ cup (25g) walnut halves, toasted
LEMON DRESSING
1 clove garlic, crushed
2 tablespoons olive oil
1 tablespoon lemon juice

1 Boil, steam or microwave asparagus until just tender; drain.
2 Meanwhile, combine ingredients for lemon dressing in small bowl.
3 Place asparagus, mint, beetroot, 75g of the cheese, nuts and dressing in serving bowl; toss gently to combine. Top with remaining cheese.
nutritional count per serving 19.4g total fat (5.4g saturated fat); 932kJ (223 cal); 4.7g carbohydrate; 6.9g protein; 2.4g fibre

sweet lime mangoes

preparation time 5 minutes
cooking time 8 minutes
serves 4

4 small mangoes (1.2kg)
1 tablespoon finely grated lime rind
1 tablespoon lime juice
1 tablespoon brown sugar
½ cup (140g) plain yogurt

1 Slice cheeks from mangoes; score each in shallow criss-cross pattern.
2 Combine rind and juice; drizzle over each mango cheek. Sprinkle with sugar.
3 Cook mangoes, flesh-side down, on heated barbecue flat plate until browned lightly. Serve with yogurt.
nutritional count per serving 1.7g total fat (0.7g saturated fat); 798kJ (191 cal); 35.8g carbohydrate; 4.1g protein; 4.1g fibre

You are invited to a
Picnic

Pack the croquet set and move the feast outside...

French

potted pork with
witlof and cornichons

—

salade composé

—

caramelised onion and
beetroot tart

—

sugar and spice palmiers

Bring a little *joie de vivre* to the picnic rug.

potted pork with belgian endive and cornichons

preparation time 30 minutes
cooking time 2 hours 30 minutes
serves 6

¼ cup (60ml) water
800g boned belly of pork, rind removed,
    diced into 5cm pieces
3 bay leaves
2 cloves garlic, chopped coarsely
¼ cup (60ml) dry white wine
2 teaspoons salt
1 teaspoon ground black pepper
1 small red onion (100g), chopped finely
1 tablespoon finely chopped fresh flat-leaf parsley
⅔ cup (120g) drained cornichons
6 belgian endives (750g), trimmed, leaves separated

1 Preheat oven to 150°C/130°C fan-assisted.
2 Combine the water, pork, bay leaves, garlic, wine, salt and pepper in large shallow baking dish. Cook about 2½ hours or until pork is very tender.
3 Discard bay leaves; using two forks, shred pork finely in dish with pan juices. Stir in onion and parsley. Serve pork with cornichons and belgian endive.
nutritional count per serving 9.4g total fat (3.1g saturated fat); 861kJ (206 cal); 1.6g carbohydrate; 25.9g protein; 2.8g fibre

salade composé

preparation time 15 minutes
cooking time 20 minutes
serves 6

1 small french bread stick
2 cloves garlic, crushed
¼ cup (60ml) olive oil
6 rashers rindless bacon (360g), sliced thickly
150g mixed salad leaves
6 medium plum tomatoes (450g), sliced thinly
4 hard-boiled eggs, halved lengthways

RED WINE VINAIGRETTE
¼ cup (60ml) red wine vinegar
3 teaspoons dijon mustard
⅓ cup (80ml) extra virgin olive oil

1 Preheat grill.
2 Cut bread into 1cm slices. Brush both sides with combined garlic and oil; toast under preheated grill.
3 Cook bacon in large frying pan until crisp; drain on absorbent paper.
4 Meanwhile, place ingredients for red wine vinaigrette in screw-top jar; shake well.
5 Layer bread and bacon in large bowl with salad leaves and tomato, top with egg; drizzle with vinaigrette.
nutritional count per serving 33.7g total fat (7.1g saturated fat); 1788kJ (434 cal); 13.4g carbohydrate; 19g protein; 2.5g fibre

caramelised onion and beetroot tart

preparation time 20 minutes (plus freezing time)
cooking time 45 minutes
serves 6

50g butter
4 medium red onions (680g), halved, sliced thinly
1 tablespoon red wine vinegar
1 teaspoon fresh thyme leaves
3 medium beetroot (500g), trimmed
1 sheet ready-rolled butter puff pastry
cooking-oil spray
120g baby rocket leaves

CHIVE OIL
½ cup coarsely chopped fresh chives
¾ cup (180ml) olive oil
1 ice cube

HORSERADISH CREAM
¾ cup (180ml) double cream
1 tablespoon horseradish cream

1 Melt butter in medium frying pan; cook onion, stirring occasionally, over medium heat about 30 minutes or until caramelised. Stir in vinegar and thyme.
2 Meanwhile, boil, steam or microwave unpeeled beetroot until just tender; drain. When cool enough to handle, peel then slice beetroot thinly.
3 Preheat oven to 240°C/220°C fan-assisted.
4 Place pastry sheet on flat surface; cut a 24cm circle out of pastry. Place on oiled oven tray, prick all over with fork; freeze 10 minutes. Bake about 5 minutes or until browned.
5 Make chive oil. Make horseradish cream.
6 Spread onion mixture over pastry; top with slightly overlapping beetroot slices. Spray tart lightly with oil; bake 10 minutes.
7 Meanwhile, combine rocket in medium bowl with half of the chive oil.
8 Serve tart cut into wedges with rocket, remaining chive oil and horseradish cream.
CHIVE OIL
Blend or process ingredients until smooth.
HORSERADISH CREAM
Beat cream in small bowl with electric mixer until soft peaks form; fold in horseradish cream.
nutritional count per serving 54.4g total fat (20.6g saturated fat); 2558kJ (612 cal) 24.2g carbohydrate; 5.8g protein; 4.6g fibre

sugar and spice palmiers

preparation time 20 minutes
cooking time 15 minutes
makes 30

2 tablespoons raw sugar
1 sheet ready-rolled puff pastry
1 teaspoon ground nutmeg
300ml whipping cream
2 teaspoons honey

1 Preheat oven to 180°C/160°C fan-assisted. Grease two oven trays; line with baking parchment.
2 Sprinkle board with a little of the sugar. Roll pastry on sugared board into 20cm x 40cm rectangle; trim edges. Sprinkle pastry with nutmeg and remaining sugar.
3 Starting from long side, loosely roll one side at a time into the middle of the rectangle, so the two long sides meet.
4 Cut pastry into 5mm-thick pieces. Place, cut-side up, about 5cm apart, on trays. Spread pastry open slightly at folded ends to make a V-shape.
5 Bake palmiers about 15 minutes or until golden brown; transfer to wire rack to cool.
6 Beat cream and honey in small bowl with electric mixer until firm peaks form. Serve palmiers with honey cream.
nutritional count per serving 5g total fat (3.1g saturated fat); 259kJ (62 cal); 3.8g carbohydrate; 0.5g protein; 0.1g fibre

All-time Favourites

old-fashioned chicken salad

~

caramelised onion and
prosciutto glazed meatloaf

~

potato salad

~

chocolate chip cookies

Tried and true favourites keep every picnicker happy.

old-fashioned chicken salad

preparation time 40 minutes
cooking time 15 minutes
serves 6

1 litre (4 cups) boiling water
1 litre (4 cups) chicken stock
700g chicken breast fillets
1 long french bread stick, sliced thinly
2 tablespoons olive oil
⅓ cup (90g) mayonnaise
½ cup (120g) soured cream
2 tablespoons lemon juice
4 trimmed celery stalks (400g), sliced thinly
1 medium white onion (150g), chopped finely
3 large dill pickles (150g), sliced thinly
2 tablespoons finely chopped fresh flat-leaf parsley
1 tablespoon finely chopped fresh tarragon
1 large butterhead lettuce, leaves separated

1 Bring the water and stock to the boil in large frying pan; poach chicken, covered, about 10 minutes or until cooked through. Cool chicken in liquid 10 minutes; slice thinly. Discard liquid.
2 Meanwhile, brush both sides of bread slices with oil; toast under preheated grill until browned lightly both sides.
3 Whisk mayonnaise, cream and juice in small bowl. Combine chicken with celery, onion, pickle and herbs in large bowl; toss gently to combine. Place lettuce leaves on serving platter; top with salad and bread, drizzle with mayonnaise mixture.
nutritional count per serving 27.3g total fat (8.3g saturated fat); 2215kJ (530 cal); 34.6g carbohydrate; 34.4g protein; 4.3g fibre

caramelised onion and prosciutto glazed meatloaf

preparation time 30 minutes
cooking time 1 hour 30 minutes
serves 6

1 tablespoon olive oil
2 large brown onions (400g), sliced thinly
¼ cup (55g) brown sugar
¼ cup (60ml) cider vinegar
12 slices prosciutto (180g)
1kg minced beef
1 egg, beaten lightly
1 cup (70g) stale breadcrumbs
2 tablespoons tomato paste
1 clove garlic, crushed
2 tablespoons tomato sauce
2 tablespoons barbecue sauce
1 tablespoon wholegrain mustard
1 tablespoon brown sugar, extra

1 Heat oil in large frying pan; cook onion, stirring, about 5 minutes or until onion softens and browns lightly. Add sugar and vinegar; cook, stirring, about 15 minutes or until onion is caramelised. Cool.

2 Meanwhile, preheat oven to 200°C/180°C fan-assisted. Grease 14cm x 21cm loaf tin; line base and long sides of tin with prosciutto slices, allowing 7cm overhang on long sides of tin.

3 Combine mince, egg, breadcrumbs, paste and garlic in large bowl. Press two-thirds of the beef mixture into tin; fill with onion mixture, cover with remaining beef mixture. Fold prosciutto slices over to cover beef mixture.

4 Bake meatloaf, covered, 40 minutes then remove from oven. Drain excess juices from tin. Turn tin upside-down onto foil-lined oven tray; remove tin.

5 Combine sauces, mustard and extra sugar in small bowl. Brush loaf with sauce mixture; bake, uncovered, basting occasionally with sauce mixture, for further 20 minutes or until cooked through. Stand loaf 10 minutes; slice thickly.

nutritional count per serving 17.8g total fat (6.2g saturated fat); 1898kJ (454 cal); 28.6g carbohydrate; 43.5g protein; 2.1g fibre

potato salad

preparation time 20 minutes (plus refrigeration time)
cooking time 20 minutes
serves 6

1.5kg salad potatoes, peeled
2 tablespoons cider vinegar
6 spring onions, sliced thinly
¼ cup finely chopped fresh flat-leaf parsley

MAYONNAISE
2 egg yolks
1 teaspoon dijon mustard
2 teaspoons lemon juice
¾ cup (180ml) vegetable oil
2 tablespoons hot water, approximately

1 Cut potatoes into 1.5cm pieces. Place potato in large saucepan, barely cover with cold water; cover saucepan, bring to the boil. Reduce heat; simmer, uncovered, stirring occasionally, until just tender. Drain, spread potato on a tray; sprinkle with vinegar. Cool 10 minutes. Refrigerate, covered, until cold.
2 Meanwhile, make mayonnaise.
3 Place potato in large bowl with mayonnaise, onion and parsley; mix gently to combine.
MAYONNAISE
Blend or process egg yolks, mustard and juice until smooth. With motor operating, gradually add oil in a thin, steady stream; process until mixture thickens. Add as much of the hot water as required to thin mayonnaise.
nutritional count per serving 29.7g total fat (4.1g saturated fat); 1722kJ (412 cal); 28.4g carbohydrate; 6.4g protein; 3.8g fibre

chocolate chip cookies

preparation time 40 minutes (plus refrigeration time)
cooking time 15 minutes
makes 40

250g butter, softened
1 teaspoon vanilla extract
¾ cup (165g) sugar
¾ cup (165g) firmly packed brown sugar
1 egg
2¼ cups (335g) plain flour
1 teaspoon bicarbonate of soda
300g dark eating chocolate, chopped coarsely

1 Preheat oven to 180°C/160°C fan-assisted. Grease oven trays.
2 Beat butter, extract, sugars and egg in small bowl with electric mixer until light and fluffy. Transfer to large bowl.
3 Stir combined sifted flour and soda, in two batches, into egg mixture; stir in chocolate. Cover; refrigerate 1 hour.
4 Roll level tablespoons of the dough into balls; place on trays 3cm apart. Bake about 12 minutes. Cool cookies on trays.
nutritional count per cookie 7.6g total fat (5.5g saturated fat); 627kJ (150 cal); 18.5g carbohydrate; 1.4g protein; 0.7g fibre

Waterside

anchovy and parmesan sticks

‑

seafood platter

‑

picnic loaf

‑

lettuce wedges with
dill mustard dressing

‑

nectarine and apricot tarts

Keep your cool and dip into the fruits of the sea.

anchovy and parmesan sticks

preparation time 10 minutes (plus freezing time)
cooking time 15 minutes
makes 24

3 drained anchovy fillets, chopped finely
1 clove garlic, crushed
2 teaspoons pine nuts, toasted, chopped finely
2 teaspoons finely chopped flat-leaf parsley
¼ teaspoon dried chilli flakes
1 sheet ready-rolled butter puff pastry
1 egg yolk
1 tablespoon finely grated parmesan cheese

1 Combine anchovy, garlic, nuts, parsley and chilli to taste in small bowl.
2 Cut pastry sheet in half; brush each half lightly with egg yolk. Spread anchovy mixture over one pastry half; sprinkle with parmesan. Top with remaining pastry and press down firmly. Place pastry on oven tray; freeze 15 minutes or until firm enough to cut.
3 Preheat oven to 200°C/180°C fan-assisted. Grease oven tray; line with baking parchment.
4 Using a sharp knife, cut pastry crossways into 5mm strips. Place pastry sticks 3cm apart on tray. Bake about 15 minutes or until browned. Cool on tray.
nutritional count per stick 2.1g total fat (1g saturated fat); 138kJ (33 cal); 2.5g carbohydrate; 0.8g protein; 0.1g fibre

seafood platter

preparation time 35 minutes
serves 8

2 cooked lobsters (2.4kg)
4 cooked crayfish tails (800g)
1kg cooked medium king prawns
24 oysters, on the half shell

PARSLEY AND ROCKET SAUCE
1 cup (160g) blanched almonds, toasted
1 clove garlic
1½ cups firmly packed flat-leaf parsley
60g rocket
1 teaspoon sea salt
½ cup (125ml) extra virgin olive oil
⅓ cup (80ml) white wine vinegar
¼ cup (60ml) water

ROASTED PEPPER AND TOMATO SALSA
250g roasted red pepper, drained, chopped finely
3 medium plum tomatoes (225g), deseeded,
    chopped finely
1 tablespoon baby capers, rinsed, drained
¼ cup finely shredded fresh basil
¼ cup (60ml) extra virgin olive oil
1 tablespoon red wine vinegar

1 Make parsley and rocket sauce. Make roasted pepper and tomato salsa.
2 Hold lobster in one hand firmly, twist head away; discard head. Using kitchen scissors, cut the softer under-shell away, leaving the tail meat whole. Carefully remove meat from the shell and slice thickly. Repeat with remaining lobster.
3 Using a sharp knife, cut one crayfish tail in half lengthways; remove centre vein from tail. Repeat with remaining crayfish tails.
4 Arrange lobster, crayfish tails, prawns and the oysters on a large platter. Serve seafood with sauce, salsa and lemon wedges, if desired.
PARSLEY AND ROCKET SAUCE
Process nuts, garlic, parsley, rocket and salt until finely chopped. With motor operating, add combined oil and vinegar in thin stream until combined. Stir in water.
ROASTED PEPPER AND TOMATO SALSA
Combine all ingredients in small bowl.
nutritional count per serving 34.2g total fat (4.2g saturated fat); 1969kJ (471 cal); 3.2g carbohydrate; 36.8g protein; 3.3g fibre

One of the simplest ways to make a picnic feel like
a grand occasion is a beautifully arranged seafood platter.
The key is day-fresh produce and tasty accompaniments.
Serve on ice cubes to keep the chill in the food.

picnic loaf

preparation time 20 minutes
cooking time 15 minutes
serves 8

675g sourdough bread loaf
150g rocket
200g sliced smoked salmon
1 small red onion (80g), sliced thinly
1 tablespoon baby capers
1 medium avocado (250g), sliced thickly
½ cucumber (130g), sliced lengthways into ribbons
3 hard-boiled eggs, peeled, cooled, sliced

1 Cut a lid from top of loaf; remove soft bread inside loaf, leaving a 2cm shell.
2 Place half of the rocket inside bread shell; top with salmon, onion, capers, avocado, cucumber, egg and remaining rocket. Replace lid; press down firmly. Wrap loaf tightly with kitchen string and cling film; refrigerate until required.
nutritional count per serving 10.4g total fat (2.2g saturated fat); 1371kJ (328 cal); 39.5g carbohydrate; 16.5g protein; 4.8g fibre

lettuce wedges with dill mustard dressing

preparation time 10 minutes
serves 8

1 tablespoon dijon mustard
1 egg yolk
1 teaspoon honey
1 cup groundnut oil
2 tablespoons lemon juice
⅓ cup (80ml) water
1 tablespoon dill
2 baby cos lettuces, rinsed, trimmed, quartered

1 Whisk mustard, egg yolk and honey in medium bowl until combined.
2 Gradually whisk in oil in a thin steady stream, whisking constantly until thick. Stir in juice, the water and dill.
3 Serve dressing with wedges of cos lettuce.
nutritional count per serving 29.3g total fat (5.4g saturated fat); 1141kJ (273 cal); 1.8g carbohydrate; 1.1g protein; 1g fibre

nectarine and apricot tarts

preparation time 25 minutes
cooking time 20 minutes
serves 8

60g butter, softened
⅓ cup (75g) caster sugar
1 egg
¾ cup (75g) ground hazelnuts
2 tablespoons plain flour
2 sheets ready-rolled butter puff pastry
4 medium nectarines (480g), sliced thinly
4 large apricots (320g), sliced thinly
¼ cup (80g) apricot jam, warmed, sieved

1 Beat butter and sugar in small bowl with electric mixer until creamy; beat in egg. Stir in nuts and flour.
2 Preheat oven to 220°C/200°C fan-assisted. Grease two oven trays.
3 Cut pastry sheets in half; place on trays. Spread nut mixture thinly over pastry pieces, leaving a 2cm border. Arrange fruit, overlapping slightly, on nut mixture.
4 Bake tarts about 15 minutes or until pastry is browned lightly. Brush fruit with jam.
nutritional count per serving 22.2g total fat (9.6g saturated fat); 1626kJ (389 cal); 39.9g carbohydrate; 5.8g protein; 3.8g fibre.

These tarts are the perfect expression of summer. When cooked, the nectarines and apricots soften and slightly caramelise, becoming the perfect foil to the buttery crunch of the pastry and the nuts.

You are invited to a
Tea Party

Finger food for elegant, low-key entertaining...

Garden

pink limeade
—
mini chicken and leek pies
—
finger sandwiches
—
strawberry jelly cakes
—
mini passionfruit cakes

Frock up and savour these girly petite treats.

pink limeade

preparation time 10 minutes (plus refrigeration time)
makes 2 litres (8 cups)

1 cup (250ml) lime juice
½ cup (125ml) vodka
2½ cups (625ml) water
1 litre (4 cups) cranberry juice

1 Combine ingredients in large jug.
2 Cover; refrigerate until chilled.
nutritional count per 250ml 0.1g total fat (0g saturated fat);
535kJ (128 cal); 16.5g carbohydrate; 0.5g protein; 0.1g fibre

mini chicken and leek pies

preparation time 40 minutes
cooking time 40 minutes
makes 16

1 cup (250ml) chicken stock
170g chicken breast fillet
1 tablespoon olive oil
1 small leek (200g), sliced thinly
½ trimmed celery stick (50g), chopped finely
2 teaspoons plain flour
2 teaspoons fresh thyme leaves
¼ cup (60ml) double cream
1 teaspoon wholegrain mustard
2 sheets ready-rolled shortcrust pastry
1 sheet ready-rolled puff pastry
1 egg yolk
2 teaspoons sesame seeds

1 Bring stock to the boil in small saucepan. Add chicken; return to the boil. Reduce heat; simmer, covered, about 10 minutes or until chicken is just cooked through. Remove from heat; stand chicken in poaching liquid 10 minutes. Remove chicken; chop finely. Reserve ¼ cup of the poaching liquid; discard remainder (or keep for another use).
2 Heat oil in medium saucepan; cook leek and celery, stirring, until leek softens. Add flour and half of the thyme; cook, stirring, 1 minute. Gradually stir in reserved liquid and cream; cook, stirring, until mixture boils and thickens. Stir in chicken and mustard. Cool 10 minutes.
3 Preheat oven to 220°C/200°C fan-assisted. Oil eight holes in each of two 12-hole patty tins.
4 Using 7cm cutter, cut 16 rounds from shortcrust pastry; press one round into each patty hole. Spoon 1 tablespoon of the chicken mixture into each pastry case. Using 6cm cutter, cut 16 rounds from puff pastry; top chicken pies with puff pastry lids. Brush lids with yolk; sprinkle with remaining thyme and sesame seeds. Using sharp knife, make two small slits in each lid.
5 Bake pies about 20 minutes or until browned lightly.
nutritional count per pie 11.5g total fat (5.6g saturated fat); 740kJ (177 cal); 13.5g carbohydrate; 5.1g protein; 1g fibre

finger sandwiches

prosciutto, blue brie and fig

preparation time 10 minutes
makes 12

50g blue brie, softened
8 slices light rye bread
6 slices prosciutto (90g), halved widthways
4 medium figs (240g), sliced thinly

1 Spread cheese over four bread slices; top with prosciutto, fig and remaining bread.
2 Remove and discard crusts; cut sandwiches into three strips.
nutritional count per finger 2.5g total fat (1.1g saturated fat); 368kJ (88 cal); 12g carbohydrate; 4.5g protein; 1.9g fibre
TIP Remove cheese from fridge 30 minutes before making sandwiches.

From left to right: Prosciutto, blue brie and fig finger sandwiches; Chicken, capers and mayonnaise finger sandwiches

chicken, capers and mayonnaise

preparation time 10 minutes
makes 12

2 cups (320g) coarsely shredded barbecued chicken
2 tablespoons drained capers, chopped coarsely
2 tablespoons finely chopped fresh chives
⅓ cup (100g) whole-egg mayonnaise
8 slices brown bread
½ cucumber (130g), sliced thinly

1 Combine chicken, capers, chives and ¼ cup of the mayonnaise in medium bowl.
2 Spread chicken mixture over four bread slices; top with cucumber. Spread remaining mayonnaise over remaining bread; place on top of cucumber.
3 Remove and discard crusts; cut sandwiches into three strips.
nutritional count per finger 4.3g total fat (0.7g saturated fat); 422kJ (101 cal); 9.9g carbohydrate; 5.7g protein; 1.2g fibre

strawberry jelly cakes

preparation time 45 minutes
cooking time 25 minutes (plus refrigeration time)
makes 36

125g butter, softened
½ teaspoon vanilla extract
½ cup (110g) caster sugar
2 eggs
1½ cups (225g) self-raising flour
⅓ cup (80ml) milk
80g packet strawberry jelly
3 cups (150g) flaked coconut
½ cup (125ml) whipping cream

1 Preheat oven to 180°C/160°C fan-assisted. Grease deep 23cm-square cake tin; line base with baking parchment.
2 Beat butter, extract and sugar in small bowl with electric mixer until light and fluffy. Beat in eggs; stir in flour and milk until smooth. Spread mixture into tin.
3 Bake cake, uncovered, about 25 minutes. Stand cake in tin 5 minutes; turn, top-side up, onto wire rack to cool.
4 Meanwhile, make jelly according to manufacturer's instructions. Refrigerate until set to the consistency of unbeaten egg white.
5 Cut cake into 36 squares; dip each square into jelly then coconut. Cover; refrigerate 30 minutes.
6 Meanwhile, beat cream in small bowl with electric mixer until firm peaks form. Serve cakes with cream.
nutritional count per cake 7.3g total fat (5.3g saturated fat); 460kJ (110 cal); 10g carbohydrate; 1.6g protein; 0.9g fibre

mini passionfruit cakes

preparation time 25 minutes
cook time 20 minutes
makes 16

2 tablespoons passionfruit pulp
60g butter, chopped
1 teaspoon finely grated lemon rind
¼ cup (55g) caster sugar
1 egg
½ cup (75g) self-raising flour
¼ cup (60ml) buttermilk

ICING
½ cup (80g) icing sugar
1 teaspoon milk

1 Preheat oven to 180°C/160°C fan-assisted. Grease eight holes in each of two 12-hole mini (1-tablespoon/20ml) muffin tins.
2 Strain passionfruit pulp over small bowl; reserve seeds and juice separately.
3 Beat butter, rind and sugar in small bowl with electric mixer until light and fluffy. Beat in egg. Fold in flour, passionfruit juice and buttermilk. Spoon mixture into muffin tin holes.
4 Bake cakes about 20 minutes. Stand cakes 5 minutes; turn, top-side up, onto wire rack to cool.
5 Meanwhile, stir icing sugar, milk and reserved seeds in small bowl until combined. Top cakes with icing.
nutritional count per cake 3.6g total fat (2.2g saturated fat; 351kJ (84 cal); 12.1g carbohydrate; 1.2g protein; 0.5g fibre

From back to front: Strawberry jelly cakes; Mini passionfruit cakes

Country

sausage rolls
—
coco-chocolate squares
—
buttermilk scones with
strawberries and cream
—
featherlight sponge

There is no match for home-made tea-time treats.

sausage rolls

preparation time 25 minutes
cooking time 25 minutes
makes 48

750g sausagemeat
1 medium white onion (150g), chopped finely
1 cup (70g) stale breadcrumbs
1 teaspoon dried mixed herbs
1 egg, beaten lightly
4 sheets ready-rolled puff pastry
1 egg, beaten lightly, extra

1 Preheat oven to 200°C/180°C fan-assisted. Oil two oven trays.
2 Combine sausagemeat, onion, breadcrumbs, herbs and egg in large bowl. Cut each sheet of pastry in half.
3 Spoon filling into piping bag. Pipe filling along one long side of each pastry sheet. Brush opposite edge of pastry with egg; roll up pastry from filled edge to enclose filling. Cut into six even pieces, place on trays. Brush with egg; cut small slits in top of each roll.
4 Bake rolls about 25 minutes or until well browned.
nutritional count per roll 7.1g total fat (1.9g saturated fat); 426kJ (102 cal); 6.6g carbohydrate; 3.1g protein; 0.6g fibre

coco-chocolate squares

preparation time 30 minutes
cooking time 1 hour
makes 36

250g butter, softened
2 cups (440g) caster sugar
6 eggs
¾ cup (180g) soured cream
2 cups (300g) plain flour
¼ cup (35g) self-raising flour
2½ cups (200g) desiccated coconut

CHOCOLATE ICING
4 cups (500g) icing sugar
½ cup (50g) cocoa powder
20g butter, melted
⅔ cup (160ml) milk

1 Preheat oven to 160°C/140°C fan-assisted. Grease deep 23cm-square cake tin; line base with baking parchment.
2 Beat butter and sugar in large bowl with electric mixer until light and fluffy. Beat in eggs; stir in soured cream and sifted flours, in two batches. Spread mixture into tin.
3 Bake cake about 55 minutes. Stand cake 10 minutes; turn, top-side up, onto wire rack to cool.
4 Meanwhile, make chocolate icing.
5 Trim cold cake so top is level; cut into 36 squares. Dip squares in icing, drain off excess then coat in coconut; place cakes on wire rack to set.
CHOCOLATE ICING
Sift icing sugar and cocoa into large heatproof bowl; stir in butter and milk. Stir icing over large saucepan of simmering water until it is of a coating consistency.
nutritional count per cake 13.1g total fat (9.1g saturated fat); 1120kJ (268 cal); 33.9g carbohydrate; 3g protein; 1.2g fibre

buttermilk scones with strawberries and cream

preparation time 20 minutes
cooking time 20 minutes
makes 15

3 cups (450g) self-raising flour
2 tablespoons caster sugar
40g unsalted butter
2 cups (500ml) buttermilk
2 tablespoons buttermilk, extra
300ml whipping cream
250g strawberries, halved

1 Preheat oven to 240°C/220°C fan-assisted. Grease 20cm x 30cm baking tin.
2 Sift flour and sugar into large bowl; rub in butter with fingertips. Add buttermilk; use knife to "cut" buttermilk through the mixture to form a soft, sticky dough. Knead dough lightly on floured surface until smooth.
3 Press dough out to an even 2.5cm thickness. Dip 6.5cm cutter into flour; cut as many rounds as possible from the dough. Place scones side by side, just touching, in tin.
4 Gently knead scraps of dough together; repeat pressing and cutting of dough, place in tin. Brush tops with extra buttermilk; bake about 20 minutes or until scones sound hollow when tapped firmly on the top.
5 Meanwhile, beat cream in small bowl with electric mixer until soft peaks form. Serve scones with whipped cream and strawberries.
nutritional count per scone 9.9g total fat (6.3g saturated fat); 869kJ (208 cal); 24.4g carbohydrate; 4.8g protein; 1.4g fibre

featherlight sponge

preparation time 20 minutes
cooking time 20 minutes
serves 12

4 eggs
¾ cup (165g) caster sugar
⅔ cup (150g) wheaten cornflour
¼ cup (30g) custard powder
1 teaspoon cream of tartar
½ teaspoon bicarbonate of soda
300ml whipping cream
1 teaspoon vanilla extract
¼ cup (80g) strawberry jam
250g strawberries, sliced thinly

ICING
1 cup (160g) icing sugar
10g butter, softened
1½ tablespoons milk, approximately
pink food colouring

1 Preheat oven to 200°C/180°C fan-assisted. Grease and flour two deep 22cm-round cake tins; shake out any excess flour.
2 Beat eggs and sugar in small bowl with electric mixer about 7 minutes or until thick and creamy. Transfer mixture to large bowl.
3 Sift dry ingredients together twice onto paper. Sift flour mixture a third time evenly over egg mixture. Using whisk or large metal spoon, quickly and lightly fold flour mixture through egg mixture until incorporated. Spread mixture evenly into tins.
4 Bake sponges about 20 minutes or until they spring back when touched lightly in the centre. Turn immediately, top-side up, onto wire racks to cool.
5 Meanwhile, make icing.
6 Beat cream and extract in small bowl with electric mixture until firm peaks form. Place one un-iced sponge on serving plate, spread with jam and whipped cream; top with sliced strawberries.
7 Spread warm icing over remaining sponge; place on top of strawberries. Stand about 15 minutes or until set.
ICING
Sift icing sugar into medium heatproof bowl; stir in butter and enough milk to form a firm paste. Tint with a few drops of food colouring. Stir over simmering water until icing is a pouring consistency.
nutritional count per serving 11.9g total fat (11.2g saturated fat); 1275kJ (305 cal); 45.5g carbohydrate; 3.2g protein; 0.6g fibre

Funky

spiced tea punch

—

tomato, feta and
pancetta frittata

—

roasted red pepper and
goats' cheese terrine

—

iced marshmallow butterflies

—

pistachio and polenta cake
with blood orange syrup

Rival the Mad Hatter's tea party with this twist.

spiced tea punch

preparation time 10 minutes (plus refrigeration time)
cooking time 10 minutes
makes 3 litres (12 cups)

1 litre (4 cups) water
4 tea bags
1 cinnamon stick
2 cardamom pods
4 whole cloves
1 cup (220g) caster sugar
1½ cups (375ml) cold water, extra
½ cup (125ml) fresh lemon juice
2 cups (500ml) fresh orange juice
1 medium lemon (140g), sliced
¼ cup coarsely chopped fresh mint
1 litre (4 cups) mineral water
ice cubes

1 Bring the water to the boil in large saucepan. Add tea bags, spices and sugar, stir over low heat about 3 minutes or until sugar is dissolved. Discard teabags. Refrigerate until cold.
2 Discard spices then stir in the extra water, juices, lemon and mint.
3 Just before serving, stir in mineral water and ice cubes.
nutritional count per 250ml 0.1g total fat (0g saturated fat); 376kJ (90 cal); 22g carbohydrate; 0.4g protein; 0.3g fibre

tomato, feta and pancetta frittata

preparation time 10 minutes
cooking time 25 minutes
makes 6

6 slices (100g) thinly sliced pancetta, chopped coarsely
100g feta cheese, crumbled
¼ cup (20g) finely grated parmesan cheese
⅓ cup coarsely chopped fresh basil
6 eggs, beaten lightly
⅔ cup (160ml) double cream
9 cherry tomatoes (150g), halved

1 Preheat oven to 180°C/160°C fan-assisted. Grease six-hole large (¾-cup/180ml) muffin tin; line bases with baking parchment.
2 Layer pancetta, cheeses and basil in muffin tin holes. Whisk egg and cream in medium bowl; pour into muffin tin holes. Arrange three tomato halves on top of each frittata.
3 Bake, uncovered, about 25 minutes or until frittata is set. Stand in pan 5 minutes before turning out.
nutritional count per frittata 24.1g total fat (13.3g saturated fat); 1170kJ (280 cal); 1.6g carbohydrate; 14.9g protein; 0.4g fibre

roasted red pepper and goats' cheese terrine

preparation time 30 minutes (plus refrigeration time)
cooking time 15 minutes
makes 6

4 large red peppers (1.4kg)
1½ cups (360g) ricotta cheese, chopped coarsely
250g firm goats' cheese, chopped coarsely
¼ cup finely chopped fresh chives
2 tablespoons lemon juice
1 clove garlic, crushed

SPINACH AND WALNUT PESTO
100g baby spinach leaves
¼ cup (25g) roasted walnuts
1 clove garlic, quartered
¼ cup (20g) finely grated parmesan cheese
¼ cup (60ml) olive oil
2 tablespoons lemon juice
1 tablespoon water

1 Preheat oven to 250°C/230°C fan-assisted. Grease six holes of eight-hole (½-cup/125ml) individual loaf tin. Line base and two long sides of each hole with a strip of baking parchment, extending 2cm over sides.
2 Halve peppers; discard seeds and membrane. Place on oven tray; roast; skin-side up, about 15 minutes or until skin blisters and blackens. Cover pepper in plastic or paper 5 minutes; peel away skin. Cut each pepper in half lengthways into 2cm-wide strips. Arrange strips, crossways, over base and two long sides of loaf tin holes, extending 2cm over edges.
3 Combine remaining ingredients in medium bowl; spoon cheese mixture into loaf tin holes, pressing down firmly. Fold pepper strips over to enclose filling. Cover; refrigerate 1 hour.
4 Meanwhile, make spinach and walnut pesto.
5 Carefully remove terrines from tin; serve topped with spinach and walnut pesto.
SPINACH AND WALNUT PESTO
Process spinach, nuts, garlic and cheese until chopped finely. With motor operating, gradually add combined oil, juice and water, in a thin, steady stream until pesto is smooth.
nutritional count per terrine (with pesto) 26.9g total fat (10.8g saturated fat); 1478kJ (354 cal); 9.7g carbohydrate; 17.4g protein; 3.2g fibre

iced marshmallow butterflies

preparation time 35 minutes
cooking time 15 minutes
makes 16

125g butter, softened
¾ cup (165g) caster sugar
1 egg
1½ cups (225g) plain flour
¼ cup (35g) self-raising flour
½ cup (40g) desiccated coconut
⅓ cup (25g) desiccated coconut, extra

TOPPING
¼ cup (80g) strawberry jam, warmed, strained, cooled
160 mini pink marshmallows
160 mini white marshmallows

1 Beat butter, sugar and egg in small bowl with electric mixer until light and fluffy. Stir in sifted flours and coconut, in two batches.
2 Knead dough on floured surface until smooth. Roll dough between sheets of baking parchment until 5mm thick; refrigerate 30 minutes.
3 Preheat oven to 180°C/160°C fan-assisted. Grease oven trays; line with baking parchment.
4 Using 11.5cm butterfly cutter, cut 16 shapes from dough. Place about 3cm apart on trays. Bake about 12 minutes.
5 Press marshmallows onto hot butterfly wings. Brush marshmallows with a little water; sprinkle with extra coconut. Bake about 1 minute or until marshmallows soften slightly.
6 Pipe jam down centre of each butterfly. Cool on wire racks.
nutritional count per biscuit 9.6g total fat (6.7g saturated fat); 1137kJ (272 cal); 42.3g carbohydrate; 3.3g protein; 1.3g fibre

pistachio and polenta cake with blood orange syrup

preparation time 10 minutes
cooking time 1 hour 15 minutes
serves 12

300g soured cream
125g butter, softened
1 cup (220g) caster sugar
2 cups (300g) self-raising flour
½ teaspoon bicarbonate of soda
⅔ cup (110g) polenta
1 teaspoon finely grated blood orange rind
¾ cup (180ml) water
⅔ cup (100g) toasted shelled pistachios

BLOOD ORANGE SYRUP
1 cup (250ml) blood orange juice
1 cup (220g) caster sugar
1 cinnamon stick

1 Preheat oven to 160°C/140°C fan-assisted. Grease deep 20cm-round cake tin; line base and side with baking parchment.
2 Make blood orange syrup.
3 Place soured cream, butter, sugar, sifted flour and soda, polenta, rind and the water in large bowl; beat on low speed with electric mixer until just combined. Increase speed to medium and beat until mixture changes to a slightly paler colour. Stir in nuts. Spread mixture into tin.
4 Bake cake about 1 hour. Stand in tin 10 minutes; turn cake, top-side up, onto wire rack to cool. Serve cake warm or cold with strained blood orange syrup.
BLOOD ORANGE SYRUP
Combine ingredients in small saucepan; bring to the boil, stirring. Reduce heat; simmer, uncovered, about 15 minutes or until syrup thickens. Cool to room temperature.
nutritional count per serving 15.2g total fat (7.6g saturated fat); 1714kJ (412 cal); 64.3g carbohydrate; 5.6g protein; 2.1g fibre
TIP If blood oranges are not available, use ordinary oranges.

With the sweet-tart flesh and brilliant hue of the blood orange, the exotic flavour of cinnamon and the crunch of the pistachio, this cake is about as dramatic as they come.

You are invited to
Dinner
with
Friends

What better excuse to entertain than friendship...

Italian

roasted pepper soup with fried
provolone polenta

—

italian sausage and
three-cheese lasagne

—

rocket, parmesan and
semi-dried tomato salad

—

clove panna cotta with
fresh figs

Be inspired by the Italian flag – green, white and red.

roasted pepper soup with fried provolone polenta

preparation time 15 minutes (plus refrigeration time)
cooking time 1 hour 15 minutes serves 6

4 medium red peppers (800g)
2 cloves garlic, unpeeled
1 tablespoon olive oil
1 medium brown onion (150g), chopped finely
1 teaspoon sweet paprika
3 cups (750ml) water
1 litre (4 cups) chicken stock
½ cup (125ml) double cream
2 teaspoons white sugar
1 tablespoon finely chopped fresh chives

PROVOLONE POLENTA
3½ (875ml) cups water
1 cup (170g) polenta
20g butter
1 cup (120g) coarsely grated provolone cheese

1 Make provolone polenta.
2 Quarter pepeprs, discard seeds and membranes. Roast peppers and garlic under grill or in very hot oven, skin-side up, until skin blisters and blackens.

Cover pepepr pieces in plastic or paper for 5 minutes, peel away skin. Peel garlic; chop coarsely.
3 Heat oil in large saucepan; cook onion, stirring, until softened. Add paprika; cook, stirring, until fragrant. Add the water, stock, pepper and garlic; bring to the boil. Reduce heat; simmer, uncovered, 40 minutes. Cool 15 minutes.
4 Meanwhile, turn polenta onto board, trim edges; halve lengthways, cut each half into 9 finger-sized slices. Cook polenta, in batches, in heated oiled frying pan until browned.
5 Blend or process soup, in batches, until smooth. Return soup to same cleaned pan, add cream and sugar; stir over medium heat until hot.
6 Sprinkle bowls of soup with chives, serve with polenta.
PROVOLONE POLENTA
Oil 20cm x 30cm baking tin; line base and two long sides with baking parchment, extending paper 5cm over long sides. Bring the water to the boil in medium saucepan. Gradually add polenta, stirring constantly. Reduce heat; simmer, stirring, 10 minutes or until thickened. Stir in butter and cheese. Spread polenta into tin, cover; refrigerate about 3 hours or until firm.
nutritional count per serving 21.6g total fat (12g saturated fat); 1484kJ (355 cal); 27.2g carbohydrate; 11.7g protein; 3.3g fibre

italian sausage and three-cheese lasagne

preparation time 1 hour
cooking time 1 hour 40 minutes
serves 6

500g italian sausages
250g frozen chopped spinach, thawed, drained
250g ricotta cheese
¼ teaspoon ground nutmeg
½ cup (40g) finely grated parmesan cheese
1 egg
6 sheets fresh lasagne
250g mozzarella cheese, sliced thinly

TOMATO SAUCE
1 tablespoon olive oil
1 medium onion (150g), chopped finely
1 medium carrot (120g), chopped finely
1 trimmed celery stalk (100g), chopped finely
5 x 8cm long parsley stalks, crushed
2 cloves garlic, crushed
½ cup (125ml) dry red wine
¼ cup (70g) tomato paste
700g bottled tomato pasta sauce

CHEESE SAUCE
50g butter
⅓ cup (50g) plain flour
2 cups (500ml) milk
1½ cups (120g) finely grated parmesan cheese

1 Make tomato sauce. Make cheese sauce.
2 Preheat oven to 200°C/180°C fan-assisted.
3 Cook sausages in oiled large frying pan until browned all over; drain then slice thinly.
4 Combine spinach, ricotta, nutmeg, parmesan and egg in medium bowl.
5 Spread ½ cup of the cheese sauce over base of 20cm x 30cm ovenproof dish. Top with two pasta sheets then spread with half the spinach mixture. Sprinkle with half the sausage; cover with 1 cup of the tomato sauce then half the remaining cheese sauce.
6 Top with two pasta sheets. Spread remaining spinach mixture over pasta; sprinkle with remaining sausage. Spread with 1 cup tomato sauce, then remaining cheese sauce. Top with remaining pasta, then half the remaining tomato sauce. Top with mozzarella; spread with remaining tomato sauce.
7 Bake lasagne, covered, 30 minutes. Uncover, bake further 10 minutes or until browned. Stand 10 minutes before serving.
TOMATO SAUCE
Heat oil in large saucepan, add onion, carrot, celery and parsley; cook, stirring occasionally, until vegetables soften. Add garlic; cook, stirring, 1 minute. Add wine; cook, stirring, until almost evaporated. Discard parsley stalks. Add paste; cook, stirring, 3 minutes. Add sauce; simmer, uncovered, about 15 minutes.
CHEESE SAUCE
Melt butter in medium saucepan, add flour; cook, stirring, until mixture thickens and bubbles. Gradually add milk; stir until mixture boils and thickens. Reduce heat; cook, stirring, 1 minute, remove from heat. Add cheese, stir until melted.
nutritional count per serving 62.4g total fat (30.9g saturated fat); 4305kJ (1030 cal); 58.6g carbohydrate; 52.5g protein; 7.3g fibre

rocket, parmesan and semi-dried tomato salad

preparation time 10 minutes
serves 6

2 tablespoons balsamic vinegar
2 tablespoons olive oil
150g baby rocket leaves
¼ cup (40g) roasted pine nuts
60g drained semi-dried tomatoes, chopped coarsely
½ cup (40g) shaved parmesan cheese

1 Place ingredients in large bowl; toss gently to combine.
nutritional count per serving 13.5g total fat (2.6g saturated fat); 681kJ (163 cal); 4.4g carbohydrate; 5.2g protein; 2.2g fibre

clove panna cotta with fresh figs

preparation time 20 minutes (plus cooling and refrigeration time)
cooking time 10 minutes
serves 6

1 teaspoon whole cloves
1⅔ cups (410ml) whipping cream
1 cup (250ml) milk
3 teaspoons gelatine
¼ cup (55g) caster sugar
1 teaspoon vanilla extract
6 medium fresh figs (360g)
¼ cup (90g) honey

1 Grease six ½-cup (125ml) moulds.
2 Place cloves, cream and milk in medium saucepan; stand 10 minutes.
3 Sprinkle gelatine and sugar over cream mixture; stir over low heat, without boiling, until gelatine and sugar dissolve. Stir in extract. Strain mixture into medium jug; cool to room temperature.
4 Divide mixture among moulds, cover; refrigerate 3 hours or until set.
5 Quarter figs. Stir honey in small saucepan until warm.
6 Turn panna cotta onto serving plates; serve with figs drizzled with warmed honey.
nutritional count per serving 29.3g total fat (19.2g saturated fat); 1639kJ (392 cal); 29.1g carbohydrate; 5.1g protein; 1.3g fibre

Panna cotta is Italian for 'cooked cream'. This light, silky egg custard is a luxurious way to treat your friends. Make the panna cotta in advance for a stress-free evening and simply warm the honey just before serving.

Indian

spicy dhal

—

beef vindaloo

—

raita

—

mango chutney

Slow-cooked and aromatic, this menu is made to share.

spicy dhal

preparation time 15 minutes
cooking time 40 minutes
serves 4

2 tablespoons vegetable oil
2 cloves garlic, crushed
1cm piece fresh ginger (5g), grated finely
1 medium brown onion (150g), chopped finely
3 teaspoons chilli powder
2 teaspoons white sugar
2 teaspoons garam masala
2 teaspoons ground turmeric
½ teaspoon ground coriander
1 tablespoon ground cumin
1 cup (200g) red lentils
400g can crushed tomatoes
1 trimmed celery stick (100g), sliced thinly
2 tablespoons lemon juice
2½ cups (625ml) vegetable stock
⅓ cup (80ml) double cream
2 tablespoons coarsely chopped fresh coriander

1 Heat oil in large heavy-based saucepan; cook garlic, ginger and onion, stirring, until onion softens. Add chilli, sugar, garam masala, turmeric, coriander and cumin; cook, stirring, until fragrant.
2 Add lentils, undrained tomatoes, celery, juice and stock; bring to the boil. Reduce heat; simmer, covered, about 30 minutes or until lentils are tender.
3 Blend or process dhal mixture, in batches, until pureed; return to pan. Add cream and coriander; cook, stirring, until heated through.
nutritional count per serving 20g total fat (7.4g saturated fat); 1584kJ (379 cal); 29g carbohydrate; 16.1g protein; 9.8g fibre

Clockwise from left: Pappadums (purchased); Raita; Beef Vindaloo; Mango chutney; Spicy dhal

beef vindaloo

preparation time 25 minutes (plus refrigeration time)
cooking time 1 hour 30 minutes
serves 4

2 teaspoons cumin seeds
2 teaspoons garam masala
4 cardamom pods, bruised
4cm piece fresh ginger (20g), grated finely
6 cloves garlic, crushed
8 fresh small red thai chillies, chopped finely
2 tablespoons white vinegar
1 tablespoon tamarind concentrate
1.5kg braising steak, diced into 3cm pieces
2 tablespoons ghee
2 large brown onions (400g), chopped finely
1 cinnamon stick
6 cloves
2 teaspoons plain flour
3 cups (750ml) beef stock

1 Dry-fry cumin, garam masala and cardamom in large heated frying pan, strring over low heat until fragrant.
2 Combine roasted spices, ginger, garlic, chilli, vinegar, tamarind and beef in large bowl. Cover; refrigerate 1 hour or overnight.
3 Melt ghee in large frying pan; cook onion, cinnamon and cloves, stirring, until onion is browned lightly.
4 Add beef mixture; cook, stirring, until beef is browned all over. Stir in flour; cook, stirring, 2 minutes. Gradually add stock; bring to the boil, stirring. Reduce heat; simmer, uncovered, 1 hour or until beef is tender.
5 Serve vindaloo with spicy dhal, raita and, if desired, a bowl of crisp pappadums.
nutritional count per serving 26.2g total fat (13.1g saturated fat); 2500kJ (598 cal); 8.9g carbohydrate; 80.1g protein; 2.5g fibre

raita

preparation time 10 minutes
serves 4

½ cucumber (130g), deseeded, grated
  coarsely, drained
1 small brown onion (80g), chopped finely
400g plain yogurt
¼ teaspoon chilli powder
1 teaspoon toasted black mustard seeds
1 tablespoon coarsely chopped fresh coriander
1 tablespoon coarsely chopped fresh mint

1 Combine ingredients in medium bowl.
*nutritional count per tablespoon 0.5g total fat
(0.3g saturated fat); 46kJ (11 cal); 0.8g carbohydrate;
0.7g protein; 0.1g fibre*

mango chutney

*preparation time 25 minutes (plus standing and
cooling time)*
cooking time 1 hour
makes 8 cups

6 medium mangoes (2.6kg), peeled, chopped coarsely
1½ cups (330g) caster sugar
2 cups (500ml) brown vinegar
8cm piece fresh ginger (40g), grated
2 cloves garlic, crushed
¾ cup (120g) raisins
½ teaspoon chilli powder
1 teaspoon ground cinnamon
1 teaspoon ground cumin

1 Place mango, sugar and vinegar in large saucepan;
stir over low heat until sugar dissolves.
2 Add remaining ingredients; simmer, uncovered, stirring
occasionally, about 45 minutes or until mixture is thick.
3 Pour chutney into hot sterilised jars; seal immediately.
*nutritional count per tablespoon 0.1g total fat (0g saturated
fat); 125kJ (30 cal); 6.8g carbohydrate; 0.2g protein;
0.4g fibre*

Yum Cha

pork, peanut and kaffir lime
spring rolls

—

prawn dumplings

—

salt and pepper squid

—

steamed asian greens with
char siu sauce

—

singapore noodles

Make pots of hot chinese tea and let the banquet begin.

pork, peanut and kaffir lime spring rolls

preparation time 50 minutes (plus standing time)
cooking time 20 minutes
makes 20

4 dried shiitake mushrooms
½ cup (75g) roasted unsalted peanuts, chopped finely
2 spring onions, chopped finely
1 medium red pepper (200g), chopped finely
3 fresh kaffir lime leaves, shredded finely
2cm piece fresh ginger (10g), grated
500g minced pork
1 tablespoon soy sauce
2 tablespoons oyster sauce
1 tablespoon chinese cooking wine
20 x 21.5cm square spring roll wrappers (300g)
groundnut oil, for deep frying

1 Cover mushrooms with boiling water in small heatproof bowl. Cover; stand 20 minutes. Drain. Discard stems; chop caps finely.
2 Combine mushrooms in medium bowl with nuts, onion, pepper, lime leaves, ginger, pork, sauces and wine.
3 Spoon rounded tablespoons of the pork filling onto a corner of one wrapper; roll once toward opposing corner to cover filling then fold in two remaining corners to enclose filling. Continue rolling; brush seam with a little water to seal. Repeat process with remaining wrappers and filling.
4 Heat oil in wok; deep-fry spring rolls, in batches, until golden and cooked through. Drain on absorbent paper.
nutritional count per roll 6.9g total fat (1.5g saturated fat); 506kJ (121 cal); 7.1g carbohydrate; 7.3g protein; 0.8g fibre

prawn dumplings

preparation time 40 minutes
cooking time 10 minutes
makes 24

1kg uncooked prawns
¼ cup (50g) bamboo shoots, chopped finely
1 tablespoon finely chopped fresh chives
2 teaspoons sesame oil
2 teaspoons cornflour
24 gow gee wrappers

1 Shell and devein prawns; chop finely.
2 Combine prawns in large bowl with bamboo shoots, chives, oil and cornflour. Blend or process half of the prawn mixture until just smooth. Return to large bowl with remaining prawn mixture; stir to combine.
3 Place one wrapper on your hand; place one heaped teaspoon of the prawn mixture into centre of wrapper. Gently cup your hand and gather sides of wrapper to form pleats, leaving top open. Press base of wrapper on bench to flatten. Repeat with remaining wrappers and prawn mixture.
4 Place dumplings, without touching, in oiled steamer; steam, in batches, over large saucepan of boiling water about 10 minutes.
5 Serve hot with light soy sauce.
nutritional count per dumpling 0.6g total fat (0.1g saturated fat); 105kJ (25 cal); 0.4g carbohydrate; 4.3g protein; 0.1g fibre

salt and pepper squid

preparation time 15 minutes
cooking time 5 minutes
serves 8

500g squid hoods
¾ cup (110g) plain flour
1 tablespoon salt
2 tablespoons ground black pepper
vegetable oil, for deep-frying

CHILLI DRESSING
½ cup (125ml) sweet chilli sauce
1 teaspoon fish sauce
¼ cup (60ml) lime juice
1 clove garlic, crushed

1 Cut squid in half lengthways; score inside surface of each piece. Cut into 2cm-wide strips.
2 Combine flour, salt and pepper in large bowl; add squid. Coat squid in flour mixture; shake off excess.
3 Heat oil in wok; deep-fry squid, in batches, until tender and browned all over, drain on absorbent paper.
4 Make chilli dressing.
5 Serve squid with chilli dressing.
CHILLI DRESSING
Place ingredients in screw-top jar; shake well.
nutritional count per serving 5.6g total fat (0.9g saturated fat); 669kJ (160 cal); 13.7g carbohydrate; 12.6g protein; 2.1g fibre

steamed asian greens with char siu sauce

preparation time 5 minutes
cooking time 10 minutes
serves 8

1 fresh long red chilli, sliced thinly
350g tenderstem broccoli, trimmed
150g mangetout, trimmed
2 baby pak choy (300g), halved
2 tablespoons char siu sauce
2 teaspoons sesame oil
1 tablespoon groundnut oil
1 tablespoon toasted sesame seeds

1 Layer chilli, broccoli, mangetout and pak choy in baking-parchment-lined bamboo steamer. Steam, covered, over wok of simmering water about 5 minutes or until vegetables are just tender.
2 Combine vegetables, sauce and sesame oil in large bowl.
3 Heat groundnut oil in small saucepan until hot; pour oil over vegetable mixture then toss to combine.
4 Serve greens sprinkled with seeds.
nutritional count per serving 4.7g total fat (0.7g saturated fat); 318kJ (76 cal); 3.5g carbohydrate; 3.3g protein; 3.3g fibre

singapore noodles

preparation time 5 minutes
cooking time 10 minutes
serves 8

450g fresh singapore noodles
1 teaspoon groundnut oil
1 small brown onion (80g), sliced finely
2 rashers rindless bacon (130g), chopped finely
3cm piece fresh ginger (15g), grated
1 tablespoon mild curry powder
3 cups (480g) shredded barbecued chicken
6 spring onions, sliced thinly
1½ tablespoons light soy sauce
⅓ cup (80ml) sweet sherry

1 Place noodles in large heatproof bowl, cover with boiling water; separate with fork, drain.
2 Heat oil in wok; stir-fry brown onion, bacon and ginger, about 2 minutes or until onion softens and bacon is crisp. Add curry powder; stir-fry until fragrant.
3 Add noodles and remaining ingredients; stir-fry until hot.
nutritional count per serving 7.6g total fat (2.2g saturated fat); 966kJ (231 cal); 16.4g carbohydrate; 20.7g protein; 1.6g fibre
TIPS You need to purchase a large barbecued chicken weighing about 900g to get the amount of shredded meat needed for this recipe.
Some of the varieties of fresh wheat noodles sold in supermarkets look very similar to one another, the main difference sometimes being only in width. Singapore noodles are a thinner version of hokkien, about the size of cooked spaghetti.

Mezze

pickled cauliflower

—

mini lamb pies

—

spinach filo triangles

—

labne

—

tabbouleh

Mezze is the perfect do-ahead easy entertainer.

pickled cauliflower

preparation time 15 minutes
cooking time 5 minutes
makes 4½ cups

3 cups (750ml) water
1½ cups (375ml) white wine vinegar
¼ cup (55g) table salt
½ small cauliflower (500g), cut into florets
1 medium white turnip (230g), cut into 1cm wedges
8 baby beetroots (200g), unpeeled, cut into wedges
1 clove garlic, sliced thinly

1 Combine the water, vinegar and salt in medium saucepan; bring to the boil. Boil, uncovered, for 3 minutes.
2 Pack vegetables and garlic into hot sterilised 1.5-litre (6-cup) glass jar with tight-fitting lid; pour in enough boiling vinegar mixture to leave 1cm space between vegetable pieces and top of jar. Seal while hot.
3 Store in cool, dark place for at least 3 days before eating; once opened, store jar in refrigerator.
nutritional count per ¼ cup 0.1g total fat (0g saturated fat); 50kJ (12 cal); 1.6g carbohydrate; 0.8g protein; 1g fibre
TIP Serve mezze with purchased baba ghanoush, hummus and pitta bread, if desired.

Clockwise from left: Pickled cauliflower; Mini lamb pies; Spinach fillo triangles; Baba ghanoush (purchased); Tabbouleh; Hummus (purchased); Labne.

mini lamb pies

preparation time 30 minutes (plus standing time)
cooking time 10 minutes
makes 20

1 cup (150g) plain flour
1 teaspoon (4g) dry yeast
½ teaspoon sea salt flakes
1 tablespoon olive oil
½ cup (125ml) warm water
cooking-oil spray

SPICED LAMB TOPPING
100g minced lamb
1 medium tomato (150g), chopped finely
1 teaspoon ground cumin
1 teaspoon ground coriander
1 tablespoon finely chopped fresh coriander
2 teaspoons toasted pine nuts, chopped coarsely

1 Process flour, yeast, salt, oil and enough of the warm water until mixture forms a ball. Place ball of dough in oiled medium bowl; coat dough with oil. Cover; stand in warm place about 1 hour or until dough doubles in size.
2 Meanwhile, make spiced lamb topping.
3 Preheat oven to 200°C/180°C fan-assisted. Oil oven tray.
4 Knead dough on floured surface 5 minutes; roll dough to 2mm thickness. Using 7cm cutter, cut 20 rounds from dough; place rounds on tray. Divide topping among rounds, spreading to edge to completely cover round.
5 Bake pies about 10 minutes or until cooked through.
SPICED LAMB TOPPING
Combine ingredients in small bowl.
nutritional count per pie 1.7g total fat (0.4g saturated fat); 188kJ (45 cal); 5.2g carbohydrate; 2g protein; 0.4g fibre

spinach filo triangles

preparation time 45 minutes
cooking time 15 minutes
makes 16

400g spinach, trimmed, shredded finely
2 teaspoons sumac
2 spring onions, chopped finely
1 tablespoon lemon juice
4 sheets filo pastry
cooking-oil spray

1 Preheat oven to 200°C/180°C fan-assisted. Oil oven tray.
2 Boil, steam or microwave spinach until wilted; drain, squeeze out as much excess liquid as possible. Combine spinach in small bowl with sumac, onion and juice.
3 Cut each pastry sheet lengthways into four strips. Place one strip on board; cover remaining strips with baking parchment, then with damp tea towel.
4 Spray strip with oil; place 1 rounded teaspoon of spinach filling on one corner, 5mm from edge, flatten slightly. Fold opposite corner of strip diagonally across filling to form triangle; continue folding to end of strip, retaining triangular shape. Place filo triangle on tray, seam-side down. Repeat process with remaining strips and filling.
5 Spray tops of filo triangles with oil; bake, uncovered, about 10 minutes or until just crisp and browned lightly.
nutritional count per triangle 0.8g total fat (0.1g saturated fat); 88kJ (21 cal); 2.1g carbohydrate; 1g protein; 0.8g fibre

labne

preparation time 20 minutes (plus refrigeration time)
makes 24 balls

3 cups (840g) greek-style plain yogurt
3 teaspoons salt
¼ cup (60ml) olive oil

1 Combine yogurt and salt in medium bowl; pour into muslin-lined large sieve or colander set over large bowl. Gather corners of muslin together, twist, then tie with kitchen string. Place heavy can on muslin to weight yogurt mixture; refrigerate 24 to 36 hours until yogurt thickens (yogurt will lose about half its weight in water; discard water in bowl).
2 Place thickened yogurt in small bowl; discard muslin. Roll level tablespoons of yogurt into balls; place balls on platter, drizzle with oil.
nutritional count per ball 3.6g total fat (1.1g saturated fat); 188kJ (45 cal); 1.6g carbohydrate; 1.6g protein; 0g fibre
TIP This recipe must be prepared at least 2 days before you want to serve the mezze.
Labne will keep for up to 2 months in the refrigerator; pack balls into clean glass jar with tight-fitting lid, cover with olive oil, seal jar tightly before refrigerating.

tabbouleh

preparation time 30 minutes (plus refrigeration time)
makes 4½ cups

¼ cup (40g) bulgar wheat
3 medium tomatoes (450g)
3 cups coarsely chopped fresh flat-leaf parsley
2 spring onions, chopped finely
¼ cup finely chopped fresh mint
¼ cup (60ml) lemon juice
¼ cup (60ml) extra virgin olive oil

1 Place bulgar wheat in small shallow bowl. Halve tomatoes; using small spoon, scoop pulp from tomato halves over bulgar wheat. Chop remaining tomato flesh finely; spread over bulgar wheat so surface is completely covered with tomato. Cover bowl; refrigerate 1 hour.
2 Place bulgar wheat mixture in large bowl with remaining ingredients; toss gently to combine.
nutritional count per ¼ cup 3.3g total fat (0.5g saturated fat); 180kJ (43 cal); 2.2g carbohydrate; 0.8g protein; 1.3g fibre
TIP Chop the mint just before assembling the tabbouleh in the bowl as it has a tendency to blacken and go limp after it's cut.

After Work

sang choy bow

—

baked mussels infused with
asian flavours

—

coconut rice with mango

Don't fear after-work entertaining; just keep it simple.

sang choy bow

preparation time 15 minutes
cooking time 15 minutes
serves 6

1 tablespoon sesame oil
1 medium brown onion (150g), chopped finely
2 cloves garlic, crushed
3cm piece fresh ginger (15g), grated
750g lean minced pork
¼ cup (60ml) water
150g shiitake mushrooms, chopped finely
¼ cup (60ml) light soy sauce
¼ cup (60ml) oyster sauce
2 tablespoons lime juice
3 cups beansprouts (240g)
6 spring onions, sliced thinly
⅓ cup coarsely chopped fresh coriander
18 large butterhead lettuce leaves

1 Heat oil in wok; stir-fry brown onion, garlic and ginger until onion softens. Add pork; stir-fry until changed in colour.
2 Add the water, mushrooms, sauces and juice; stir-fry until mushrooms are tender. Remove from heat. Add beansprouts, spring onion and coriander; toss to combine.
3 Spoon filling into lettuce leaves to serve.
nutritional count per serving 13.5g total fat (3.8g saturated fat); 1150kJ (275 cal); 6g carbohydrate; 30.8g protein; 3.6g fibre
TIP The size of the butterhead lettuce available will determine whether you buy one or two of them in order to get 18 large leaves. You could also use large iceberg leaves.

baked mussels infused with asian flavours

preparation time 20 minutes
cooking time 20 minutes
serves 6

2kg large black mussels
8cm piece fresh ginger (40g), cut into matchsticks
2 cloves garlic, sliced thinly
3 kaffir lime leaves, shredded finely
2 fresh long red chillies, sliced thinly
1 large carrot (180g), cut into matchsticks
1 large red pepper (250g), cut into matchsticks
⅓ cup (80ml) water
⅓ cup (80ml) kecap manis
⅓ cup (80ml) lime juice
1 cup beansprouts (80g)
⅔ cup loosely packed fresh coriander leaves

1 Preheat oven to 220°C/200°C fan-assisted.
2 Scrub mussels; remove beards. Combine mussels in large baking dish with ginger, garlic, lime leaves, chilli, carrot, pepper, the water, kecap manis and juice.
3 Cook mussels, covered, in oven about 20 minutes or until mussels open (discard any that do not). Stir in beansprouts and coriander.
nutritional count per serving 1.4g total fat (0.4g saturated fat); 364kJ (87 cal); 7.2g carbohydrate; 10.2g protein; 2.2g fibre

coconut rice with mango

preparation time 15 minutes
serves 6

You will need to cook about 1 cup of medium-grain white rice for this recipe.

1¾ cups (430ml) whipping cream
¾ cup (180ml) coconut cream
½ cup (80g) icing sugar
3 cups (450g) cooked medium-grain white rice
2 medium mangoes (860g), chopped coarsely
¾ cup (35g) toasted flaked coconut

1 Beat cream, coconut cream and sugar in small bowl with electric mixer until soft peaks form.
2 Place rice in large bowl; fold in cream mixture. Cover; refrigerate while preparing mango.
3 Blend or process three-quarters of the mango until smooth; slice remaining mango into thin strips.
4 Divide rice mixture and mango puree, in alternate layers, among six 1-cup (250ml) glasses; top with mango strips and coconut.
nutritional count per serving 37g total fat (26.3g saturated fat); 2349kJ (562 cal); 50.9g carbohydrate; 5.2g protein; 3.5g fibre

Games Night

ginger beer fizz

—

falafel rolls

—

mini moroccan pies

—

turkish-style pizza with
minted yogurt

Casual and relaxed is the name of the game.

ginger beer fizz

preparation time 5 minutes
serves 1

15ml vodka
15ml white rum
15ml white tequila
15ml gin
10ml Cointreau
1 tablespoon lime juice
½ cup ice cubes
½ cup (125ml) ginger beer

1 Combine vodka, rum, tequila, gin, Cointreau, juice, and ice in cocktail shaker; shake vigorously.
2 Pour into 250ml highball glass. Top with ginger beer; garnish with lime slice, if desired.
nutritional count per serving 0.1g total fat (0g saturated fat); 1016kJ (243 cal); 24.2g carbohydrate; 0.2g protein; 0g fibre
TIP When making several serves, make up to three quantities of recipe in cocktail shaker at a time.

falafel rolls

preparation time 25 minutes
cooking time 45 minutes
serves 6

1 teaspoon olive oil
1 medium brown onion (150g), chopped finely
1 clove garlic, crushed
2 teaspoons ground cumin
1 teaspoon ground coriander
½ teaspoon chilli powder
420g can chickpeas, rinsed, drained
1 cup coarsely chopped fresh flat-leaf parsley
2 teaspoons plain flour
2 teaspoons olive oil, extra
6 slices lavash bread (150g) (or flatbread)
2 cups tabbouleh

BABA GHANOUSH
1 small aubergine (230g)
cooking-oil spray
2 teaspoons tahini
1 tablespoon lemon juice
1 tablespoon water
1 clove garlic, crushed

1 Preheat oven to 200°C/180°C fan-assisted.
2 Make baba ghanoush.
3 Meanwhile, heat oil in small frying pan; cook onion and garlic, stirring, until onion softens. Add spices; cook, stirring, until fragrant.
4 Blend or process chickpeas until chopped finely. Add onion mixture and parsley; blend until combined. Stir in flour.
5 Using hands, shape mixture into twelve patties. Place on oiled oven tray; brush with extra oil. Cook, uncovered, in oven about 20 minutes or until browned both sides.
6 Roll each piece of lavash into a cone; secure with a toothpick. Divide tabbouleh and patties among cones. Serve with baba ghanoush.

BABA GHANOUSH
Pierce aubergine all over with fork. Place aubergine on oiled oven tray; spray with oil. Roast, uncovered, about 40 minutes or until tender. When cool enough to handle, peel aubergine. Blend or process aubergine flesh with remaining ingredients until smooth.

nutritional count per serving 13.7g total fat (2.2g saturated fat); 1074kJ (257 cal); 21.4g carbohydrate; 7.9g protein; 8.7g fibre

Use the tabbouleh recipe on page 150 – or save yourself some time and buy freshly prepared tabbouleh from a deli or from a large supermarket.

mini moroccan pies

preparation time 25 minutes
cooking time 35 minutes
makes 24

1 tablespoon vegetable oil
1 small brown onion (80g), chopped finely
1 clove garlic, crushed
400g minced lamb
2 teaspoons ground cumin
1 cup (280g) undrained crushed tomatoes
¼ cup (40g) toasted pine nuts
2 tablespoons finely chopped raisins
2 tablespoons finely chopped fresh coriander
3 sheets ready-rolled shortcrust pastry
2 sheets ready-rolled puff pastry
1 egg, beaten lightly

1 Heat oil in medium frying pan; cook onion and garlic, stirring, until onion softens. Add mince; cook, stirring, until mince changes colour. Add cumin; cook, stirring, until fragrant. Add tomato; bring to the boil. Reduce heat; simmer, uncovered, about 10 minutes or until thickened slightly. Stir in nuts, raisins and coriander; cool.
2 Preheat oven to 200°C/180°C fan-assisted. Grease two 12-hole deep flat-based patty tins.
3 Cut 24 rounds from shortcrust pastry using 7cm-round cutter; press one round into each patty tin hole. Spoon lamb mixture into pastry cases.
4 Cut 24 rounds from puff pastry using 6cm-round cutter; top pies with puff pastry lids. Press edges firmly to seal; brush lids with a little beaten egg. Using sharp knife, cut a small slit into top of each pie. Bake, uncovered, about 20 minutes or until browned lightly.
nutritional count per pie 12.2g total fat (5.5g saturated fat); 828kJ (198 cal); 15.6g carbohydrate; 6.2g protein; 0.9g fibre

turkish-style pizza with minted yogurt

preparation time 15 minutes
cooking time 35 minutes
serves 6

1 tablespoon olive oil
1 medium onion (150g), chopped finely
1 clove garlic, crushed
500g minced beef
¼ teaspoon cayenne pepper
2 teaspoons ground cumin
½ teaspoon ground cinnamon
1½ teaspoons mixed spice
1 teaspoon grated lemon rind
2 tablespoons lemon juice
1 cup (250ml) beef stock
2 medium tomatoes (280g), chopped finely
⅓ cup (50g) toasted pine nuts
¼ cup coarsely chopped fresh parsley
¼ cup coarsely chopped fresh mint
2 x 500g turkish bread
200g plain yogurt
1 tablespoon chopped fresh mint, extra

1 Preheat oven to 220°C/200°C fan-assisted.
2 Heat oil in large frying pan; cook onion and garlic, stirring, until onion is soft. Add mince; cook until browned. Add pepper and spices; stir until fragrant.
3 Add rind, juice, stock and tomatoes to pan; cook, stirring, over medium heat until most of the liquid is evaporated. Remove from heat; stir in pine nuts and herbs.
4 Place bread on oven trays; press mince mixture evenly over the top of the bread, leaving a 3cm border.
5 Cover pizzas with foil; bake for 10 minutes. Remove foil; bake another 10 minutes until browned lightly.
6 Serve cut into thick slices topped with combined yogurt and extra mint.
nutritional count per serving 22g total fat (5.4g saturated fat); 2809kJ (672 cal); 79g carbohydrate; 35.6g protein; 6.2g fibre

You are invited to a

Formal Dinner Party

British

beef and barley soup

–

roast beef with
yorkshire puddings

–

hasselback potatoes

–

leeks, courgettes and asparagus
with chive butter

–

steamed ginger pudding

Satisfyingly traditional British goodness.

beef and barley soup

preparation time 30 minutes
cooking time 1 hour 45 minutes
serves 6

1 tablespoon olive oil
500g braising steak, trimmed, diced into 2cm pieces
2 cloves garlic, crushed
2 medium brown onions (300g), chopped finely
¾ cup (150g) pearl barley
3 cups (750ml) beef stock
1.5 litres (6 cups) water
1 bay leaf
1 sprig fresh rosemary
1 sprig fresh thyme
2 medium potatoes (400g), diced into 1cm pieces
2 medium carrots (240g), diced into 1cm pieces
2 medium courgettes (240g), diced into 1cm pieces
2 medium yellow patty-pan squash (60g), diced into
1cm pieces
100g chestnut mushrooms, chopped coarsely
½ cup finely chopped fresh flat-leaf parsley

1 Heat half the oil in large saucepan; cook beef, in batches, until browned.
2 Heat remaining oil in same pan; cook garlic and onion, stirring, until onion softens. Return beef to pan with barley, stock, the water, bay leaf, rosemary and thyme, bring to the boil. Reduce heat; simmer, covered, about 1 hour or until beef and barley are tender, skimming fat occasionally.
3 Add potato, carrot, courgette, squash and mushrooms to soup; simmer, covered, about 25 minutes or until vegetables are softened. Remove and discard bay leaf, rosemary and thyme.
4 Serve bowls of soup sprinkled with parsley.
nutritional count per serving 8.8g total fat (2.6g saturated fat); 1350kJ (323 cal); 30g carbohydrate; 26.9g protein; 7.8g fibre

roast beef with yorkshire puddings

preparation time 35 minutes (plus refrigeration and standing time)
cooking time 2 hours
serves 8

2kg corner piece beef topside roast
2 cups (500ml) dry red wine
2 bay leaves
6 black peppercorns
¼ cup (70g) wholegrain mustard
4 cloves garlic, sliced
4 sprigs fresh thyme
1 medium brown onion (150g), chopped coarsely
2 medium carrots (240g), chopped coarsely
1 large leek (500g), chopped coarsely
2 trimmed celery stalks (200g), chopped coarsely
2 tablespoons olive oil
2 tablespoons plain flour
1½ cups (375ml) beef stock

YORKSHIRE PUDDINGS
1 cup (150g) plain flour
½ teaspoon salt
2 eggs, beaten lightly
½ cup (125ml) milk
½ cup (125ml) water

1 Combine beef, wine, bay leaves, peppercorns, mustard, garlic, thyme and onion in large bowl, cover; refrigerate 3 hours or overnight.
2 Preheat oven to 180°C/160°C fan-assisted.
3 Drain beef over medium bowl; reserve 1 cup (250ml) of marinade. Combine carrot, leek and celery in large baking dish, top with beef; brush beef with oil. Bake, uncovered, about 1½ hours or until browned and cooked as desired.
4 Make batter for yorkshire puddings.
5 Remove beef from dish, wrap in foil; stand 20 minutes before serving. Remove vegetables with slotted spoon; discard vegetables. Pour pan juices into jug, stand 2 minutes, then pour off excess oil; reserve 1½ tablespoons oil for yorkshire puddings and 2 tablespoons of pan juices for gravy.
6 Increase oven temperature to 200°C/180°C fan-assisted.
7 Divide reserved oil for puddings among 16 holes of mini (1½ tablespoons/30ml) muffin tins; heat in oven for 2 minutes. Divide pudding batter among muffin tin holes; bake about 10 minutes or until puddings are puffed and golden.
8 Meanwhile, heat reserved pan juices for gravy in same baking dish, add flour; cook, stirring, until bubbling. Gradually add reserved marinade and stock; cook, stirring, until mixture boils and thickens, strain gravy into jug.
9 Serve beef with yorkshire puddings and gravy, and roasted potatoes and greens, if desired.
YORKSHIRE PUDDINGS
Sift flour and salt into bowl, make well in centre; add combined egg, milk and water all at once. Using wooden spoon, gradually stir in flour from side of bowl until batter is smooth; cover, stand 30 minutes.
nutritional count per serving 2.8g total fat (0.9g saturated fat); 397kJ (95 cal); 3.9g carbohydrate; 11.2g protein; 0.7g fibre

hasselback potatoes

preparation time 20 minutes
cooking time 1 hour 10 minutes
serves 6

1.5kg desiree potatoes, peeled, halved horizontally
50g butter, melted
2 tablespoons olive oil
¼ cup (25g) packaged breadcrumbs
½ cup (60g) finely grated cheddar cheese

1 Preheat oven to 180°C/160°C fan-assisted.
2 Place one potato half, cut-side down, on chopping board; place a chopstick on board along each side of potato. Slice potato thinly, cutting through to chopsticks to prevent cutting all the way through. Repeat with remaining potato halves.
3 Coat potato halves in combined butter and oil in medium baking dish; place, rounded-side up, in single layer. Roast, uncovered, 45 minutes, brushing frequently with oil mixture. Continue roasting without brushing about 15 minutes or until potatoes are cooked through.
4 Sprinkle combined breadcrumbs and cheese over potatoes; roast, uncovered, further 10 minutes or until topping is browned.
nutritional count per serving 15.2g total fat (6.6g saturated fat); 1070kJ (256 cal); 22.1g carbohydrate; 6.7g protein; 2.5g fibre

leeks, courgettes and asparagus with chive butter

preparation time 10 minutes
cooking time 8 minutes
serves 6

1 litre (4 cups) vegetable stock
6 small leeks (1.2kg), halved lengthways
8 small courgettes (720g), halved lengthways
200g asparagus, trimmed
50g butter
1 clove garlic, crushed
2 tablespoons chopped fresh chives

1 Bring stock to the boil in large shallow frying pan; add leeks and courgettes. Reduce heat; simmer gently, uncovered, 3 minutes.
2 Add asparagus, simmer, 3 minutes or until vegetables are just tender, turning occasionally. Drain.
3 Melt butter in same frying pan, add garlic and chives. Return vegetables to pan; toss to coat in butter mixture.
nutritional count per serving 7.9g total fat (4.8g saturated fat); 460kJ (110 cal); 4.3g carbohydrate; 4.2g protein; 2.7g fibre

steamed ginger pudding

preparation time 15 minutes
cooking time 1 hour
serves 6

60g butter
¼ cup (90g) golden syrup
½ teaspoon bicarbonate of soda
1 cup (150g) self-raising flour
2 teaspoons ground ginger
½ cup (125ml) milk
1 egg

SYRUP
⅓ cup (115g) golden syrup
2 tablespoons water
30g butter

1 Grease 1.25-litre (5-cup) pudding basin.
2 Stir butter and syrup in small saucepan over low heat until smooth. Remove from heat, stir in soda; transfer mixture to medium bowl. Stir in sifted dry ingredients then combined milk and egg, in two batches.
3 Spread mixture into basin. Cover with pleated baking parchment and foil; secure with lid.
4 Place basin in large saucepan with enough boiling water to come halfway up side of basin; cover pan with tight fitting lid. Boil 1 hour, replenishing water as necessary to maintain level. Stand pudding 5 minutes before turning onto plate.
5 Meanwhile, make syrup.
6 Serve pudding topped with syrup and, if desired, cream or custard.
SYRUP
Stir ingredients in small saucepan over heat until smooth; bring to the boil. Reduce heat; simmer, uncovered, 2 minutes.
nutritional count per serving 14.3g total fat (9g saturated fat); 1367kJ (327 cal); 44.5g carbohydrate; 4.5g protein; 1g fibre

"And the root of all happiness? The humble art of cooking."

Mrs McKee, former cook to Her Majesty, Queen Elizabeth II

Modern

tuna, whitefish and
salmon carpaccio

—

roast butternut squash and
goats' curd salad

—

pork belly and spicy sausage
with braised lettuce

—

nougat semifreddo in
white chocolate cones

Contemporary influences from around the world.

tuna, whitefish and salmon carpaccio

*preparation time 50 minutes (plus freezing and
refrigeration times)*
serves 6

350g piece sashimi tuna
350g piece sashimi white fish
350g piece sashimi salmon
⅓ cup (80ml) lime juice
⅔ cup (160ml) lemon juice
4cm piece fresh ginger (20g), grated finely
¼ cup (60ml) soy sauce
1 baby fennel (130g)
⅓ cup (80ml) extra virgin olive oil
1 tablespoon drained baby capers, rinsed
½ small red onion (50g), sliced thinly
1 teaspoon finely chopped fresh dill

1 Tightly wrap fish, separately, in cling film; freeze about
1 hour or until slightly firm.
2 Unwrap fish then slice as thinly as possible. Arrange
slices on separate serving platters; drizzle tuna with lime
juice, drizzle white fish and salmon with lemon juice. Cover
platters; refrigerate 1 hour.
3 Meanwhile, combine ginger and sauce in small jug;
stand while fish is under refrigeration. Finely chop enough
fennel leaves to make 1 level tablespoon; discard remaining
leaves. Chop fennel bulb finely.
4 Drain excess juice from platters. To serve, divide fish
among serving plates: drizzle tuna with strained sauce
mixture; sprinkle white fish with fennel, leaves and half of the
oil; sprinkle salmon with capers, onion, dill and remaining oil.
Serve carpaccio with crusty bread, if desired.
*nutritional count per serving 21.1g total fat (4.5g saturated
fat); 1488kJ (356 cal); 2.3g carbohydrate; 39.1g protein;
0.6g fibre*

roast butternut squash and goats' curd salad

preparation time 15 minutes
cooking time 15 minutes
serves 6

500g butternut squash, chopped finely
2 tablespoons olive oil
2 cloves garlic, sliced thinly
2 tablespoons finely chopped fresh sage
½ cup (70g) pecans, chopped coarsely
6 radicchio treviso leaves
125g goats' cheese
2 tablespoons olive oil, extra
1½ tablespoons lemon juice

1 Preheat oven to 220°C/200°C fan-assisted.
2 Toss squash and oil on an oven tray; roast about 10 minutes. Add garlic and sage; roast further 5 minutes or until squash is tender. Stir in pecans.
3 Divide squash mixture among treviso leaves; top with cheese. Drizzle with combined extra oil and juice, and top with extra sage, if desired.
nutritional count per serving 24.2g total fat (4.7g saturated fat); 1120kJ (268 cal); 6.4g carbohydrate; 5.8g protein; 2.3g fibre

pork belly and spicy sausage with braised lettuce

preparation time 40 minutes (plus refrigeration time)
cooking time 40 minutes
serves 6

4 merguez sausages (320g)
200g minced pork
1 teaspoon finely chopped fresh thyme
500g boned belly of pork, rind removed
1 cup (220g) sugar
½ cup (125ml) apple juice
1¼ cup (310ml) chicken stock
20g butter
2 large butterhead lettuces (1kg), trimmed, shredded finely

1 Using sharp knife, slit sausage skins; discard skins. Combine sausagemeat in medium bowl with minced pork and thyme. Roll mixture into sausage shape measuring about 5cm in diameter and 20cm in length. Wrap sausage tightly in baking parchment then foil, twisting ends tightly to seal. Wrap sausage once again, this time in cling film, twisting ends tightly; refrigerate 1 hour.
2 Meanwhile, cut pork belly, across grain, into 1cm slices; cut each slice in half. Cook pork in large non-stick frying pan about 10 minutes, pressing down with back of spoon until browned and crisp. Drain on absorbent paper.
3 Cook sausage in large saucepan of boiling water, covered, 30 minutes.
4 Meanwhile, combine sugar and apple juice in large heavy-based saucepan. Stir over heat, without boiling, until sugar dissolves; bring to the boil. Reduce heat; simmer, uncovered, without stirring, about 10 minutes or until mixture is browned lightly. Gradually add 1 cup of the stock, stirring until apple sauce is smooth.
5 Melt butter in large saucepan; cook lettuce, stirring, 5 minutes. Add remaining stock; cook, uncovered, until stock evaporates.
6 Reheat apple sauce until almost boiling; add pork, stir about 2 minutes or until pork is heated through.
7 Remove sausage from wrapping; cut into 12 slices. Divide lettuce mixture, sausage and pork among serving plates; drizzle with apple sauce.
nutritional count per serving 35.9g total fat (13.9g saturated fat); 2002kJ (479 cal); 8.1g carbohydrate; 30.3g protein; 3.5g fibre

nougat semifreddo in white chocolate cones

preparation time 35 minutes (plus freezing time)
cooking time 5 minutes
makes 6

250g white eating chocolate, melted
2 eggs
¼ cup (55g) caster sugar
1½ cups (375ml) whipping cream, whipped
1 teaspoon vanilla extract
100g almond nougat, chopped finely
100g caramelised almonds, chopped coarsely

DARK CHOCOLATE SAUCE
⅔ cup (160ml) double cream
200g good-quality dark eating chocolate,
    chopped finely

1 Fold six 30cm squares of baking parchment in half diagonally to form a triangle. Twist each triangle to make a cone shape. Secure with a staple at least 7cm from where the corners meet at the top. Trim rim evenly. Cones should measure 15cm in height.
2 Using a long-stemmed teaspoon, coat inside of paper cone with white chocolate. Stand each cone in a tall glass to set.
3 Beat eggs and sugar in small bowl with electric mixer until thick and foamy. Transfer to large bowl; fold in whipped cream and vanilla, then nougat and three-quarters of the almonds. Spoon mixture into white chocolate cones; freeze several hours or overnight, until set.
4 Make dark chocolate sauce.
5 To unmould semi-freddo, carefully remove staple and baking parchment from cones, place each in centre of serving plate; stand for up to 15 minutes.
6 Serve semi-freddo drizzled with warm chocolate sauce and sprinkled with remaining almonds.
DARK CHOCOLATE SAUCE
Bring cream to the boil in small saucepan; pour over chocolate in medium bowl, whisk until smooth.
nutritional count per serving 67.3g total fat (38.4g saturated fat); 3954kJ (946 cal); 74g carbohydrate; 11.6g protein; 1.5g fibre

Fusion

vodka-cured gravlax

—

seafood ravioli with
sesame dressing

—

braised sweet ginger duck

—

chocolate gulab jaman with
orange cinnamon syrup

Combine culinary traditions for a showstopping meal.

vodka-cured gravlax

preparation time 10 minutes (plus refrigeration time)
makes 12

2 teaspoons sea salt
½ teaspoon finely ground black pepper
2 teaspoons sugar
2 teaspoons vodka
150g salmon fillet, skin on
12 mini toasts
SOUR CREAM SAUCE
2 tablespoons soured cream
1 teaspoon drained baby capers, rinsed
1 teaspoon lemon juice
1 teaspoon finely chopped drained cornichons
¼ small red onion (25g), chopped finely

1 Combine salt, pepper, sugar and vodka in small bowl.
2 Remove bones from fish; place fish, skin-side down, on piece of cling film. Spread vodka mixture over flesh side of fish; enclose securely in cling film. Refrigerate overnight, turning parcel several times.
3 Combine ingredients for the soured cream sauce in a small bowl.
4 Slice fish thinly; spread sauce on toasts, top with fish.
nutritional count per serving 2.4g total fat (1.1g saturated fat); 234kJ (56 cal); 4.7g carbohydrate; 3.2g protein; 0.2g fibre

seafood ravioli with sesame dressing

preparation time 30 minutes
cooking time 10 minutes
serves 6

400g uncooked prawns, peeled, chopped coarsely
150g red snapper fillets, chopped coarsely
2 cloves garlic, crushed
3cm piece fresh ginger (15g), grated finely
1 teaspoon sesame oil
18 scallops on the shell
36 wonton wrappers
1 egg white, beaten lightly
1 cup loosely packed coriander leaves
3 spring onions, sliced thinly
SESAME DRESSING
¼ cup (60ml) kecap manis
2 tablespoons rice wine vinegar
1 teaspoon sesame oil
1 long red chilli, sliced thinly

1 Process prawns, fish, garlic, ginger and oil until almost smooth. Remove scallops from shells.
2 Place a heaped teaspoon of the prawn filling in the centre of 18 wonton wrappers, then one scallop on top of the filling. Lightly brush edges with egg white. Place another wrapper on top, pressing edges firmly to seal.
3 Using the blunt edge of a 5.5cm round cutter, gently press around the filling to seal. Then, using a 7cm cutter, cut the wontons into rounds; discard excess wonton pastry. Transfer rounds to tea-towel-lined tray.
4 Place ingredients for sesame dressing in screw-top jar; shake well.
5 Cook ravioli, in two batches, in large saucepan of simmering water about 3 minutes or until seafood is just cooked through. Remove ravioli with slotted spoon; drain on absorbent paper.
6 Divide ravioli among serving plates, drizzle with dressing and top with combined coriander and onion.
nutritional count per serving 2.9g total fat (0.6g saturated fat); 468kJ (112 cal); 2.3g carbohydrate; 18.6g protein; 0.5g fibre

braised sweet ginger duck

preparation time 20 minutes
cooking time 1 hour 50 minutes
serves 6

2.4kg duck
3½ cups (875ml) water
¾ cup (180ml) chinese cooking wine
½ cup (125ml) soy sauce
⅓ cup (75g) firmly packed brown sugar
2 whole star anise
3 spring onions, halved
3 cloves garlic, quartered
10cm piece fresh ginger (50g), unpeeled, chopped coarsely
2 teaspoons sea salt
1 teaspoon five-spice powder
800g baby pak choy, halved

1 Preheat oven to 180°C/160°C fan-assisted.
2 Discard neck from duck, wash duck; pat dry with absorbent paper. Score duck in thickest parts of skin; cut duck in half through breastbone and along both sides of backbone, discard backbone. Tuck wings under duck.
3 Place duck, skin-side down, in medium shallow baking dish; add combined water, wine, soy, sugar, star anise, onion, garlic and ginger. Cook, covered, in oven about 1 hour or until duck is cooked as desired.
4 Increase oven temperature to 240°C/220°C fan-assisted.
5 Remove duck from braising liquid; strain liquid through muslin-lined sieve into large saucepan. Place duck, skin-side up, on wire rack in same dish. Rub combined salt and five-spice all over duck; roast duck about 30 minutes or until skin is crisp.
6 Skim fat from surface of braising liquid; bring to the boil. Reduce heat; simmer, uncovered, 10 minutes. Add pak choy; simmer, covered, 5 minutes or until pak choy is just tender.
7 Cut duck halves into two pieces; divide pak choy, braising liquid and duck among plates. Serve with steamed jasmine rice, if desired.
nutritional count per serving 84.5g total fat (25.3g saturated fat); 4025kJ (963 cal); 15.6g carbohydrate; 32.6g protein; 2.3g fibre

chocolate gulab jaman with orange cinnamon syrup

preparation time 20 minutes
cooking time 10 minutes
serves 6

2 cups (500ml) water
2 cups (440g) caster sugar
4 x 5cm strips orange rind
1 cinnamon stick
1 tablespoon orange-flavoured liqueur
⅓ cup (50g) self-raising flour
2 tablespoons full-cream milk powder
1 tablespoon cocoa powder
100g cream cheese, softened
18 chocolate-coated raisins
vegetable oil, for deep-frying

1 Stir the water, sugar, rind and cinnamon in medium saucepan over heat, without boiling, until sugar dissolves. Bring to the boil; boil, uncovered, without stirring, 5 minutes. Remove syrup from heat; stir in liqueur. Cool.
2 Sift flour, milk powder and cocoa into medium bowl; add cheese, mix to a soft dough with hand. Turn onto floured surface; knead 10 minutes. Roll one heaped teaspoon of dough around each chocolate raisin.
3 Heat oil in deep pan or wok; deep-fry balls, in batches, about 2 minutes or until browned. Drain on absorbent paper. Place gulab jaman in syrup; stand 1 hour before serving.
nutritional count per serving 10g total fat (4.7g saturated fat); 1885kJ (451 cal); 84.4g carbohydrate; 3.7g protein; 0.5g fibre

"Indian sweetmeats and sweet makers are a world unto themselves, a world that draws anyone who has a very sweet tooth into a spiral of temptation."
Charmaine Solomon, *Asian Food*

Thai Banquet

tom ka gai

—

spicy thai beef salad with
nam jim dressing

—

chicken panang curry

—

pad thai

—

yellow coconut rice

A delicate balancing act of hot, sweet, salty and sour.

tom ka gai

preparation time 15 minutes
cooking time 35 minutes
serves 12

1.5 litres (6 cups) chicken stock
4cm piece fresh galangal (20g), sliced thinly
2 x 10cm sticks fresh lemongrass (40g),
    cut into 5cm pieces
2 fresh kaffir lime leaves
2 teaspoons coarsely chopped coriander root and stem
600g chicken thigh fillets, sliced thinly
200g canned straw mushrooms, rinsed, drained
1½ cup (375ml) coconut milk
2 tablespoons lime juice
2 tablespoons fish sauce
2 teaspoons grated palm sugar
⅓ cup loosely packed fresh coriander leaves
3 fresh small red thai chillies, sliced thinly
2 fresh kaffir lime leaves, extra, shredded finely
10cm stick fresh lemongrass (20g), extra, sliced thinly

1 Bring stock, galangal, lemongrass pieces, whole lime leaves and coriander root and stem mixture to the boil in large saucepan. Reduce heat; simmer, covered, 5 minutes. Remove from heat; stand 10 minutes. Strain broth through muslin-lined sieve or colander into large heatproof bowl; discard solids.
2 Return broth to same cleaned pan, add chicken and mushrooms; bring to the boil. Reduce heat; simmer, uncovered, 5 minutes or until chicken is cooked through.
3 Stir in coconut milk, juice, sauce and sugar; cook, stirring, until hot (do not allow to boil). Remove from heat; stir in coriander leaves, chilli, shredded lime leaf and sliced lemongrass.
nutritional count per serving 10.7g total fat (7g saturated fat); 656kJ (157 cal); 2.9g carbohydrate; 12.1g protein; 1g fibre

spicy thai beef salad with nam jim dressing

preparation time 15 minutes
cooking time 10 minutes
serves 12

600g beef rump steak
1 tablespoon macadamia oil
200g herb salad mix
1 cucumber (260g), deseeded, sliced thinly
3 purple shallots (75g), sliced thinly
¾ cup (120g) toasted cashews
¼ cup firmly packed coriander leaves

NAM JIM DRESSING
4 spring onions, sliced thinly
1 clove garlic, peeled, quartered
1 fresh small red thai chilli, chopped finely
2 teaspoons finely chopped coriander root
1 tablespoon brown sugar
2 teaspoons fish sauce
2 tablespoons lime juice
¼ cup (60ml) macadamia oil

1 Rub steak with oil; cook on heated oiled grill plate (or grill or barbecue) over high heat until cooked as desired. Transfer steak to plate, stand, covered, 10 minutes; slice thinly.
2 Make nam jim dressing.
3 Arrange salad leaves, cucumber, shallots, steak and cashews on a serving platter. Drizzle with dressing and, if desired, top with coriander leaves.
NAM JIM DRESSING
Blend or process ingredients until smooth.
nutritional count per serving 14.5g total fat (3.3g saturated fat); 844kJ (202 cal); 3.9g carbohydrate; 13.6g protein; 1.5g fibre

chicken panang curry

preparation time 30 minutes
cooking time 25 minutes
serves 12

2 x 400ml cans coconut milk
2 tablespoons grated palm sugar
2 tablespoons fish sauce
2 fresh kaffir lime leaves, torn
2 tablespoons groundnut oil
1.2kg chicken thigh fillets, quartered
150g green beans, chopped coarsely
½ cup firmly packed fresh thai basil leaves
½ cup (75g) coarsely chopped roasted
   unsalted peanuts
2 fresh long red thai chillies, sliced thinly

PANANG CURRY PASTE
25 dried long red chillies
1 teaspoon ground coriander
2 teaspoons ground cumin
2 large cloves garlic, quartered
8 spring onions, chopped coarsely
2 x 10cm sticks fresh lemongrass (40g),
   sliced thinly
2 teaspoons finely chopped fresh galangal
2 teaspoons shrimp paste
½ cup (75g) roasted unsalted peanuts
2 tablespoons groundnut oil

1 Make panang curry paste.
2 Place coconut milk, ¼ cup of the curry paste, sugar, sauce and lime leaves in wok; bring to the boil. Reduce heat; simmer, stirring, about 15 minutes or until curry sauce mixture reduces by about a third.
3 Meanwhile, heat oil in large frying pan; cook chicken, in batches, until browned lightly. Drain on absorbent paper.
4 Add beans, chicken and half of the basil to curry sauce mixture; cook, uncovered, stirring occasionally, about 5 minutes or until beans are just tender and chicken is cooked through.
5 Place curry in serving bowl; sprinkle with peanuts, chilli and remaining basil.

PANANG CURRY PASTE
Place chillies in small heatproof jug, cover with boiling water; stand 15 minutes, drain. Meanwhile, dry-fry ground coriander and cumin over medium heat in small frying pan until fragrant. Process chillies and roasted spices with remaining ingredients, except for oil, until mixture forms a paste. With motor operating, gradually add oil to paste, processing until mixture is smooth.

nutritional count per serving 25.9g total fat (14.5g saturated fat); 1501kJ (359 cal); 6g carbohydrate; 24.6g protein; 2.8g fibre

TIP Store remaining curry paste in refrigerator for up to 3 weeks.

pad thai

preparation time 20 minutes (plus standing time)
cooking time 10 minutes
serves 12

40g tamarind pulp
½ cup (125ml) boiling water
2 tablespoons grated palm sugar
⅓ cup (80ml) sweet chilli sauce
⅓ cup (80ml) fish sauce
375g rice stick noodles
12 uncooked medium prawns (500g)
2 cloves garlic, crushed
2 tablespoons finely chopped preserved turnip
2 tablespoons dried shrimp
1 tablespoon grated fresh ginger
2 fresh small red thai chillies, chopped coarsely
1 tablespoon groundnut oil
250g minced pork
3 eggs, beaten lightly
2 cups (160g) beansprouts
4 green onions, sliced thinly
⅓ spring coarsely chopped fresh coriander
¼ cup (35g) coarsely chopped
   roasted unsalted peanuts
1 lime, quartered

1 Soak tamarind pulp in the boiling water for 30 minutes. Pour tamarind into fine strainer over small bowl; push as much tamarind pulp through strainer as possible, scraping underside of strainer occasionally. Discard any tamarind solids left in strainer; reserve pulp liquid in bowl. Mix sugar and sauces into bowl with tamarind; reserve.
2 Meanwhile, place noodles in large heatproof bowl, cover with boiling water, stand until noodles just soften; drain.
3 Shell and devein prawns, leaving tails intact.
4 Blend or process (or crush using mortar and pestle) garlic, turnip, shrimp, ginger and chilli until mixture forms a paste.
5 Heat oil in wok; stir-fry spice paste until fragrant. Add pork; stir-fry until just cooked through. Add prawns; stir-fry 1 minute. Add egg; stir-fry until egg just sets. Add noodles, tamarind mixture, beansprouts and half of the onion; stir-fry, tossing gently until combined. Remove wok from heat; toss through remaining spring onion, coriander and nuts. Serve with lime wedges.
nutritional count per serving 6.6g total fat (1.5g saturated fat); 932kJ (223 cal); 25.3g carbohydrate; 14.3g protein; 1.9g fibre

yellow coconut rice

preparation time 5 minutes (plus standing time)
cooking time 15 minutes
serves 12

2¼ cups (450g) long-grain white rice
1¾ cups (410ml) water
2 cups (500ml) coconut cream
1 teaspoon salt
1 teaspoon sugar
½ teaspoon ground turmeric
pinch saffron threads

1 Soak rice in large bowl of cold water for 30 minutes. Pour rice into strainer; rinse under cold water until water runs clear. Drain.
2 Place rice and remaining ingredients in large heavy-based saucepan; cover, bring to the boil, stirring occasionally. Reduce heat; simmer, covered, about 15 minutes or until rice is tender.
3 Remove pan from heat; stand, covered, 5 minutes.
nutritional count per serving 8.8g total fat (7.6g saturated fat); 928kJ (222 cal); 31.6g carbohydrate; 3.3g protein; 1g fibre

Japanese

mixed sashimi

—

udon and prawn soup

—

vegetarian sukiyaki

—

japanese-style duck with
wombok and daikon salad

Fresh produce and an eye for detail are essential.

mixed sashimi

preparation time 45 minutes
serves 6

½ small daikon (200g)
300g piece sashimi tuna
300g piece sashimi salmon
300g piece sashimi white fish
1 teaspoon wasabi paste
2 tablespoons japanese pink pickled ginger
⅓ cup (80ml) japanese soy sauce

1 Shred daikon finely; place in bowl of iced water. Reserve.
2 Place tuna on chopping board; using sharp knife, cut 6mm slices at right angles to grain of tuna, holding tuna with your fingers and slicing with the knife almost vertical to the board. Repeat with salmon and white fish.
3 Divide drained daikon and fish among serving plates; serve with wasabi, ginger and soy sauce.
nutritional count per serving 7.7g total fat (2.4g saturated fat); 886kJ (212 cal); 1.6g carbohydrate; 33.5g protein; 0.7g fibre

udon and prawn soup

preparation time 10 minutes
cooking time 20 minutes
serves 6

1 litre (4 cups) fish stock
1 litre (4 cups) water
10cm stick fresh lemongrass (20g), chopped coarsely
4 fresh kaffir lime leaves, shredded
8cm piece fresh ginger (40g), sliced thinly
2 fresh small red thai chillies, chopped coarsely
2 tablespoons fish sauce
1kg uncooked medium king prawns
300g fresh udon noodles
230g can sliced bamboo shoots, rinsed, drained
150g fresh shiitake mushrooms, sliced thickly
80g baby spinach leaves

1 Combine stock, the water, lemongrass, lime leaves, ginger, chilli and sauce in large saucepan; bring to the boil. Reduce heat, simmer broth, uncovered, 10 minutes.
2 Meanwhile, shell and devein prawns.
3 Strain broth through sieve into large bowl; discard solids. Return broth to pan with prawns, noodles, bamboo shoots and mushrooms. Simmer, uncovered, about 5 minutes or until prawns are changed in colour and noodles are cooked as desired. Remove from heat; stir in spinach.
nutritional count per serving 1.2g total fat (0.3g saturated fat); 652kJ (156 cal); 13.4g carbohydrate; 21.5g protein; 1.9g fibre

vegetarian sukiyaki

preparation time 15 minutes
cooking time 15 minutes
serves 6

440g fresh udon noodles
8 fresh shiitake mushrooms
4 spring onions, cut into 3cm lengths
100g baby spinach leaves
230g can bamboo shoots, drained
½ small wombok (350g), chopped coarsely
150g enoki mushrooms, trimmed
1 small leek (200g), chopped coarsely
2 medium carrots (240g), sliced thickly
350g firm tofu, diced into 2cm pieces
6 eggs

BROTH
1 cup (250ml) soy sauce
½ cup (125ml) cooking sake
½ cup (125ml) mirin
1 cup (250ml) water
½ cup (110g) white sugar

1 Rinse noodles under hot water; drain. Cut noodles into random lengths.
2 Cook ingredients for broth in medium saucepan over medium heat, stirring, until sugar dissolves.
3 Meanwhile, remove and discard shiitake stems; cut a cross in the top of caps.
4 Arrange all ingredients, except eggs, on platters or in bowls. Place broth in medium bowl.
5 Break eggs into individual bowls; beat lightly.
6 Pour broth into sukiyaki (or electric frying pan) pan. Heat pan on portable gas cooker at the table; cook a quarter of the noodles and a quarter of the remaining ingredients in broth, uncovered, until just tender. Dip cooked ingredients into egg before eating. Repeat process until all the remaining noodles and ingredients are cooked.
nutritional count per serving 7.9g total fat (1.7g saturated fat); 1542kJ (369 cal); 43.4g carbohydrate; 19.4g protein; 6.3g fibre

japanese-style duck with wombok and daikon salad

preparation time 45 minutes (plus standing time)
cooking time 1 hour 10 minutes
serves 6

15 dried shiitake mushrooms
3 litres (12 cups) water
2 litres (8 cups) chicken stock
¼ cup (310ml) cooking sake
1¼ cup (310ml) mirin
⅓ cup (80ml) tamari
½ cup (125ml) soy sauce
6 spring onions, halved
3 cloves garlic, quartered
5cm piece fresh ginger (25g), unpeeled,
    chopped coarsely
¾ cup (165g) firmly packed dark brown sugar
2.4kg duck
2 tablespoons teriyaki sauce
1 tablespoon soy sauce, extra

WOMBOK AND DAIKON SALAD
2 medium carrots (240g), cut into matchsticks
½ medium daikon (300g), halved lengthways,
    sliced thinly
½ medium wombok (chinese cabbage)
    (500g), shredded finely
6 spring onions, chopped coarsely
1 fresh long red chilli, sliced thinly
2 tablespoons white miso
2 tablespoons mirin
1 tablespoon cooking sake
1 tablespoon white sugar
¼ cup (60ml) rice vinegar
1 teaspoon soy sauce

1 Place mushrooms in small heatproof bowl, cover with boiling water, stand 20 minutes; drain. Discard stems; slice caps thickly.
2 Combine mushrooms, the water, stock, sake, mirin, tamari, soy sauce, onion, garlic, ginger and sugar in stock pot. Add duck; bring to the boil. Reduce heat; simmer, uncovered, about 1 hour or until duck is cooked through. Remove from heat; stand duck in cooking liquid about 2 hours or until cool. Remove duck from cooking liquid; stand on wire rack 2 hours (discard cooking liquid). Cut duck into quarters.
3 Make wombok and daikon salad.
4 Combine teriyaki and extra soy sauce in small bowl; brush over duck skin. Cook duck, skin-side down, on heated oiled grill plate (or grill or barbecue), 5 minutes. Turn duck skin-side up; brush with remaining teriyaki mixture. Cover; cook about 5 minutes or until duck is heated through. Serve duck with salad.
WOMBOK AND DAIKON SALAD
Place carrot, daikon, wombok, onion and chilli in medium bowl. Stir miso, mirin, sake and sugar in small saucepan over heat until sugar dissolves. Remove from heat; stir in vinegar and soy sauce. Add dressing to salad; toss gently to combine.
nutritional count per serving 86.2g total fat (26.1g saturated fat); 4824kJ (1154 cal); 42.2g carbohydrate; 38.1g protein; 3.9g fibre

Moroccan

harira
—
beef and prune tagine
—
roasted vegetables with
harissa yogurt
—
spinach couscous
—
semolina slice

Spicy, piquant and hearty – North-African specialties.

harira

preparation time 25 minutes (plus standing time)
cooking time 2 hours 15 minutes
serves 8

1 cup (200g) dried chickpeas
20g butter
2 medium brown onions (300g), chopped finely
2 trimmed celery stalks (200g), chopped finely
2 cloves garlic, crushed
4cm piece fresh ginger (20g), grated
1 teaspoon ground cinnamon
½ teaspoon ground black pepper
pinch saffron threads
500g diced lamb
3 large tomatoes (750g), deseeded, chopped coarsely
2 litres (8 cups) hot water
½ cup (100g) brown lentils
2 tablespoons plain flour
½ cup (100g) white long-grain rice
½ cup firmly packed fresh coriander leaves
2 tablespoons lemon juice

1 Place chickpeas in medium bowl, cover with water; stand overnight, drain. Rinse under cold water; drain.
2 Heat butter in large saucepan; cook onion, celery and garlic, stirring, until onion softens. Add ginger, cinnamon, pepper and saffron; cook, stirring, about 2 minutes or until fragrant. Add lamb; cook, stirring, about 5 minutes or until lamb is browned.
3 Add chickpeas and tomato; cook, stirring, about 5 minutes or until tomato softens.
4 Stir in the water; bring to the boil. Reduce heat; simmer, covered, 45 minutes. Add lentils; simmer, covered, 1 hour.
5 Blend flour with ½ cup of the slightly cooled cooking liquid in small bowl; stir into lamb mixture with rice. Cook, stirring, until mixture boils and thickens. Stir coriander and juice into harira just before serving. If desired, garnish each bowl with extra coriander leaves.
nutritional count per serving 9.5g total fat (4.1g saturated fat); 1283kJ (307 cal); 29g carbohydrate; 22.7g protein; 6.7g fibre

beef and prune tagine

preparation time 20 minutes
cooking time 2 hours 30 minutes
serves 8

3 large red onions (900g), chopped finely
¼ cup (60ml) olive oil
2 teaspoons cracked black pepper
pinch saffron threads
1½ teaspoons ground cinnamon
½ teaspoon ground ginger
1.8 kg braising steak, diced into 4cm pieces
80g butter, chopped
800g can diced tomatoes
1½ cups (375ml) water
2 tablespoons white sugar
1 cup (140g) roasted slivered almonds
1¾ cups (290g) pitted prunes
2 teaspoons finely grated lemon rind
¼ teaspoon ground cinnamon, extra

1 Combine onion, oil, pepper, saffron, cinnamon and ginger in large bowl with beef; toss beef to coat in mixture.
2 Place beef mixture in large deep saucepan with butter, undrained tomatoes, the water, half of the sugar and half of the nuts; bring to the boil. Reduce heat; simmer, covered, 1½ hours. Remove 1 cup cooking liquid; reserve. Simmer tagine, uncovered, 30 minutes.
3 Meanwhile, place prunes in small bowl, cover with boiling water; stand 20 minutes, drain. Place prunes in small saucepan with rind, extra cinnamon, remaining sugar and reserved cooking liquid; bring to the boil. Reduce heat; simmer, uncovered, about 15 minutes or until prunes soften. Stir into tagine.
4 Serve tagine sprinkled with remaining nuts.
nutritional count per serving 39.8g total fat (13.3g saturated fat); 2884kJ (690 cal); 26g carbohydrate; 54g protein; 7.1g fibre

Cooking in a tagine produces fragrant and meltingly tender meat infused with exotic Northern African spices and spiked with sour lemon and sweet prunes.

roasted vegetables with harissa yogurt

preparation time 15 minutes
cooking time 50 minutes
serves 8

1.5kg jap (kent) pumpkin
4 medium beetroot (700g), halved
2 large parsnips (700g), peeled, halved lengthways
400g baby carrots, trimmed
2 medium red onions (320g), halved
¼ cup (60ml) olive oil
50g butter, chopped
1 teaspoon sea salt flakes
1 cup (280g) greek-style plain yogurt
1 tablespoon harissa

1 Preheat oven to 220°C/200°C fan-assisted.
2 Cut pumpkin into thin wedges. Place vegetables in two large baking dishes; drizzle with oil and dot with butter. Sprinkle with salt.
3 Roast vegetables for 40 minutes, turning once. Remove vegetables as they cook, onto trays; return trays to oven for a further 10 minutes or until all vegetables are browned and tender.
4 Meanwhile, combine yogurt and harissa in small bowl. Serve roasted vegetables with harissa yogurt.
nutritional count per serving 12.9g total fat (6g saturated fat); 1104kJ (264 cal); 26.3g carbohydrate; 7.5g protein; 6.5g fibre

spinach couscous

preparation time 10 minutes
serves 8

2 cups (400g) couscous
2 cups (500ml) boiling water
80g finely shredded baby spinach leaves

1 Combine couscous with boiling water in large heatproof bowl, cover; stand for about 5 minutes or until water is absorbed, fluffing with fork occasionally. Stir in spinach.
nutritional count per serving 0.3g total fat (0.1g saturated fat); 782kJ (187 cal); 38.4g carbohydrate; 6.6g protein; 0.7g fibre

semolina slice

preparation time 15 minutes (plus refrigeration time)
cooking time 1 hour 50 minutes
makes 28

1kg coarsely ground semolina
2½ cups (550g) sugar
1 cup (250ml) milk
125g butter
¼ cup (40g) blanched almonds

SUGAR SYRUP
3 cups (750ml) water
2 teaspoons lemon juice
1½ cups (330g) caster sugar
2 teaspoons orange flower water

1 Make sugar syrup.
2 Preheat oven to 160°C/140°C fan-assisted. Grease 20cm x 30cm baking tin.
3 Combine semolina and sugar in large bowl. Stir milk and butter in small saucepan over low heat until butter melts. Pour into semolina mixture; stir to combine.
4 Spread mixture into tin; smooth surface with wet hand. Score slice into 4cm diamond shapes; centre one almond on each diamond. Bake about 1 hour 20 minutes or until slice is golden brown and slightly firm to the touch.
5 Cut through diamond shapes to bottom of slice; gradually pour cooled syrup over hot slice. Cool in tin.
SUGAR SYRUP
Bring the water, juice and sugar to the boil in medium saucepan. Reduce heat; simmer, uncovered, about 20 minutes or until syrup reduces to about 2½ cups. Cool to room temperature. Add orange flower water, cover; refrigerate 3 hours or overnight.
nutritional count per piece 5.2g total fat (2.8g saturated fat); 1125kJ (293 cal); 55.6g carbohydrate; 4.4g protein; 1.3g fibre
TIP Cover slice loosely with foil if it starts to overbrown during cooking.

Chinese New Year

quick peking duck

—

pork dumplings

—

whole fried fish with
chilli bean sauce

—

crisp five-spice pork belly

—

broccoli and mangetout
in oyster sauce

—

fortune cookies

Celebrate Chinese New Year with a special banquet.

quick peking duck

preparation time 10 minutes
cooking time 15 minutes
makes 16

½ cucumber (130g)
6 spring onions
2 cups (320g) shredded barbecued duck meat
16 peking duck pancakes
⅔ cup (160ml) hoisin sauce

1 Preheat oven to 180°C/ 160°C fan-assisted.
2 Halve cucumber lengthways; remove seeds. Slice cucumber and spring onions into thin, 8cm-long strips.
3 Place duck in baking dish covered with foil; heat in oven about 10 minutes or until duck is hot.
4 Meanwhile, cook pancakes, in batches, in a dry, non-stick frying pan over medium heat until browned lightly on both sides. Wrap pancakes in foil as they are cooked to keep warm and prevent drying out.
5 Spread each pancake with 2 teaspoons of sauce; top with cucumber, onion and duck. Roll up to enclose filling.
nutritional count per pancake 5.9g total fat (1.7g saturated fat); 439kJ (105 cal); 7.5g carbohydrate; 4.8g protein; 1.5g fibre
TIP It is easier to place all ingredients on a platter, so guests can assemble their own pancakes. The duck and pancakes (found in asian food stores) are best heated just before serving.

pork dumplings

preparation time 20 minutes
cooking time 15 minutes
makes 24

450g minced pork
¼ cup finely chopped garlic chives
3 spring onions, chopped finely
2cm piece fresh ginger (10g), grated coarsely
1 teaspoon sugar
2 tablespoons light soy sauce
1 tablespoon chinese cooking wine
2 teaspoons sesame oil
24 round gow gee wrappers
2 tablespoons groundnut oil
1¼ cups (310ml) water
1 spring onion, extra, sliced thinly

DIPPING SAUCE
2 tablespoons light soy sauce
1 tablespoon rice vinegar
1 spring onion, sliced thinly

1 Combine pork, chives, onion, ginger, sugar, sauce, wine and sesame oil in large bowl. Place 1 level tablespoon of filling in centre of each wrapper. Moisten edges of wrappers with a little water; press and pleat sides together to seal.
2 Heat half of the groundnut oil in large frying pan. Add half of the dumplings; cook until bases are dark brown. Add half of the water, taking care, as it will bubble up and steam; cook, covered, 5 minutes. Remove lid; cook until water has evaporated. Remove from pan; cover to keep warm. Repeat with remaining dumplings, oil and water.
3 Meanwhile, combine ingredients for dipping sauce in small bowl.
4 Serve dumplings with dipping sauce, topped with extra sliced onion.
nutritional count per dumpling 3.3g total fat (0.8g saturated fat); 263kJ (63 cal); 3.5g carbohydrate; 4.5g protein; 0.2g fibre

whole fried fish with chilli bean sauce

preparation time 20 minutes (plus refrigeration time)
cooking time 20 minutes
serves 8

750g whole fish, cleaned, scaled
2 teaspoons coarse cooking salt
2 tablespoons chinese cooking wine
2 tablespoons soy sauce
¼ cup (60ml) groundnut oil
4cm piece fresh ginger (20g), grated finely
3 cloves garlic, chopped finely
1 tablespoon chilli bean sauce
¾ cup (180ml) water
1 teaspoon brown sugar
3 spring onions, sliced finely

1   Using kitchen scissors, trim fins from fish. Dip a piece of damp absorbent paper in salt and wipe out cavity. Rinse fish in cold water; pat dry with absorbent paper. Make three diagonal slits across the thickest part of the fish, on both sides.
2   Combine wine and half of the soy sauce in medium shallow dish. Add fish; turn to coat in mixture. Cover; refrigerate 30 minutes.
3   Heat oil in large flameproof baking dish. Cook drained fish, covered, over medium heat, about 6 minutes each side or until browned and cooked through. Transfer fish to serving platter; cover to keep warm.
4   Remove all but 1 tablespoon of the oil from the dish; cook ginger and garlic, stirring, until fragrant. Add bean sauce, the water, remaining soy sauce and sugar; bring to the boil. Simmer, uncovered, until thickened slightly.
5   Serve fish on platter with sauce mixture and onion.
nutritional count per serving 8g total fat (1.6g saturated fat); 518kJ (124 cal); 1.6g carbohydrate; 10.6g protein; 0.5g fibre

crisp five-spice salt pork belly

preparation time 15 minutes (plus refrigeration time)
cooking time 2 hours 30 minutes
serves 8

1.2kg piece boned pork belly, skin on
1½ teaspoons fine sea salt
½ teaspoon five-spice powder
1 tablespoon groundnut oil
¼ cup (60ml) light soy sauce
1 fresh small red chilli, chopped finely

1   Pat pork rind dry with absorbent paper; rub in combined salt, five-spice and oil. Place on wire rack over large shallow baking dish; cover, refrigerate 1 hour.
2   Preheat oven to 240°C/220°C fan-assisted.
3   Roast pork 1 hour or until rind begins to crisp.
4   Reduce oven temperature to 160°C/140°C fan-assisted; cook pork further 1½ hours or until tender. Stand, uncovered, 15 minutes.
5   Cut pork into thick slices; serve with combined soy sauce and chilli.
nutritional count per serving 31g total fat (10.2g saturated fat); 1555kJ (372 cal); 0.2g carbohydrate; 23.8g protein; 0g fibre

broccoli and mangetout in oyster sauce

preparation time 10 minutes
cooking time 10 minutes
serves 8

2 cups (500ml) chicken stock
1 litre (4 cups) water
2 bunches tenderstem broccoli, halved crossways
400g mangetout, trimmed
¼ cup (60ml) oyster sauce
2 teaspoons sesame oil

1 Bring stock and the water to the boil in deep frying pan or saucepan. Add broccoli; simmer, uncovered, 2 minutes.
2 Add mangetout, simmer, uncovered, about 1 minute or until mangetout and broccoli are just tender. Drain.
3 Arrange broccoli and mangetout on serving platter; drizzle with oyster sauce and sesame oil.
nutritional count per serving 1.7g total fat (0.3g saturated fat); 247kJ (59 cal); 5g carbohydrate; 4.5g protein; 2.9g fibre

fortune cookies

preparation time 25 minutes
cooking time 5 minutes
makes 12

2 egg whites
⅓ cup (75g) caster sugar
⅓ cup (50g) plain flour
1 teaspoon coconut essence
30g butter, melted
½ teaspoon finely grated lime rind
2 tablespoons desiccated coconut
12 small paper messages

1 Preheat oven to 160°C/140°C fan-assisted. Grease oven tray; line with baking parchment. Mark two 9cm circles on paper.
2 Beat egg whites in small bowl with electric mixer until soft peaks form; gradually beat in sugar, beating until dissolved between additions. Fold in sifted flour, essence, butter and rind.
3 Drop one level tablespoon of mixture into centre of each circle on tray, spread evenly to cover circle completely; sprinkle with a little coconut. Bake about 5 minutes.
4 Working quickly, loosen cookies from tray, place message in the centre of cookies; fold in half then gently bend cookies over edge of a glass. Transfer to wire rack to cool. Repeat with remaining cookie mixture and coconut.
nutritional count per serving 3.5g total fat (2.1g saturated fat); 3001kJ (72 cal); 9.4g carbohydrate; 1.2g protein; 0.3g fibre

French

salmon and green
peppercorn rillettes

—

french onion soup with
gruyère croutons

—

roast beef rib with
mustard béarnaise

—

crisp roasted potatoes

—

green bean and lentil salad

—

pear tarte tartin

Treat your guests to a French feast.

salmon and green peppercorn rillettes

preparation time 20 minutes
cooking time 20 minutes (plus cooling time)
serves 6

1 long french bread stick
3 cups (750ml) water
½ cup (125ml) dry white wine
1 small brown onion (80g), chopped coarsely
1 bay leaf
1 teaspoon black peppercorns
300g salmon fillets
100g smoked salmon, sliced thinly
60g butter, softened
2 teaspoons finely grated lemon rind
1 tablespoon green peppercorns in brine, rinsed,
    drained, chopped coarsely

1 Preheat oven to 160°C/140°C fan-assisted.
2 Cut bread into 1cm slices, place on oven tray, in single layer; toast in oven about 15 minutes or until bread is dry.
3 Meanwhile, bring the water, wine, onion, bay leaf and black peppercorns to the boil in medium saucepan. Add salmon fillets, reduce heat; simmer, uncovered, 5 minutes or until almost cooked through. Remove from heat; cool fillets in liquid 5 minutes then drain. Discard cooking liquid.
4 Discard any skin and bones from salmon fillets; place flesh in medium bowl, flake with fork. Add smoked salmon, butter, rind and green peppercorns; stir to combine rillettes.
5 Divide rillettes among six ⅓-cup (80ml) dishes; cool to room temperature. Serve with bread slices.
nutritional count per serving 14.4g total fat (6.6g saturated fat); 1371kJ (328 cal); 27g carbohydrate; 18.2g protein; 2g fibre

french onion soup with gruyère croûtons

preparation time 30 minutes
cooking time 50 minutes
serves 6

80g butter
5 large brown onions (1kg), halved, sliced thinly
¾ cup (180ml) dry white wine
1 litre (4 cups) water
1.5 litres (6 cups) beef stock
1 bay leaf
1½ tablespoons plain flour
1 teaspoon fresh thyme leaves

GRUYERE CROUTONS
1 small french bread stick
60g gruyère cheese, grated finely

1 Melt butter in large saucepan; cook onion, stirring, about 30 minutes or until caramelised.
2 Meanwhile, bring wine to the boil in large saucepan; boil 1 minute. Stir in the water, stock and bay leaf; return to the boil. Remove from heat.
3 Stir flour into onion mixture; cook, stirring, 2 minutes. Gradually add hot broth mixture, stirring, until mixture boils and thickens slightly. Reduce heat; simmer, uncovered, stirring occasionally, 20 minutes. Discard bay leaf; stir in thyme.
4 Meanwhile, make gruyère croûtons.
5 Serve bowls of soup topped with croûtons.
GRUYERE CROUTONS
Preheat grill. Cut bread into 1.5cm slices; discard end pieces. Toast slices one side then turn and sprinkle equal amounts of cheese over untoasted sides; grill croûtons until cheese browns lightly.
nutritional count per serving 15.4g total fat (9.5g saturated fat); 1212kJ (290 cal); 21g carbohydrate; 10.5g protein; 3.1g fibre

"The onions for an onion soup need a long, slow cooking … to develop the deep, rich flavour which characterises a perfect brew."

Julia Child, *Mastering the Art of French Cooking*

roast beef rib with mustard béarnaise

preparation time 30 minutes (plus 20 mins standing time)
cooking time 1 hour 15 minutes
serves 6

2kg standing rib of beef (bone in rib or baron of beef)
1 tablespoon olive oil
sea salt flakes

MUSTARD BEARNAISE
1 small shallot, chopped finely
1 tablespoon coarsely chopped fresh tarragon
1 teaspoon whole black peppercorns
1½ tablespoons white wine vinegar
2 egg yolks
200g unsalted butter, melted
1 tablespoon finely chopped fresh tarragon, extra
1 tablespoon wholegrain mustard

1 Preheat oven to 220°C/200°C fan-assisted.
2 Tie beef with kitchen string at 2cm intervals. Place beef in large roasting dish, brush beef with oil; sprinkle with salt.
3 Roast beef for 15 minutes. Reduce oven temperature to 180°C/160°C fan-assisted. Roast, uncovered, about 1 hour for medium rare or until beef is cooked as desired. Stand beef, covered with foil, 20 minutes.
4 Meanwhile, make mustard béarnaise.
5 Serve beef with béarnaise and crisp roasted potoates.
MUSTARD BEARNAISE
Bring shallot, tarragon, peppercorns and vinegar to the boil in small saucepan. Reduce heat; simmer, uncovered, until reduced by half. Strain into medium heatproof bowl. Place bowl over medium saucepan of simmering water (ensuring base of the bowl does not touch the water); add egg yolks. Whisk vigorously until egg yolks are frothy. Slowly whisk in melted butter until mixture thickens. Stir in extra tarragon and mustard.
nutritional count per serving 48.6g total fat (26g saturated fat); 2450kJ (586 cal); 0.6g carbohydrate; 37.8g protein; 0.2g fibre

crisp roasted potatoes

preparation time 15 minutes
cooking time 40 minutes
serves 6

1.5kg desiree potatoes, peeled, quartered
40g duck fat, melted
1 teaspoon sea salt flakes

1 Preheat oven to 180°C/160°C fan-assisted.
2 Boil potatoes in large saucepan for 5 minutes; drain. Return potatoes to pan; toss over low heat to dry out.
3 Toss potatoes with duck fat in shallow baking dish; arrange in single layer. Sprinkle with salt. Roast with beef for last 20 minutes of cooking time.
4 When beef is removed from the oven, increase oven temperature to 240°C/220°C fan-assisted. Roast potatoes for about 20 minutes or until browned and crisp, turning once. Sprinkle with a little more salt.
nutritional count per serving 6.9g total fat (3.3g saturated fat); 840kJ (201 cal); 27.8g carbohydrate; 5.1g protein; 3.4g fibre
TIP Duck fat is available in jars and cans from larger supermarkets and delicatessens. You can substitute 30g melted butter and 1 tablespoon olive oil, if preferred.

green bean and lentil salad

preparation time 20 minutes
cooking time 20 minutes
serves 6

⅔ cup (130g) french-style green lentils
500g baby green beans, trimmed
2 medium tomatoes (240g), deseeded, chopped
¼ cup finely chopped fresh chives

VINAIGRETTE
1 shallot, chopped finely
1 tablespoon dijon mustard
2 tablespoons white wine vinegar
2 tablespoons olive oil

1 Cook lentils, uncovered, in medium saucepan of boiling water for about 15 minutes or until just tender; drain.
2 Meanwhile, make vinaigrette.
3 Cook beans, uncovered, in large saucepan of boiling water until just tender; drain.
4 Place lentils and beans in medium bowl with tomatoes, chives and vinaigrette; toss well to combine.
VINAIGRETTE
Combine shallot, mustard and vinegar in small bowl; gradually whisk in oil.
nutritional count per serving 6.8g total fat (0.9g saturated fat); 619kJ (148 cal); 11.3g carbohydrate; 7.8g protein; 5.9g fibre

pear tarte tatin

preparation time 20 minutes (plus refrigeration time)
cooking time 1 hour 15 minutes (plus cooling time)
serves 6

3 large firm pears (990g)
90g butter, chopped
½ cup (110g) firmly packed brown sugar
⅔ cup (160ml) double cream
¼ cup (35g) roasted pecans, chopped coarsely

PASTRY
1¼ cups (175g) plain flour
⅓ cup (55g) icing sugar
90g butter, chopped
1 egg yolk
1 tablespoon water

1 Peel and core pears; cut lengthways into quarters.
2 Melt butter with brown sugar in large frying pan. Add cream, stirring, until sugar dissolves; bring to the boil. Add pear; reduce heat, simmer, turning occasionally, about 45 minutes or until tender.
3 Meanwhile, make pastry.
4 Preheat oven to 240°C/220°C fan-assisted.
5 Place pear, round-side down, in deep 22cm-round cake tin; pour caramelised pan liquid over pear, sprinkle with nuts.
6 Roll pastry between sheets of baking parchment until slightly larger than circumference of tin. Remove top paper, turn pastry onto pears. Remove remaining paper; tuck pastry between pears and side of tin.
7 Bake tarte tatin about 25 minutes or until pastry is browned lightly. Cool 5 minutes; turn tart onto serving plate, serve with cinnamon-scented whipped cream, if desired.
PASTRY
Blend or process flour, icing sugar and butter until mixture is crumbly. Add egg yolk and the water; process until ingredients just come together. Enclose in cling film; refrigerate 30 minutes.
nutritional count per serving 16.9g total fat (9.9g saturated fat); 1095kJ (262 cal); 24.8g carbohydrate; 2.2g protein; 1.6g fibre

Slow Food

mediterranean fish soup

—

braised beef cheeks in red wine
with cheesy polenta

—

caramelised carrots

—

broccoli and beans with
garlic and anchovies

—

coffee and pecan puddings
with caramel sauce

—

rich mocha fudge

Slow cooking coaxes the rich flavours out of food.

mediterranean fish soup

preparation time 25 minutes
cooking time 30 minutes serves 6

1 tablespoon olive oil
1 clove garlic, crushed
1 small leek (200g), halved, sliced thinly
1 small red pepper (150g), cut into 1cm pieces
1 small red onion (100g), halved, sliced thinly
1 trimmed celery stick (100g), cut into 1cm pieces
1 small carrot (70g), cut into 1cm pieces
½ teaspoon finely grated orange rind
¼ teaspoon dried chilli flakes
2 tablespoons tomato paste
3 cups (750ml) water
3 cups (750ml) fish stock
¼ cup (60ml) dry white wine
2 large plum tomatoes (180g), chopped coarsely
250g uncooked small king prawns
250g skinless white fish fillet, chopped coarsely
200g skinless ocean trout fillet, chopped coarsely
¼ teaspoon finely chopped fresh thyme
1 tablespoon finely chopped fresh dill

1 Heat oil in large saucepan; cook garlic, leek, pepper, onion, celery, carrot, orange rind and chilli, stirring, until vegetables soften.
2 Add paste, the water, stock, wine and tomato; bring to the boil. Reduce heat; simmer, uncovered, 20 minutes.
3 Meanwhile, shell and devein prawns; chop meat coarsely. Add prawn meat, fish, thyme and half the dill to soup; simmer, uncovered, about 3 minutes or until prawn and fish are cooked.
4 Serve bowls of soup sprinkled with remaining dill.
nutritional count per serving 5.1g total fat (0.9g saturated fat); 652kJ (156 cal); 5.7g carbohydrate; 18.9g protein; 2.5g fibre

braised beef cheeks in red wine with cheesy polenta

preparation time 20 minutes
cooking time 3 hours 10 minutes
serves 6

2 tablespoons olive oil
1.8kg beef cheeks, trimmed
1 large brown onion (250g), chopped coarsely
2 medium carrot (240g), chopped coarsely
3 cups (750ml) dry red wine
¼ cup (60ml) red wine vinegar
2 x 400g cans whole tomatoes
¼ cup (55g) firmly packed brown sugar
2 sprigs fresh rosemary
6 black peppercorns
2 tablespoons fresh oregano leaves
1 large fennel bulb (550g), cut into thin wedges
400g spring onions, trimmed, halved
250g chestnut mushrooms

CHEESY POLENTA
2½ cups (625ml) water
2½ cups (625ml) milk
1¼ cup (210g) polenta
½ cup (50g) finely grated parmesan cheese
40g butter

1 Preheat oven to 160°C/140°C fan-assisted.
2 Heat half of the oil in large flameproof casserole dish; cook beef, in batches, until browned all over.
3 Heat remaining oil in same dish; cook brown onion and carrot, stirring, until onion softens. Return beef to dish with wine, vinegar, undrained tomatoes, sugar, rosemary, peppercorns, oregano and fennel; bring to the boil. Cover; cook in oven 2 hours.
4 Stir in spring onion and mushrooms; cook 45 minutes or until beef is tender.
5 Meanwhile, make cheesy polenta.
6 Serve beef with cheesy polenta and, if desired, sprinkle with extra rosemary leaves.
CHEESY POLENTA
Bring the water and milk to the boil in large saucepan. Gradually add polenta, stirring constantly. Reduce heat; simmer, stirring, about 10 minutes or until polenta thickens. Stir in cheese and butter.
nutritional count per serving 43.3g total fat (19.2g saturated fat); 4167kJ (997 cal); 50.5g carbohydrate; 76.8g protein; 7.6g fibre

caramelised carrots

preparation time 10 minutes
cooking time 20 minutes
serves 6

1 tablespoon olive oil
20g butter
4 medium carrots (480g), sliced thickly
1 tablespoon white sugar
1 tablespoon finely chopped fresh flat-leaf parsley
2 teaspoons balsamic vinegar

1 Heat oil and butter in large frying pan; cook carrots, covered, over low heat until just tender.
2 Add sugar; cook, stirring constantly, about 10 minutes or until carrots caramelise. Stir in parsley and vinegar.
nutritional count per serving 5.8g total fat (2.2g saturated fat); 351kJ (84 cal); 6.5g carbohydrate; 0.6g protein; 2.1g fibre
TIP This recipe can be made several hours ahead; reheat just before serving.

broccoli and beans with garlic and anchovies

preparation time 10 minutes
cooking time 10 minutes
serves 6

350g tenderstem broccoli, trimmed
250g baby green beans, trimmed
2 tablespoons olive oil
2 cloves garlic, chopped finely
4 drained anchovies, chopped finely

1 Boil, steam or microwave broccoli and beans, separately, until just tender; drain.
2 Heat oil in large frying pan; cook garlic and anchovies until garlic softens.
3 Add beans and broccoli; toss gently to combine.
nutritional count per serving 6.5g total fat (0.9g saturated fat); 368kJ (88 cal); 1.5g carbohydrate; 4.4g protein; 3.7g fibre

coffee and pecan puddings with caramel sauce

preparation time 15 minutes
cooking time 40 minutes
serves 6

¾ cup (90g) coarsely chopped roasted pecans
300ml double cream
1½ cups (330g) firmly packed brown sugar
100g cold butter, chopped
125g butter, softened
1 teaspoon vanilla extract
½ cup (110g) caster sugar
2 eggs
1 cup (150g) self-raising flour
¼ cup (35g) plain flour
¼ cup (60ml) milk
1 tablespoon finely ground espresso coffee

1 Preheat oven to 180ºC/160ºC fan-assisted. Grease six ¾-cup (180ml) metal moulds or ovenproof dishes; line bases with baking parchment.
2 Divide nuts among moulds; place moulds on oven tray.
3 Stir cream, brown sugar and chopped butter in small saucepan over heat, without boiling, until sugar dissolves. Reduce heat; simmer, uncovered, without stirring, about 5 minutes or until mixture thickens slightly. Spoon 2 tablespoons of the sauce over nuts in each mould; reserve remaining sauce.
4 Beat softened butter, extract and caster sugar in small bowl with electric mixer until light and fluffy. Beat in eggs; stir in sifted flours, milk and coffee. Divide mixture among moulds; bake about 30 minutes. Stand puddings 5 minutes before turning onto serving plates.
5 Reheat reserved sauce. Serve puddings with sauce.
nutritional count per serving 62.2g total fat (33.8g saturated fat); 3921kJ (938 cal); 91.3g carbohydrate; 8.3g protein; 2.5g fibre

rich mocha fudge

preparation time 20 minutes
cooking time 15 minutes (plus cooling and refrigeration time)
makes 30 pieces

1 cup (220g) caster sugar
⅔ cup (160g) soured cream
2 tablespoons glucose syrup
250g dark cooking chocolate, chopped finely
100g packet white marshmallows, chopped coarsely
2 tablespoons coffee-flavoured liqueur
2 tablespoons dry instant coffee
2 teaspoons boiling water
30 chocolate-coated coffee beans

1 Grease 8cm x 25cm cake tin; line base and two long sides with baking parchment.
2 Stir sugar, soured cream and glucose in small saucepan over low heat, without boiling, until sugar dissolves. Using pastry brush dipped in hot water, brush down side of pan to dissolve any sugar crystals; bring to the boil. Boil, uncovered, without stirring, about 10 minutes or until syrup reaches 155ºC when measured on a sugar thermometer.
3 Remove from heat; add chocolate and marshmallow, stir until melted. Stir in combined liqueur, coffee and the boiling water.
4 Spread fudge mixture into tin; cool. Cover; refrigerate until firm.
5 Cut fudge into 30 small squares; top each square with a chocolate-coated coffee bean.
nutritional count per piece 4.9g total fat (3g saturated fat); 489kJ (117 cal); 18.3g carbohydrate; 0.8g protein; 0.2g fibre
TIPS The recipe can be made up to four weeks ahead. Store, covered, in the refrigerator.
You can use a hazelnut-flavoured liqueur instead of the coffee-flavoured liqueur and top each piece with a halved hazelnut, if preferred.

You are invited to a

Romantic Dinner

Cancel the restaurant reservation...

Valentine's Day

cream soda cuba libre

—

oysters with leek confit and
salmon roe

—

roasted beef tenderloin with
rösti and mushrooms

—

chocolate volcano puddings

Turn up the heat with this luscious dinner for two.

cream soda cuba libre

preparation time 5 minutes
serves 2

90ml dark rum
1 tablespoon lemon juice
1 cup ice cubes
1 cup (250ml) cream soda

1 Divide rum, juice and ice cubes between two 300ml
highball glasses; stir to combine. Top with cream soda;
garnish with lemon wedges, if desired.
nutritional count per serving 0g total fat (0g saturated fat);
606kJ (145 cal); 13g carbohydrate; 0.1g protein; 0g fibre

oysters with leek confit and salmon roe

preparation time 10 minutes (plus standing time)
cooking time 30 minutes (plus cooling time)
serves 2

2 small leeks (400g), sliced thinly
1 teaspoon salt
12 oysters, on the half shell (300g)
25g butter
2 tablespoons water
1 tablespoon salmon roe

1 Combine leek and salt in sieve over medium bowl; stand 1 hour.
2 Meanwhile, remove oysters from shells; wash shells, dry thoroughly, reserve. Refrigerate oysters until required.
3 Rinse leek under cold water; drain. Pat dry with absorbent paper.
4 Melt butter in medium frying pan; cook leek with the water, uncovered, stirring occasionally, over low heat about 30 minutes or until leek breaks down and is almost pulpy. Cool 10 minutes.
5 Divide shells between serving plates; divide leek confit among shells. Place one oyster on leek mixture; top with roe.
nutritional count per serving 15.1g total fat (8.3g saturated fat); 1066kJ (255 cal); 5.8g carbohydrate; 22.6g protein; 3.5g fibre

Casanova, who admitted to seducing 122 women in his 18th-century memoir, *History of My Life*, often ate 50 oysters for breakfast. In 2005, science vindicated this fetish with a study showing oysters really are an aphrodisiac.

roasted beef tenderloin with rösti and mushrooms

preparation time 20 minutes
cooking time 45 minutes
serves 2

1 tablespoon olive oil
500g beef tenderloin
1 small sweet potato (250g)
1 large desirée potato (300g)
40g butter
1 tablespoon olive oil, extra
20g butter, extra
100g chestnut mushrooms, halved
100g enoki mushrooms, trimmed
100g oyster mushrooms, halved
100g crème fraîche
2 spring onions, sliced thinly
2 tablespoons firmly packed fresh flat-leaf parsley

1 Preheat oven to 220°C/200°C fan-assisted.
2 Heat oil in large shallow flameproof baking dish; cook beef, uncovered, until browned all over. Roast about 20 minutes or until cooked as desired. Cover to keep warm.
3 Meanwhile, coarsely grate sweet potato and potato into medium bowl. Using hands, squeeze out excess moisture from potato mixture; shape mixture into eight portions.
4 Heat 10g of the butter and 1 teaspoon of the extra oil in medium non-stick frying pan; spread one portion of the potato mixture over base of pan, flatten with spatula to form a firm pancake-like rösti. Cook over medium heat until browned; invert rösti onto large plate then gently slide back into pan to cook other side. Drain on absorbent paper; cover to keep warm. Repeat process with remaining butter, oil and potato mixture.
5 Heat extra butter in same cleaned pan; cook mushrooms, stirring, until just tender. Add crème fraîche; bring to the boil. Reduce heat; simmer, stirring, until sauce thickens slightly. Remove from heat; stir in onion and parsley. Serve mushrooms with rösti and sliced beef.
nutritional count per serving 73.8g total fat (36.3g saturated fat); 4502kJ (1077 cal); 34.7g carbohydrate; 65.6g protein; 9.1g fibre

chocolate volcano puddings

preparation time 10 minutes (plus standing time)
cooking time 12 minutes
makes 2

10g unsalted butter, softened
2 teaspoons cocoa powder
2 teaspoons caster sugar
50g dark chocolate, chopped
50g unsalted butter, chopped, extra
1 tablespoon raisins
2 teaspoons dark rum
1 egg
1 egg yolk
1 tablespoon caster sugar, extra
¼ cup (35g) plain flour

1 Preheat oven to 200°C/180°C fan-assisted. Grease two holes of a large (¾-cup/180ml) muffin tin with softened butter. Coat inside of holes with combined cocoa and sugar; shake away the excess.
2 Stir chocolate and extra butter in small saucepan over low heat until just melted; transfer mixture to medium bowl.
3 Place raisins and rum in small bowl; cook in microwave oven on MEDIUM (75%) for 1½ minutes, stirring every 30 seconds. Cover; stand 10 minutes.
4 Beat egg, egg yolk and extra sugar in small bowl with electric mixer until light and fluffy. Fold in sifted flour. Fold egg mixture and raisin mixture into chocolate mixture. Divide mixture between muffin tin holes.
5 Bake puddings 8 minutes. Stand cakes in tin 2 minutes; invert onto serving plates. Dust with sifted cocoa and serve with cream or ice-cream, if desired.
nutritional count per serving 37.7g total fat (22.3g saturated fat); 2395kJ (573 cal); 47.1g carbohydrate; 8.7g protein; 1.4g fibre

Anniversary

classic tom collins

—

green pea soup with
mint pistou

—

duck breasts with fig sauce
and spinach risoni

—

brandy snap and
rhubarb stacks

Rely on French cuisine for an evening to remember.

classic tom collins

preparation time 5 minutes
serves 2

120ml gin
¼ cup (60ml) lemon juice
1 tablespoon icing sugar
⅔ cup (160ml) soda water
½ cup ice cubes

1 Divide gin, juice, sugar, soda water and ice cubes
between two chilled 340ml highball glass; stir to combine.
Garnish with maraschino cherries, if desired.
nutritional count per serving 0.1g total fat (0g saturated fat);
627kJ (150 cal); 6.3g carbohydrate; 0.2g protein; 0g fibre

green pea soup with mint pistou

preparation time 10 minutes (plus cooling time)
cooking time 20 minutes
serves 2

2 teaspoons olive oil
½ small leek (100g), sliced thinly
1 clove garlic, crushed
1 large potato (300g), chopped coarsely
1½ cups (180g) frozen peas
1½ cups (375ml) water
1 cup (250ml) vegetable stock

MINT PISTOU
1 cup loosely packed fresh mint leaves
2 tablespoons finely grated parmesan cheese
2 teaspoons lemon juice
1 clove garlic, quartered
2 tablespoons olive oil

1 Heat oil in medium saucepan; cook leek and garlic, stirring, until leek softens. Add potato, peas, the water and stock; bring to the boil. Reduce heat; simmer, covered, about 10 minutes or until potato is tender. Cool 15 minutes.
2 Meanwhile, make mint pistou.
3 Blend or process soup, in batches, until smooth. Return soup to same cleaned pan; stir over medium heat until hot.
4 Serve bowls of soup topped with pistou.
MINT PISTOU
Blend or process ingredients until smooth.
nutritional count per serving 20.9g total fat (3.7g saturated fat); 1634kJ (391 cal); 32.2g carbohydrate; 12.9g protein; 12g fibre

duck breasts with fig sauce and spinach risoni

preparation time 15 minutes
cooking time 25 minutes
serves 2

2 duck breast fillets (300g)
2 sprigs fresh rosemary
2 bay leaves
100g risoni
10g butter
100g baby spinach leaves, trimmed
½ small brown onion (40g), chopped finely
3 dried figs (45g), quartered
½ cup (125ml) port
½ cup (125ml) chicken stock
10g butter, extra

1 Use fingers to make pocket between meat and fat of each duck breast; press 1 sprig rosemary and 1 bay leaf into each pocket. Prick duck skins with fork several times.
2 Cook duck, skin-side down, in heated large oiled frying pan about 8 minutes or until browned and crisp. Turn duck; cook about 5 minutes or until cooked as desired. Remove from pan; cover to keep warm.
3 Cook pasta in medium saucepan of boiling water, uncovered, until just tender; drain. Place pasta in medium bowl with butter and spinach; toss gently to combine. Cover to keep warm.
4 Meanwhile, cook onion in same frying pan as duck, stirring, until soft. Add fig, port and stock; bring to the boil. Reduce heat; simmer, stirring, about 3 minutes or until sauce thickens. Add extra butter; whisk until sauce is combined.
5 Slice duck thinly; serve with risoni and fig sauce.
nutritional count per serving 17.6g total fat (8.1g saturated fat); 2508kJ (600 cal); 56g carbohydrate; 35.5g protein; 6.5g fibre

brandy snap and rhubarb stacks

preparation time 10 minutes
cooking time 15 minutes
serves 2

1½ cups (165g) coarsely chopped rhubarb
1 tablespoon water
2 tablespoons caster sugar
10g butter
1 tablespoon brown sugar
2 teaspoons golden syrup
¼ teaspoon ground ginger
1 tablespoon plain flour
2 tablespoons plain yogurt

1 Preheat oven to 180°C/160°C fan-assisted. Grease oven tray.

2 Bring rhubarb, the water and caster sugar in medium saucepan to the boil. Reduce heat; simmer, uncovered, stirring occasionally, about 3 minutes or until rhubarb softens. Drain rhubarb mixture through sieve over medium bowl; reserve liquid. Spread rhubarb mixture onto metal tray; cover with foil, place in freezer.

3 Meanwhile, stir butter, brown sugar, syrup and ginger in same cleaned pan over low heat until butter has melted. Remove from heat; stir in flour.

4 Drop level teaspoons of mixture about 6cm apart on tray. Bake, in oven, about 7 minutes or until brandy snaps bubble and become golden brown. Cool on trays 2 minutes; transfer to wire rack to cool completely.

5 Place cooled rhubarb mixture in small bowl; add yogurt, pull skewer backwards and forwards through rhubarb mixture for marbled effect.

6 Sandwich three brandy snaps with a quarter of the rhubarb mixture; repeat with remaining brandy snaps and rhubarb mixture.

7 Place stacks on serving plates; drizzle with reserved rhubarb liquid.

nutritional count per serving 7g total fat (4.5g saturated fat); 865kJ (207 cal); 31.7g carbohydrate; 3g protein; 3.4g fibre

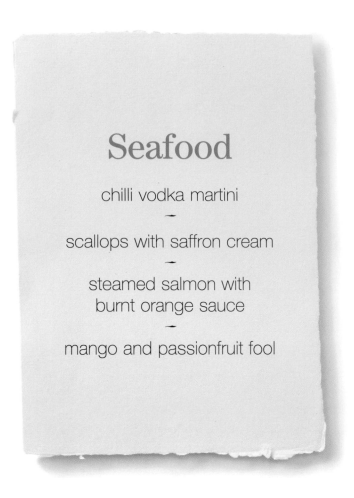

Seafood

chilli vodka martini
—
scallops with saffron cream
—
steamed salmon with
burnt orange sauce
—
mango and passionfruit fool

Nothing says love quite like a martini.

chilli vodka martini

preparation time 5 minutes
serves 2

2 fresh small red thai chillies
6 drops Tabasco sauce
90ml vodka
2 cups ice cubes

1 Divide chilli and Tabasco between two chilled 120ml
martini glasses; swirl glasses to coat in Tabasco.
2 Combine vodka and ice cubes in cocktail shaker;
shake vigorously, strain into glasses.
nutritional count per serving 0.1g total fat (0g saturated fat);
397kJ (95 cal); 0.7g carbohydrate; 0g protein; 0.2g fibre

scallops with saffron cream

preparation time 5 minutes (plus standing time)
cooking time 10 minutes
serves 2

12 scallops in half shell (480g)
1 teaspoon olive oil
1 small brown onion (80g), chopped finely
2 teaspoons finely grated lemon rind
pinch saffron threads
⅔ cup (160ml) double cream
1 tablespoon lemon juice
2 teaspoons salmon roe

1 Remove scallops from shells; wash and dry shells. Place shells, in single layer, on serving platter.
2 Rinse scallops under cold water; discard scallop roe. Gently pat scallops dry with absorbent paper.
3 Heat oil in small saucepan; cook onion, stirring, until softened. Add rind, saffron and cream; bring to the boil. Reduce heat; simmer, uncovered, about 5 minutes or until mixture has reduced to about ½ cup. Remove from heat; stand 30 minutes. Stir in juice; stand 10 minutes. Strain cream mixture into small bowl then back into same cleaned pan; stir over low heat until heated through.
4 Meanwhile, cook scallops, in batches, on heated oiled grill plate (or grill or barbecue) until browned lightly and cooked as desired.
5 Return scallops to shells; top with cream sauce and roe.
nutritional count per serving 38.3g total fat (23.6g saturated fat); 1856kJ (444 cal); 5g carbohydrate; 20.4g protein; 0.7g fibre

steamed salmon with burnt orange sauce

preparation time 10 minutes
cooking time 25 minutes
serves 2

¼ cup (55g) caster sugar
1 tablespoon water
1 teaspoon finely grated orange rind
2 tablespoons orange juice
2 teaspoons olive oil
2 teaspoons rice wine vinegar
2 x 200g salmon fillets
175g watercress, trimmed

1 Stir sugar and the water in small saucepan, without boiling, until sugar dissolves. Bring to the boil. Reduce heat; simmer, uncovered, without stirring, until mixture is a light caramel colour.
2 Remove pan from heat; allow bubbles to subside. Carefully stir in rind and juice; return pan to low heat. Stir until any pieces of caramel melt. Remove pan from heat; stir in oil and vinegar.
3 Meanwhile, place fish in large bamboo steamer set over large saucepan of simmering water; steam, covered, 15 minutes. Serve fish with watercress, drizzled with sauce.
nutritional count per serving 9.6g total fat (1.9g saturated fat); 970kJ (232 cal); 14.7g carbohydrate; 20.8g protein; 1.7g fibre

mango and passionfruit fool

preparation time 15 minutes (plus refrigeration)
serves 2

1 small mango (300g), chopped coarsely
1 tablespoon passionfruit pulp
1 egg white
2 tablespoons caster sugar
¾ cup (200g) vanilla yogurt

1 Blend or process mango until smooth. Combine mango puree and pulp in small bowl.
2 Beat egg white in small bowl with electric mixer until soft peaks form. Gradually beat in sugar until dissolved. Fold yogurt into egg-white mixture.
3 Layer mango mixture and egg-white mixture into two 1½-cup (375ml) serving glasses. Cover; refrigerate 15 minutes before serving.
nutritional count per serving 1.8g total fat (1.1g saturated fat); 491kJ (118 cal); 21g carbohydrate; 3.9g protein; 1.2g fibre
TIP Frozen mango puree can be used if mangoes are unavailable.

Fruit fools are a mixture of pureed fruit and cream (or in this case, yogurt); in the past they were sometimes thickened with eggs. They are usually served in glasses or glass dishes because their soft creamy colours are part of their charm.

You are invited to a
Girls' Lunch

Break out the bubbly and get the goss ready...

Celebration

blood orange margarita

—

fig and feta canapés

—

prosciutto-wrapped lamb
with roasted potatoes

—

green salad with
orange vinaigrette

—

chocolate cherry dacquoise

When a toast is due, the food needs to be impressive.

blood orange margarita

preparation time 5 minutes
serves 8

1½ cup (375ml) dark tequila
¾ cup (180ml) lime juice
1 cup (250ml) blood orange juice
¼ cup (55g) caster sugar
4 cups ice

1 Combine a quarter of the tequila, juices, sugar and ice cubes in cocktail shaker; shake vigorously. Strain into two salt-rimmed 150ml margarita glass. Repeat with remaining ingredients to make eight margaritas; garnish with blood orange slices, if desired.
nutritional count per serving 0.2g total fat (0g saturated fat); 1041kJ (249 cal); 32g carbohydrate; 0.4g protein; 0.1g fibre

fig and feta canapés

preparation time 10 minutes
makes 24

125g marinated feta cheese
1 tablespoon finely chopped fresh chives
24 melba toasts
3 medium fresh figs (180g)

1 Using fork, mash cheese with chives in small bowl; spread on one side of each toast.
2 Cut each fig into eight wedges; place one wedge on each toast. Sprinkle with coarsely ground black pepper, if desired.
nutritional count per canapé 1.4g total fat (0.8g saturated fat); 155kJ (37 cal); 4.2g carbohydrate; 1.7g protein; 0.4g fibre

prosciutto-wrapped lamb with roasted potatoes

preparation time 25 minutes
cooking time 30 minutes
serves 8

2kg salad potatoes, halved lengthways
1.2kg lamb fillet
4 cloves garlic, sliced finely
8 slices prosciutto (120g)
400g green beans, trimmed
3 ruby red grapefruits (1kg), segmented
1 cup coarsely chopped fresh flat-leaf parsley
150g feta cheese, crumbled
¼ cup (60ml) olive oil

1 Preheat oven to 220°C/200°C fan-assisted.
2 Place potatoes in large ovenproof dish; roast, uncovered, 15 minutes.
3 Meanwhile, cut small slits in lamb; fill each slit with a garlic slice. Wrap prosciutto around lamb. Cook lamb in heated large frying pan, in batches, 1 minute each side. Remove from pan; place on top of potatoes.
4 Roast lamb and potatoes, uncovered, about 10 minutes.
5 Meanwhile, boil, steam or microwave beans until tender. Combine beans with remaining ingredients in large bowl.
6 Slice lamb, serve with potatoes and salad.
nutritional count per serving 16.4g total fat (5.4g saturated fat); 2098kJ (502 cal); 38.1g carbohydrate; 46.4g protein; 7.5g fibre

green salad with orange vinaigrette

preparation time 20 minutes
cooking time 20 minutes
serves 8

150g sugar snap peas, trimmed
150g mangetout, trimmed
150g mizuna leaves
1 cup firmly packed fresh coriander leaves
1 cup firmly packed fresh flat-leaf parsley leaves
1 cup firmly packed fresh mint leaves
1 cup firmly packed fresh chervil sprigs
1 green oak leaf lettuce, trimmed, torn

ORANGE VINAIGRETTE
2 cups (500ml) orange juice
⅓ cup (80ml) extra virgin olive oil
1 teaspoon dijon mustard

1 Make orange vinaigrette.
2 Meanwhile, boil, steam or microwave peas until just tender; drain. Rinse under cold water; drain.
3 Combine peas in large bowl with mizuna, herbs and lettuce; drizzle salad with vinaigrette.

ORANGE VINAIGRETTE
Bring juice to the boil in medium saucepan. Boil, uncovered, about 15 minutes or until reduced to ½ cup. Combine juice in small bowl with oil and mustard.

nutritional count per serving 9.4g total fat (1.3g saturated fat); 539kJ (129 cal); 7.2g carbohydrate; 2.4g protein; 3.2g fibre

chocolate cherry dacquoise

preparation time 50 minutes (plus cooling and refrigeration time)
cooking time 45 minutes
serves 8

1 cup (120g) ground almonds
1¼ cups (275g) caster sugar
1½ tablespoons wheaten cornflour
6 egg whites
pinch cream of tartar

POACHED CHERRIES
½ cup (110g) caster sugar
½ cup (125ml) white wine
500g cherries, pitted, halved

CHOCOLATE CREAM
1¾ cups (430ml) whipping cream
200g dark eating chocolate, melted

1 Preheat the oven to 160°C/140°C fan-assisted. Grease three oven trays. Mark a 22cm circle on three sheets of baking parchment; place, upside down, on trays.
2 Combine ground almonds ¼ cup of the sugar and cornflour in small bowl.
3 Beat egg whites and cream of tartar in large bowl with electric mixer until firm peaks form. Gradually add remaining sugar; beat until dissolved between additions. Gently fold in ground almond mixture in two batches.

4 Spoon meringue mixture into piping bag fitted with plain 1.5cm tube. Pipe mixture evenly in a spiral inside circles on each tray. Bake about 30 minutes or until meringue is dry to touch. Turn off oven; cool meringues in oven with door ajar.
5 Meanwhile, make poached cherries and chocolate cream.
6 Place one meringue disc on serving plate; spread with half the chocolate cream, then top with half the well-drained poached cherries. Repeat layers, ending with a meringue disc. Cover; refrigerate at least 3 hours or overnight.
7 Serve dusted with sifted cocoa or icing sugar; top with extra cherries, if desired.

POACHED CHERRIES
Stir sugar and wine in medium saucepan over heat, without boiling, until sugar dissolves. Add cherries; bring to the boil. Simmer, covered, about 10 minutes or until cherries are tender. Using a slotted spoon, transfer cherries to medium heatproof bowl. Boil cherry liquid, uncovered, about 2 minutes or until thickened slightly. Pour liquid over cherries; cool to room temperature.

CHOCOLATE CREAM
Whip 1¼ cups (300ml) of the cream until soft peaks form. Fold whipped cream into cooled chocolate in three batches. Gently fold in remaining unwhipped cream.

nutritional count per serving 35.5g total fat (17.9g saturated fat); 2746kJ (657 cal); 72.6g carbohydrate; 8.6g protein; 2.4g fibre

Vegetarian

mushroom and rocket risotto

—

pan-fried haloumi with
green salad

—

asparagus with three toppings

—

pistachio and lime friands

Skip the meat and opt for a luscious vegie lunch.

mushroom and rocket risotto

preparation time 10 minutes
cooking time 35 minutes
serves 4

2 cups (500ml) vegetable stock
3½ cups (875ml) water
50g butter
2 tablespoons olive oil
250g button mushrooms, sliced thickly
2 cloves garlic, crushed
2 medium brown onions (300g), sliced thinly
2 cups (400g) arborio rice
¼ cup chopped fresh flat-leaf parsley
¾ cup (60g) grated parmesan cheese
30g butter, chopped, extra
250g rocket, trimmed

1 Bring stock and the water to the boil in large saucepan; reduce heat to simmer gently.
2 Meanwhile, heat half of the butter and half of the oil in another large saucepan; cook mushrooms, stirring, until browned lightly. Add garlic; cook, stirring, until fragrant. Remove from pan; cover to keep warm.
3 Heat remaining butter and remaining oil in same pan; cook onion, stirring, until soft. Add rice, stir over medium heat until rice is coated in butter mixture. Stir in ½ cup (125ml) of the simmering stock mixture; cook, stirring, over low heat until liquid is absorbed.
4 Continue adding stock mixture, in ½-cup batches, stirring after each addition until liquid is absorbed. Total cooking time should be about 20 minutes or until rice is tender.
5 Stir in mushroom mixture, parsley, cheese, extra butter and rocket. Top with shaved parmesan cheese, if desired.
nutritional count per serving 93.6g total fat (56g saturated fat); 5229kJ (1251 cal); 85.9g carbohydrate; 19.3g protein; 6.2g fibre

pan-fried haloumi with green salad

preparation time 15 minutes
cooking time 5 minutes
serves 4

150g curly endive
50g baby spinach leaves
½ cup loosely packed fresh flat-leaf parsley leaves
⅔ cup (125g) drained semi-dried tomatoes,
   chopped coarsely
250g haloumi cheese

LEMON DIJON DRESSING
¼ cup (60ml) lemon juice
1 clove garlic, crushed
1 tablespoon water
1 teaspoon white sugar
1 teaspoon dijon mustard
¼ teaspoon ground cumin
pinch cayenne pepper

1 Combine endive, spinach, parsley and tomato in
medium bowl.
2 Cut cheese into eight slices. Cook cheese in heated oiled
medium frying pan, in batches, until browned both sides.
3 Meanwhile, make lemon dijon dressing.
4 Add dressing to salad; toss gently to combine. Serve
salad topped with cheese.
LEMON DIJON DRESSING
Place ingredients in screw-top jar; shake well.
nutritional count per serving 12g total fat (7g saturated fat);
949kJ (227 cal); 11.8g carbohydrate; 17.3g protein;
5.4g fibre

asparagus with three toppings

preparation time 20 minutes
cooking time 10 minutes
serves 4

600g asparagus, trimmed

BALSAMIC DRESSING
2 tablespoons extra virgin olive oil
3 teaspoons balsamic vinegar
1 medium tomato (150g), peeled, deseeded,
   chopped finely
1 tablespoon small fresh basil leaves

PARMESAN BUTTER
25g butter, melted
2 tablespoons shaved parmesan cheese

GARLIC OIL
2 tablespoons extra virgin olive oil
1 clove garlic, sliced thinly

1 Cook asparagus on heated oiled grill plate (or grill or
barbecue) about 5 minutes or until tender.
2 Make balsamic dressing, parmesan butter and garlic oil.
3 Arrange asparagus in three piles on a serving platter.
Drizzle one pile with balsamic dressing, one with parmesan
butter and one with garlic oil.
BALSAMIC DRESSING
Combine ingredients in small bowl.
PARMESAN BUTTER
Combine melted butter and parmesan in small bowl.
GARLIC OIL
Heat oil in small frying pan; cook garlic until browned lightly.
nutritional count per serving 25.6g total fat (6.6g saturated
fat); 1037kJ (248 cal); 2.3g carbohydrate; 4.3g protein;
2.1g fibre

From left to right: Balsamic dressing; Parmesan butter; Garlic oil.

pistachio and lime friands

preparation time 15 minutes
cooking time 20 minutes
makes 12

1 cup (140g) unsalted pistachios
6 egg whites
185g butter, melted
1½ cups (240g) icing sugar
½ cup (75g) plain flour
1 tablespoon lime juice
2 teaspoons finely grated lime rind

1 Preheat oven to 200°C/180°C fan-assisted. Grease 12 x ½-cup (125ml) oval friand tins; stand on oven tray.
2 Process nuts until ground finely.
3 Place egg whites in large bowl; whisk lightly with fork until combined. Add butter, sifted icing sugar and flour, juice, rind and nuts; stir until just combined. Divide mixture among tins.
4 Bake friands, uncovered, about 20 minutes. Stand in pans 5 minutes before turning, top-side up, onto wire rack to cool.

nutritional count per friand 18.6g total fat (9g saturated fat); 1229kJ (294 cal); 26.4g carbohydrate; 4.9g protein; 1.3g fibre

TIP A friand is a small densely-textured sponge cake, popular in Australia and New Zealand. Traditionally baked in oval shapes, they are made with butter, ground nuts and a variety of flavourings. If you can't get hold of the traditional oval tins, then deep muffin tins work just as well.

In France, these little oval cakes are better known as financiers because they were originally baked in tiny, gold-bar shaped pans.

Detox

beetroot, rocket and
orange juice
—
orange, fennel and
almond salad
—
brown rice pilaf
—
papaya with
passionfruit and lime

Rejuvenate and energise your mind and body.

beetroot, rocket and orange juice

preparation time 5 minutes
makes 1 litre (4 cups)

350g beetroot, chopped coarsely
6 medium oranges (1.4kg), peeled, chopped coarsely
80g rocket leaves
⅔ cup (160ml) water
1 teaspoon finely grated orange rind

1 Push beetroot, oranges and rocket leaves through juice
extractor. Stir in water and rind.
nutritional count per 250ml 0.4g total fat (0g saturated fat);
543kJ (130 cal); 23.8g carbohydrate; 4.4g protein; 7g fibre

orange, fennel and almond salad

preparation time 10 minutes
cooking time 10 minutes
serves 4

⅔ cup (160ml) fresh orange juice
1 tablespoon almond oil
2 baby fennel bulb (260g)
2 large oranges (600g), segmented
100g baby spinach leaves
½ cup (40g) flaked almonds

1 Bring juice to the boil in small saucepan. Boil, uncovered, until juice reduces to 2 tablespoons; cool 10 minutes. Combine juice with oil in small jug.
2 Meanwhile, reserve fennel tips from fennel; slice fennel thinly.
3 Place fennel in medium bowl with orange, spinach and nuts; toss gently to combine.
4 Serve salad drizzled with dressing and sprinkled with fennel tips.
nutritional count per serving 10.4g total fat (0.7g saturated fat); 719kJ (172 cal); 13.2g carbohydrate; 4.2g protein; 4.8g fibre

This fresh salad is extremely good for you: almonds are packed with good oils, fennel acts as a diuretic and helps to settle the stomach and oranges give the ultimate vitamin C shot to help protect the body from infections and viruses.

brown rice pilaf

preparation time 25 minutes
cooking time 1 hour
serves 4

2 medium sweet potatoes (800g), chopped coarsely
cooking-oil spray
2⅓ cups (580ml) vegetable stock
1 tablespoon olive oil
1 large brown onion (200g), chopped finely
2 cloves garlic, crushed
3 trimmed celery stalks (300g), chopped finely
200g mushrooms, chopped coarsely
1½ cups (300g) brown medium-grain rice
1 tablespoon finely grated lemon rind
1 cup loosely packed fresh flat-leaf parsley leaves

1 Preheat oven to 180°C/160°C fan-assisted.
2 Place sweet potato on oiled oven trays; spray with oil. Roast, uncovered, about 25 minutes or until tender.
3 Meanwhile, bring stock to the boil in medium saucepan. Reduce heat; simmer, uncovered.
4 Heat oil in large saucepan; cook onion, garlic and celery, stirring, until onion softens. Add mushroom and rice; cook, stirring, 2 minutes. Add stock, reduce heat; simmer, covered, about 50 minutes or until stock is absorbed and rice is tender. Stir in sweet potato, rind and parsley.
nutritional count per serving 7.5g total fat (1.3g saturated fat); 2057kJ (492 cal); 86.3g carbohydrate; 14g protein; 9.8g fibre

papaya with passionfruit and lime

preparation time 20 minutes
serves 4

2 small papaya (1.3kg), cut into thick wedges
¼ cup (60ml) fresh passionfruit pulp
2 tablespoons fresh lime juice

1 Place papaya on serving plates.
2 Drizzle with passionfruit and juice.
nutritional count per serving 0.4g total fat (0g saturated fat); 560kJ (134 cal); 25.1g carbohydrate; 2.1g protein; 10.7g fibre

Grazing

white bean dip

—

caesar salad

—

smoked seafood and
mixed vegetable antipasti

—

beef carpaccio with
rocket, parmesan and aïoli

—

lemon tart

The ideal selection for an afternoon get-together.

white bean dip

preparation time 5 minutes
makes 2 cups

2 x 400g cans white beans, rinsed, drained
2 cloves garlic, crushed
2 tablespoons lemon juice
⅓ cup (80ml) olive oil
1 tablespoon fresh basil leaves

1 Blend or process beans, garlic, lemon juice and oil until almost smooth.
2 Sprinkle dip with basil.
nutritional count per tablespoon 3.1g total fat (0.4g saturated fat); 138kJ (33 cal); 0.6g carbohydrate; 0.5g protein; 0.9g fibre
TIP Many varieties of cooked white beans are available canned, among them cannellini (which is what we used), butter and haricot beans; any of these is suitable.

caesar salad

preparation time 30 minutes
cooking time 15 minutes
serves 8

½ loaf ciabatta (220g)
1 clove garlic, crushed
⅓ cup (80ml) olive oil
3 eggs
4 baby cos lettuces, trimmed, leaves separated
1 cup (80g) shaved parmesan cheese

CAESAR DRESSING
1 clove garlic, crushed
1 tablespoon dijon mustard
¼ cup (60ml) lemon juice
2 teaspoons worcestershire sauce
¼ cup (60ml) olive oil

1 Preheat oven to 180°C/160°C fan-assisted.
2 Cut bread into 2cm cubes; combine garlic and oil in large bowl with bread. Toast bread on oven tray until croûtons are browned.
3 Place ingredients for caesar dressing in screw-top jar; shake well.
4 Bring water to the boil in small saucepan, add eggs; cover pan tightly, remove from heat. Remove eggs from water after 2 minutes. When cool enough to handle, break eggs into large bowl; add lettuce, mixing gently so egg coats leaves.
5 Add cheese, croûtons and dressing to bowl; toss gently to combine.
nutritional count per serving 22.2g total fat (5g saturated fat); 1262kJ (302 cal); 14.6g carbohydrate; 10.1g protein; 2.9g fibre

smoked seafood and mixed vegetable antipasti

preparation time 35 minutes
serves 8

⅓ cup (80g) soured cream
2 teaspoons raspberry vinegar
1 tablespoon coarsely chopped fresh chives
1 clove garlic, crushed
1 large yellow courgette (150g)
1 tablespoon raspberry vinegar, extra
¼ cup (60ml) extra virgin olive oil
⅓ cup (45g) roasted slivered almonds
1 cup (150g) drained semi-dried tomatoes
1 large avocado (320g)
1 tablespoon lemon juice
300g hot-smoked ocean trout portions
250g sliced smoked salmon
16 drained caperberries (80g)
1 lemon, cut into wedges
170g packet roasted garlic bagel crisps

1 Combine soured cream, vinegar, chives and garlic in small bowl, cover; refrigerate until required.
2 Meanwhile, using vegetable peeler, slice courgette lengthways into ribbons; combine courgette in small bowl with extra vinegar and 2 tablespoons of the oil.
3 Combine nuts, tomatoes and remaining oil in another small bowl. Slice avocado thickly into a third small bowl; sprinkle with juice. Flake trout into bite-sized pieces.
4 Arrange courgette mixture, nut mixture, avocado, trout, salmon and caperberries on large platter; serve with soured cream mixture, lemon and bagel crisps.
nutritional count per serving 27.4g total fat (6.3g saturated fat); 1597kJ (382 cal); 16.1g carbohydrate; 22.3g protein; 4.4g fibre
TIP If you can't locate bagel crisps, thinly slice a couple of bagels horizontally, palce the slices on a non-stick oven tray and bake in a hot oven for 10 minutes until crisp.

beef carpaccio with rocket, parmesan and aïoli

preparation time 20 minutes (plus freezing time)
serves 8

600g piece beef fillet, trimmed
100g wild rocket leaves
150g parmesan cheese, shaved

AIOLI
2 eggs
1 clove garlic, quartered
2 tablespoons lemon juice
1 tablespoon dijon mustard
⅔ cup (160ml) olive oil

1 Wrap beef tightly in plastic wrap; place in freezer about 1 hour or until partially frozen.
2 Meanwhile, make aïoli.
3 Using sharp knife, slice unwrapped beef as thinly as possible; divide beef among serving plates.
4 Top beef with rocket and cheese; drizzle with aïoli.
AIOLI
Blend or process egg, garlic, juice and mustard until combined. With motor operating, add oil in a thin, steady stream until aïoli thickens slightly.
nutritional count per serving 28.9g total fat (8.2g saturated fat); 1509kJ (361 cal); 0.6g carbohydrate; 25.4g protein; 0.3g fibre

lemon tart

preparation time 30 minutes (plus refrigeration time)
cooking time 55 minutes
serves 8

1¼ cups (185g) plain flour
⅓ cup (55g) icing sugar
¼ cup (30g) ground almonds
125g cold butter, chopped
1 egg yolk

LEMON FILLING
1 tablespoon finely grated lemon rind
½ cup (125ml) lemon juice
5 eggs
¾ cup (165g) caster sugar
1 cup (250ml) whipping cream

1 Blend or process flour, icing sugar, ground almonds and butter until combined. Add egg yolk, process until ingredients just come together. Knead dough on floured surface until smooth. Wrap in cling film, refrigerate 30 minutes.
2 Roll pastry between sheets of baking parchment until large enough to line 24cm-round loose-based flan tin. Lift pastry into tin; press into side, trim edge. Cover; refrigerate 30 minutes.
3 Meanwhile, preheat oven to 200°C/180°C fan-assisted.
4 Place flan tin on oven tray. Line pastry case with baking parchment, fill with dried beans or rice. Bake 15 minutes. Remove paper and beans; bake about 10 minutes or until browned lightly.
5 Meanwhile, make lemon filling.
6 Reduce oven temperature to 180°C/160°C fan-assisted.
7 Pour lemon filling into pastry case; bake about 30 minutes or until filling has set slightly, cool. Refrigerate until cold. Serve dusted with sifted icing sugar, if desired.
LEMON FILLING
Whisk ingredients in medium bowl; stand 5 minutes.
nutritional count per serving 30.7g total fat (17.4g saturated fat); 2040kJ (488 cal); 45.9g carbohydrate; 8.6g protein; 1.3g fibre

Vietnamese

lemongrass and
lime spritzer

–

vietnamese prawn rolls

–

char-grilled chilli squid and
rice noodle salad

–

citrus salad with
lime and mint granita

Light and refreshing with a balance of sweet and sour.

lemongrass and lime spritzer

preparation time 10 minutes (plus refrigeration time)
cooking time 5 minutes
makes 1 litre (4 cups)

⅓ cup (90g) grated palm sugar
½ cup (125ml) water
2 tablespoons coarsely chopped fresh lemongrass
½ cup (125ml) lime juice
750ml chilled sparkling mineral water
1 cup ice cubes

1 Stir sugar and water in small saucepan over low heat, until sugar dissolves. Remove from heat; stir in lemongrass. Cover; refrigerate until chilled.
2 Combine strained sugar mixture with juice, mineral water and ice cubes in large jug.
nutritional count per 250ml 0.1g total fat (0g saturated fat); 385kJ (92 cal); 22.2g carbohydrate; 0.3g protein; 0.1g fibre

vietnamese prawn rolls

preparation time 20 minutes
makes 12

50g rice vermicelli noodles, soaked, drained
¼ small wombok (chinese cabbage) (175g),
  shredded finely
½ cup loosely packed fresh mint leaves, torn
2 teaspoons brown sugar
2 tablespoons lime juice
500g cooked medium king prawns
12 x 21cm rice paper rounds

HOISIN DIPPING SAUCE
½ cup (125ml) hoisin sauce
2 tablespoons rice vinegar

1   Coarsely chop noodles. Place noodles in medium bowl with wombok, mint, sugar and juice; toss gently to combine.
2   Shell and devein prawns; chop meat finely.
3   Meanwhile, make hoisin dipping sauce.
4   Dip one rice paper round into bowl of warm water until soft; place on tea-towel-covered board. Top with a little of the prawn meat and noodle filling. Fold and roll to enclose filling. Repeat with remaining rounds, prawn meat and noodle filling.
5   Serve rolls with hoisin dipping sauce.
HOISIN DIPPING SAUCE
Combine ingredients in small bowl.
nutritional count per roll 0.9g total fat (0.1g saturated fat); 326kJ (78 cal); 10.8g carbohydrate; 5.5g protein; 1.7g fibre

char-grilled chilli squid and rice noodle salad

preparation time 15 minutes
cooking time 15 minutes
serves 4

800g cleaned squid hoods
450g fresh wide rice noodles
1 medium red pepper (200g), sliced thinly
150g mangetout, trimmed, halved
½ cucumber (130g), deseeded, sliced thinly
1 small red onion (100g), sliced thinly
1 cup loosely packed fresh coriander leaves
⅓ cup coarsely chopped fresh mint

SWEET CHILLI DRESSING
⅓ cup (75g) caster sugar
½ cup (125ml) water
1 tablespoon white vinegar
2 fresh small red thai chillies, chopped finely

1   Cut squid down centre to open out; score the inside in a diagonal pattern. Halve squid lengthways; cut squid into 3cm pieces.
2   Make sweet chilli dressing.
3   Cook squid on heated oiled grill plate (or grill or barbecue), in batches, until tender and browned.
4   Place noodles in large heatproof bowl, cover with boiling water; separate with fork, drain. Combine noodles in large serving bowl with squid, dressing and remaining ingredients.
SWEET CHILLI DRESSING
Stir sugar and the water in small saucepan, over low heat, until sugar dissolves; bring to the boil. Reduce heat; simmer, uncovered, without stirring, about 5 minutes or until syrup thickens slightly. Stir in vinegar and chilli off the heat.
nutritional count per serving 3.1g total fat (0.8g saturated fat); 1584kJ (379 cal); 48.3g carbohydrate; 38.1g protein; 2.8g fibre

citrus salad with lime and mint granita

preparation time 15 minutes
serves 4

2 medium oranges (480g)
2 small pink grapefruits (700g)
⅓ cup finely chopped fresh mint
2 tablespoons icing sugar
1 tablespoon lime juice
2 cups ice cubes

1 Segment orange and grapefruit into medium bowl.
2 Blend or process mint, sugar, juice and ice until ice is crushed; serve with fruit segments.
nutritional count per serving 0.4g total fat (0g saturated fat); 385kJ (92 cal); 18.1g carbohydrate; 2.1g protein; 2.7g fibre

Make the lime and mint granita at the last minute – it will melt quickly if kept waiting.

You are invited to

Sunday Lunch

There's no rush – let day ease into night...

Roast

cream of sweet potato soup
with rosemary sourdough

—

roast lamb with
mustard and herbs

—

fresh peas, caraway and
parmesan

—

baby carrots with
orange maple syrup

—

apple pie

Leave the week behind with this traditional Sunday roast.

cream of sweet potato soup with rosemary sourdough

preparation time 10 minutes (plus cooling time)
cooking time 30 minutes
serves 6

1 tablespoon olive oil
2 medium sweet potatoes (800g), chopped coarsely
1 medium brown onion (150g), chopped coarsely
2 cloves garlic, quartered
2 teaspoons coarsely chopped fresh rosemary
1 teaspoon finely grated lemon rind
2 cups (500ml) vegetable stock
2 cups (500ml) water
1 tablespoon lemon juice
½ cup (125ml) double cream

ROSEMARY SOURDOUGH
1 loaf sourdough bread
2 tablespoons olive oil
2 teaspoons finely chopped fresh rosemary

1 Heat oil in large frying pan; cook sweet potatoes, onion and garlic, stirring, 10 minutes. Add rosemary, rind, stock and the water; bring to the boil. Reduce heat; simmer, covered, about 15 minutes or until sweet potatoes are soft. Cool 15 minutes.
2 Meanwhile, make rosemary sourdough.
3 Blend or process soup, in batches, until smooth. Return soup to same cleaned pan, add juice; stir over medium heat until hot. Serve bowls of soup drizzled with cream, accompanied with sourdough.
ROSEMARY SOURDOUGH
Preheat oven to 180°C/160°C fan-assisted. Cut bread into 3cm slices; combine with oil and rosemary in large bowl. Place bread on oven tray; toast, both sides, about 15 minutes.
nutritional count per serving 21.3g total fat (7.7g saturated fat); 2282kJ (546 cal); 70.9g carbohydrate; 13.2g protein; 8.8g fibre

roast lamb with mustard and herbs

preparation time 20 minutes
cooking time 1 hour 45 minutes
serves 6

1kg potatoes, sliced thickly
1 large brown onion (200g), sliced thickly
1½ cups (375ml) chicken stock
1½ tablespoons dijon mustard
3 cloves garlic, crushed
2 drained anchovy fillets, chopped
2 teaspoons finely grated lemon rind
2kg leg of lamb
½ cup coarsely chopped fresh flat-leaf parsley
2 tablespoons coarsely chopped fresh oregano

1 Preheat oven to 180°C/160°C fan-assisted.
2 Place potato and onion in large oiled baking dish; pour in stock.
3 Combine mustard, garlic, anchovies and rind in small bowl; rub all over lamb. Place lamb on top of potatoes. Bake, uncovered, about 1½ hours or until lamb is cooked as desired. Remove lamb from dish; stand, covered, for about 15 minutes.
4 Meanwhile, increase oven temperature to 250°C/230°C fan-assisted; bake potatoes for further 15 minutes or until browned.
5 Sprinkle lamb with herbs; serve with potato mixture and lemon wedges, if desired.
nutritional count per serving 14g total fat (6.1g saturated fat); 1927kJ (461 cal); 21.4g carbohydrate; 59.9g protein; 3.7g fibre

This family Sunday lunch with roast lamb and apple pie is a tradition well worth keeping.

fresh peas, caraway and parmesan

preparation time 35 minutes
cooking time 5 minutes
serves 6

You need about 1kg fresh peas for this recipe.

60g butter
1 teaspoon caraway seeds
2 teaspoons finely grated lemon rind
1 small red onion (100g), sliced thinly
3½ cups (560g) fresh peas
⅓ cup coarsely chopped fresh flat-leaf parsley
½ cup (40g) finely grated parmesan cheese

1 Melt butter in large frying pan; cook seeds, rind and onion, stirring, until onion softens.
2 Add peas; cook, stirring, until peas are just tender. Stir in parsley; sprinkle with cheese.
nutritional count per serving 8.1g total fat (5.1g saturated fat); 598kJ (143 cal); 8.5g carbohydrate; 6.8g protein; 4.8g fibre

baby carrots with orange maple syrup

preparation time 35 minutes
cooking time 20 minutes
serves 6

1.2kg baby carrots
30g butter
2 teaspoons finely grated orange rind
2 tablespoons orange juice
2 tablespoons maple syrup

1 Boil, steam or microwave carrots until just tender.
2 Melt butter in large frying pan; stir rind, juice and syrup in pan until mixture boils. Reduce heat; simmer, uncovered, until syrup mixture thickens slightly.
3 Add drained carrots to pan, stirring gently to coat in orange maple syrup.
nutritional count per serving 4.3g total fat (2.7g saturated fat); 493kJ (118 cal); 15.8g carbohydrate; 1.5g protein; 5.1g fibre

apple pie

preparation time 45 minutes (plus refrigeration time)
cooking time 35 minutes (plus cooling time)
serves 6

1½ cups (225g) plain flour
¾ cup (110g) self-raising flour
⅓ cup (50g) cornflour
½ cup (60g) custard powder
185g chilled butter, chopped
1 tablespoon white sugar
1 egg, separated
⅓ cup (80ml) iced water, approximately
2 tablespoons apricot jam
2 teaspoons white sugar, extra

FILLING
1.5kg bramley apples
½ cup (125ml) water
¼ cup (55g) white sugar
½ teaspoon ground cinnamon
1 teaspoon finely grated lemon rind

1 Make filling.
2 Sift flours and custard powder into large bowl; rub in butter, add sugar. Make well in centre, add egg yolk and enough of the water to mix to a firm dough; knead lightly. Cover; refrigerate 1 hour.
3 Preheat oven to 200°C/180°C fan-assisted.
4 Roll out just over half of the pastry, on floured surface, until just large enough to line a 23cm pie plate. Lift pastry into pie plate; press into side, trim edge. Spread base of pastry with apricot jam, top with filling.
5 Roll out remaining pastry until large enough to cover pie. Brush edges of pie with a little lightly beaten egg white; cover with pastry. Press edges together firmly, trim and decorate. Brush pastry with egg white; sprinkle with extra sugar. Cut a few slits in pastry to allow steam to escape. Bake about 25 minutes or until golden brown.
FILLING
Peel, quarter and core apples; cut each quarter in half lengthways. Combine apples in large saucepan with the water, sugar, cinnamon and rind. Bring to the boil, simmer, covered, about 5 minutes or until apples are almost tender. Remove from heat; drain, cool to room temperature.
nutritional count per serving 7.3g total fat (4.6g saturated fat); 752kJ (180 cal); 25.7g carbohydrate; 2.1g protein; 1.5g fibre

Italian

antipasti

–

vongole and chorizo linguine

–

italian braised pork

–

baby spinach and
radicchio salad

–

tiramisu

Make lunchtime last with this relaxing menu.

antipasti

preparation time 15 minutes
cooking time 20 minutes
serves 6

400g piece baked ricotta cheese
⅛ teaspoon smoked paprika
¼ teaspoon dried chilli flakes
¼ teaspoon dried oregano leaves
250g cherry tomatoes
½ cup (125ml) extra virgin olive oil
1 medium aubergine (300g), sliced thinly
2 tablespoons small fresh basil leaves
3 chorizo (400g), sliced
¼ cup lightly packed fresh flat-leaf parsley leaves
12 fresh asparagus spears, trimmed
¼ cup (20g) shaved parmesan cheese
10 trimmed red radishes (150g)
150g marinated pitted kalamata olives

1 Preheat oven to 180°C/160°C fan-assisted.
2 Place ricotta on shallow oven tray; sprinkle with paprika, chilli and oregano. Place tomatoes on same tray. Drizzle ricotta and tomatoes with 2 tablespoons of the oil; roast about 10 minutes or until tomatoes begin to split.
3 Brush aubergine slices with 2 tablespoons of the oil; cook in grill pan (or pan-fry or barbecue) until browned both sides. Drizzle aubergine with 1 tablespoon of oil; top with basil.
4 Cook chorizo in grill pan (or pan-fry or barbecue) until browned both sides; combine in small bowl with parsley.
5 Cook asparagus in large frying pan of simmering water until just tender; drain. Top asparagus with parmesan; drizzle with remaining oil.
6 Serve ricotta, tomatoes, aubergine, chorizo, asparagus, radishes and olives on large platter.
nutritional count per serving 47.9g total fat (15.1g saturated fat); 2374kJ (568 cal); 11.1g carbohydrate; 22.1g protein; 3.2g fibre

vongole and chorizo linguine

preparation time 15 minutes (plus standing time)
cooking time 15 minutes
serves 6

750g vongole (small clams)
375g linguine pasta
1 tablespoon extra virgin olive oil
1 chorizo (170g), sliced thinly
2 cloves garlic, crushed
2 long red chillies, sliced thinly
250g cherry tomatoes, halved
¾ cup loosely packed small fresh basil leaves
¼ cup (60ml) extra virgin olive oil, extra

1 Rinse vongole. Place in bowl of cold water 1 hour; drain.
2 Cook pasta in large saucepan of boiling, salted water, uncovered, until just tender; drain. Return to pan.
3 Meanwhile, heat oil in large frying pan; add chorizo, cook until crisp. Remove from pan using a slotted spoon.
4 Add vongole to same heated pan; cook, covered, about 3 minutes or until vongole open. Push vongole to one side of pan. Add garlic, chilli and tomatoes; cook, uncovered, about 2 minutes or until fragrant and softened.
5 Add chorizo and vongole mixture to hot pasta with basil and extra oil; toss gently to combine.

nutritional count per serving 21.5g total fat (5g saturated fat); 1868kJ (447 cal); 44.7g carbohydrate; 17.2g protein; 3.1g fibre

italian braised pork

preparation time 25 minutes
cooking time 2 hours 50 minutes
serves 6

2 tablespoons olive oil
1.5kg pork shoulder, rolled and tied
2 cloves garlic, crushed
1 medium brown onion (150g), chopped coarsely
½ small fennel bulb (100g), chopped coarsely
8 slices hot pancetta (120g), chopped coarsely
1 tablespoon tomato paste
½ cup (125ml) dry white wine
400g can whole tomatoes
1 cup (250ml) chicken stock
1 cup (250ml) water
2 sprigs fresh rosemary
2 large fennel bulbs (1kg), halved, sliced thickly
SPICE RUB
1 teaspoon fennel seeds
2 teaspoons dried oregano
½ teaspoon cayenne pepper
1 tablespoon cracked black pepper
1 tablespoon sea salt
2 teaspoons olive oil

1 Preheat oven to 180°C/160°C fan-assisted.
2 Heat oil in large flameproof casserole dish; cook pork, uncovered, until browned all over.
3 Meanwhile, combine ingredients for spice rub in small bowl.
4 Remove pork from dish; discard all but 1 tablespoon of the oil in dish. Cook garlic, onion, chopped fennel and pancetta in same dish, stirring, until onion softens. Add paste; cook, stirring, 2 minutes.
5 Meanwhile, rub pork with spice rub.
6 Return pork to dish with wine, undrained tomatoes, stock, the water and rosemary; bring to the boil. Cover; cook 1 hour.
7 Add sliced fennel; cook, covered, 1 hour. Remove pork from dish; discard rind. Cover to keep warm.
8 Meanwhile, cook braising liquid in dish over medium heat, uncovered, until thickened slightly. Return sliced pork to dish. Serve pork and sauce with warm italian bread, if desired.

nutritional count per serving 32.8g total fat (10.7g saturated fat); 2525kJ (604 calories); 7.5g carbohydrate; 66.5g protein; 4.6g fibre

baby spinach and radicchio salad

preparation time 15 minutes (plus standing time)
cooking time 5 minutes
serves 6

¼ cup (40g) raisins
⅓ cup (80ml) olive oil
2 tablespoons red wine vinegar
1 medium radicchio (200g)
100g baby spinach leaves
¼ cup (40g) pine nuts, roasted

1 Place raisins, oil and vinegar in small jar; shake well. Stand 1 hour.
2 Just before serving, place lettuce leaves in large bowl with pine nuts and dressing; toss gently to combine.

nutritional count per serving 17g total fat (2g saturated fat); 769kJ (184 cal); 5.5g carbohydrate; 1.9g protein; 1.8g fibre

tiramisu

preparation time 25 minutes (plus refrigeration time)
serves 6

2 tablespoons ground espresso coffee
1 cup (250ml) boiling water
½ cup (125ml) marsala
250g packet sponge finger biscuits
300ml whipping cream
¼ cup (40g) icing sugar
500g mascarpone cheese
2 tablespoons marsala, extra
50g dark eating chocolate, grated coarsely

1 Combine coffee and the boiling water in coffee plunger; stand 2 minutes before plunging. Combine coffee mixture and marsala in medium heatproof bowl; cool 10 minutes.
2 Place one-third of the biscuits, in single layer, over base of deep 2-litre (8-cup) dish; drizzle with one-third of the coffee mixture.
3 Beat cream and icing sugar in small bowl until soft peaks form; transfer to large bowl. Fold in combined cheese and extra marsala.
4 Spread one-third of the cream mixture over biscuits in dish. Submerge half of the remaining biscuits, one at a time, in coffee mixture, taking care the biscuits do not become so soggy that they fall apart; place over cream layer. Top biscuit layer with half of the remaining cream mixture. Repeat process with remaining biscuits, coffee mixture and cream mixture; sprinkle with chocolate. Cover; refrigerate 3 hours or overnight.
nutritional count per serving 70.4g total fat (45.5g saturated fat); 3536kJ (846 cal); 42.9g carbohydrate; 6.7g protein; 1.4g fibre

When translated from Italian, *tiramisu* means 'pick me up' – aptly named considering its punchy mix of caffeine and liqueur.

Old-fashioned Favourites

cream of chicken soup

—

shepherd's pie

—

green beans almondine

—

sugar-roasted pumpkin

—

bread and butter pudding

—

oat biscuits

When Sunday calls for comfort, turn to old favourites.

cream of chicken soup

preparation time 35 minutes
cooking time 2 hours 30 minutes
serves 4

2 litres (8 cups) water
1 litre (4 cups) chicken stock
1.8kg whole chicken
1 medium carrot (120g), chopped coarsely
1 trimmed celery stalk (100g), chopped coarsely
1 medium brown onion (150g), chopped coarsely
40g butter
⅓ cup (50g) plain flour
2 tablespoons lemon juice
½ cup (125ml) double cream
¼ cup finely chopped fresh flat-leaf parsley

1 Place the water and stock in large saucepan with chicken, carrot, celery and onion; bring to the boil. Reduce heat; simmer, covered, 1½ hours. Remove chicken from pan; simmer broth, covered, 30 minutes.
2 Strain broth through muslin-lined sieve or colander into large heatproof bowl; discard solids. Remove and discard chicken skin and bones; shred meat coarsely.
3 Melt butter in large saucepan, add flour; cook, stirring, until mixture thickens and bubbles. Gradually stir in broth and juice; bring to the boil, stirring. Add cream, reduce heat; simmer, uncovered, about 25 minutes, stirring occasionally. Add chicken; stir soup over medium heat until hot.
4 Serve bowls of soup sprinkled with parsley.
nutritional count per serving 58.6g total fat (14.9g saturated fat); 3327kJ (796 cal); 15.5g carbohydrate; 51.9g protein; 2.4g fibre

shepherd's pie

preparation time 20 minutes
cooking time 45 minutes
serves 4

30g butter
1 medium brown onion (150g), chopped finely
1 medium carrot (120g), chopped finely
½ teaspoon dried mixed herbs
4 cups (750g) chopped cooked lamb
¼ cup (70g) tomato paste
¼ cup (60ml) tomato sauce
2 tablespoons worcestershire sauce
2 cups (500ml) beef stock
2 tablespoons plain flour
⅓ cup (80ml) water

POTATO TOPPING
5 medium potatoes (1kg), chopped
60g butter, chopped
¼ cup (60ml) milk

1 Preheat oven to 220°C/200°C fan-assisted. Oil shallow 2.5-litre (10 cup) ovenproof dish.
2 Make potato topping.
3 Meanwhile, heat butter in large saucepan; cook onion and carrot, stirring, until tender. Add mixed herbs and lamb; cook, stirring, 2 minutes. Stir in paste, sauces and stock, then blended flour and water; stir over heat until mixture boils and thickens. Pour mixture into dish.
4 Place heaped tablespoons of potato topping on lamb mixture. Bake about 20 minutes or until browned lightly and heated through.
POTATO TOPPING
Boil, steam or microwave potatoes until tender; drain. Mash with butter and milk until smooth.
nutritional count per serving 36.2g total fat (20.2g saturated fat); 2976kJ (712 cal); 44.7g carbohydrate; 48.8g protein; 6g fibre

green beans almondine

preparation time 10 minutes
cooking time 10 minutes
serves 4

300g green beans
20g butter
1 clove garlic, crushed
2 rashers rindless bacon (130g), chopped finely
¼ cup (35g) slivered almonds

1 Boil, steam or microwave beans until just tender; drain. Rinse beans under cold water; drain.
2 Melt butter in large frying pan; cook garlic, bacon and nuts, stirring, until bacon crisps. Add beans; stir until hot.
nutritional count per serving 11.5g total fat (3.9g saturated fat); 602kJ (144 cal); 2.3g carbohydrate; 6.9g protein; 2.9g fibre

sugar-roasted pumpkin

preparation time 15 minutes
cooking time 1 hour
serves 4

1.5kg pumpkin, peeled, cut into wedges
30g butter, melted
2 tablespoons brown sugar
1 tablespoon wholegrain honey mustard

1 Preheat oven to 200°C/180°C fan-assisted.
2 Place pumpkin in large oiled baking dish; add combined butter, sugar and mustard. Toss to coat pumpkin in sugar mixture. Roast, uncovered, about 1 hour or until pumpkin is tender and slightly caramelised.
nutritional count per serving 7.5g total fat (5g saturated fat); 865kJ (207 cal); 26.2g carbohydrate; 6.7g protein; 3.8g fibre

bread and butter pudding

preparation time 20 minutes
cooking time 50 minutes
serves 4

6 slices white bread (270g)
40g butter, softened
½ cup (80g) sultanas
¼ teaspoon ground nutmeg
CUSTARD
1½ cups (375ml) milk
2 cups (500ml) double cream
⅓ cup (75g) caster sugar
½ teaspoon vanilla extract
4 eggs

1 Preheat oven to 160°C/140°C fan-assisted. Grease shallow 2-litre (8-cup) ovenproof dish.
2 Make custard.
3 Trim crusts from bread. Spread each slice with butter; cut into 4 triangles. Layer bread, overlapping, in dish; sprinkle with sultanas. Pour custard over bread; sprinkle with nutmeg.
4 Place dish in large baking dish; add enough boiling water to come halfway up sides of dish. Bake about 45 minutes or until pudding sets. Remove pudding from baking dish; stand 5 minutes before serving.
CUSTARD
Bring milk, cream, sugar and extract to the boil in medium saucepan. Whisk eggs in large bowl; whisking constantly, gradually add hot milk mixture to egg mixture.
nutritional count per serving 72.9g total fat (45.6g saturated fat); 4289kJ (1026 cal); 74g carbohydrate; 18.7g protein; 2.7g fibre

oat biscuits

preparation time 15 minutes
cooking time 20 minutes
makes 25

1 cup (90g) rolled oats
1 cup (150g) plain flour
1 cup (220g) firmly packed brown sugar
½ cup (40g) desiccated coconut
125g butter
2 tablespoons golden syrup
1 tablespoon water
½ teaspoon bicarbonate of soda

1 Preheat oven to 160°C/140°C fan-assisted. Grease oven trays; line with baking parchment.
2 Combine oats, sifted flour, sugar and coconut in large bowl. Stir butter, syrup and the water in small saucepan, over low heat until smooth; stir in soda. Stir into dry ingredients.
3 Roll level tablespoons of mixture into balls; place about 5cm apart on trays, flatten slightly.
4 Bake biscuits about 20 minutes; cool on trays.
nutritional count per serving 5.7g total fat (2.8g saturated fat); 523kJ (125 cal); 17g carbohydrate; 1.2g protein; 0.7g fibre

Spring

sparkling fruity punch

—

lemon-pepper lamb with
broad bean risoni

—

goats' cheese, pea and
mint salad

—

passionfruit buttermilk
puddings

Let your inspiration be the best of fresh spring produce.

sparkling fruity punch

preparation time 10 minutes
makes 3 litres (12 cups)

1 litre (4 cups) orange and passionfruit juice drink
1 cup (250ml) unsweetened pineapple juice
125g strawberries, chopped
¼ cup (60ml) passionfruit pulp
1 medium red apple (150g), chopped
medium orange (180g), peeled, chopped
3 cups (750ml) traditional lemonade
3 cups (750ml) cream soda
1½ cups (375ml) ginger beer
fresh mint sprigs

1 Combine orange and passionfruit juice drink, pineapple
juice and fruit in large bowl.
2 Just before serving, stir in remaining ingredients.
Serve cold.
nutritional count per 250ml 0.2g total fat (0g saturated fat);
523kJ (125 cal); 28.4g carbohydrate; 1.2g protein; 1.6g fibre

lemon-pepper lamb with broad bean risoni

preparation time 35 minutes (plus refrigeration time)
cooking time 20 minutes
serves 6

1 tablespoon finely grated lemon rind
1 tablespoon cracked black pepper
2 teaspoons sea salt
2 cloves garlic, sliced thinly
¼ cup (60ml) olive oil
6 lamb fillets (1.2kg)
500g frozen broad beans
1 cup (220g) risoni
6 spring onions, sliced thinly
1 cup coarsely chopped fresh flat-leaf parsley
½ cup coarsely chopped fresh mint
¼ cup (125ml) lemon juice

1 Combine rind, pepper, salt, garlic and half of the oil in large bowl with lamb. Cover; refrigerate 1 hour.
2 Meanwhile, place broad beans in large heatproof bowl, cover with boiling water; stand 10 minutes. Drain beans; when cool enough to handle, peel grey outer shell from beans. Discard shells; reserve beans.
3 Cook risoni in large saucepan of boiling water until just tender; drain. Rinse under cold water; drain.
4 Meanwhile, heat remaining oil in large frying pan; cook lamb, uncovered, until cooked as desired. Cover lamb, stand 5 minutes; slice lamb thickly.
5 Cook onion, stirring, in same pan until just softened. Add risoni and beans; cook, stirring, until heated through. Remove from heat; stir in herbs and juice.
6 Serve lamb with broad bean risoni.
nutritional count per serving 23.7g total fat (7.9g saturated fat); 2358kJ (564 cal); 32.1g carbohydrate; 52.3g protein; 6.2g fibre

goats' cheese, pea and mint salad

preparation time 25 minutes
cooking time 5 minutes
serves 6

1 cup (160g) shelled fresh peas
4 small celery sticks (150g), sliced thinly
½ cup loosely packed celery leaves
1 small curly endive, trimmed
1 small radicchio, leaves separated
3 trimmed red radishes (45g), sliced thinly
1 medium red apple (150g), sliced thinly
½ cup loosely packed fresh mint leaves
220g goats' cheese, sliced

HONEY MUSTARD DRESSING
1 teaspoon wholegrain mustard
1 tablespoon lemon juice
1 tablespoon honey
1 tablespoon olive oil

1 Boil, steam or microwave peas until just tender; drain. Refresh under cold water, drain.
2 Meanwhile make honey mustard dressing by combining ingredients in a screw-top jar; shake well.
3 Combine the peas with the remaining ingredients in a large bowl.
4 Just before serving, drizzle with honey mustard dressing.
nutritional count per serving 9.2g total fat (4.3g saturated fat); 688kJ (165 cal); 10.5g carbohydrate; 7.9g protein; 4.8g fibre

passionfruit buttermilk puddings

preparation time 20 minutes (plus refrigeration time)
cooking time 5 minutes
serves 6

3 cups (750ml) buttermilk
½ cup (110g) caster sugar
½ teaspoon vanilla bean paste
3 teaspoons gelatine
1 tablespoon water
6 passionfruit, approximately
¼ small canteloupe melon (250g)
¼ small honeydew melon (250g)
¼ small pineapple (250g)
1 passionfruit, extra

1 Heat buttermilk, sugar and vanilla in small saucepan over low heat until sugar dissolves. Remove from heat.
2 Meanwhile, sprinkle gelatine over water in small heatproof jug; place jug in small saucepan of simmering water, stir until gelatine dissolves. Cool slightly.
3 Stir gelatine mixture into buttermilk mixture. Strain through fine sieve into a jug; cool to room temperature.
4 Scoop pulp from passionfruit. Press pulp in a sieve over a bowl. You will need ⅓ cup (80ml) passionfruit juice. Stir juice into buttermilk mixture; pour into six greased ⅔-cup (160ml) dariole moulds. Cover; refrigerate 6 hours or overnight until firm.
5 Slice melons and pineapple; remove pulp from extra passionfruit.
6 Turn puddings out onto serving plates. Serve puddings with fruit.
nutritional count per serving 2.9g total fat (1.7g saturated fat); 874kJ (209 cal); 33g carbohydrate; 8.8g protein; 7.5g fibre

315

You are invited to a

Kids' Party

Choose a theme and let your imagination run wild...

Sugar and Spice

strawberry ice punch
-
heart-shaped hamwiches
-
strawberry and cream
meringues
-
sweetheart cake

Ages 2-5

... and all things nice – that's what little girls are made of.

strawberry ice punch

preparation time 15 minutes (plus freezing time)
serves 12

250g strawberries, sliced
½ cup (110g) caster sugar
pink food colouring
1 egg white, beaten lightly
1 litre (4 cups) chilled apple and strawberry juice
1 litre (4 cups) chilled mineral water
1 litre (4 cups) chilled lemonade

1 Place one strawberry slice into each hole of 12-hole ice-cube tray. Fill with water; freeze.
2 Combine sugar and a few drops of colouring in a small plastic bag; rub together until sugar is coloured pink. Place pink sugar on a saucer; place egg white on another saucer. Dip rim of each glass into beaten egg white then into sugar.
3 Just before serving, combine juice, mineral water and lemonade in large serving bowl; tint pink with a few drops of colouring. Add strawberries and strawberry ice cubes.
nutritional count per serving 0g total fat (0g saturated fat); 477kJ (114 cal); 27.2g carbohydrate; 0.7g protein; 0.5g fibre

heart-shaped hamwiches

preparation time 30 minutes
makes 18

18 large slices white bread
⅓ cup (80g) spreadable cream cheese
100g wafer-thin ham

1 Using 7.5cm heart cutter, cut two hearts from each slice of bread. Using 4cm heart cutter, cut out a smaller heart from the centre of half the large hearts.
2 Spread one side of the large uncut hearts with some of the cream cheese; top with ham. Spread the remaining cream cheese on one side of the remaining hearts; place on top of ham.
nutritional count per serving 2g total fat (1.1g saturated fat); 213kJ (51 cal); 5.6g carbohydrate; 2.5g protein; 0.4g fibre

strawberry and cream meringues

preparation time 25 minutes (plus cooling time)
cooking time 30 minutes
makes 12

2 egg whites
½ cup (110g) caster sugar
1 teaspoon white vinegar
2 teaspoons icing sugar
pink food colouring
½ cup (125ml) whipping cream, whipped
3 large strawberries, sliced thinly

1 Preheat oven to 120°C/100°C fan-assisted. Grease two oven trays; dust with cornflour, shake off excess.
2 Beat egg whites in small bowl with electric mixer until soft peaks form. Gradually add caster sugar, 1 tablespoon at a time, beating until dissolved between additions. Fold in vinegar, sifted icing sugar and a few drops of colouring.
3 Drop rounded tablespoons of meringue mixture, 3cm apart, on oven trays. Using the back of a teaspoon, make a small hollow in each meringue.
4 Bake meringues about 30 minutes. Cool meringues in oven with door ajar.
5 Just before serving, fill meringues with cream and top with strawberries.
nutritional count per serving 3.9g total fat (2.5g saturated fat); 330kJ (79 cal); 10.1g carbohydrate; 0.9g protein; 0.1g fibre

sweetheart cake

preparation time 50 minutes (plus standing and cooking time)
cooking time 20 minutes
makes 48 cupcakes

2 x 340g packets sponge mix
2 quantities buttercream (see below)
pink and red food colourings
48cm x 55cm cake board

BUTTERCREAM
125g butter, softened
1½ cups (240g) icing sugar
2 tablespoons milk

DECORATIONS
pink and white mini marshmallows, halved
raspberry jellies
small red jubes, cut in half
red fruit rings
red jelly beans
pink and white marshmallows
pink jelly beans
pink candy sticks

1 Preheat oven to 180°C/160°C fan-assisted. Line four 12-hole (⅓-cup/80ml) muffin tins with red paper cake cases.
2 Make cakes according to directions on packets; divide mixture evenly among cases. Bake about 20 minutes. Stand cakes 5 minutes before transferring to wire racks to cool.
3 Make buttercream; tint one-third of the buttercream pink, tint another third red and leave remaining third plain.
4 Spread one-third of the cakes with pink buttercream, another third with red buttercream and remaining cakes with plain buttercream.
5 Using picture as a guide, decorate cakes with sweets, as desired.
6 Arrange cupcakes, side by side, on prepared board, in the shape of a heart. Use candy sticks to outline the heart shape.
BUTTERCREAM
Beat butter in small bowl with electric mixer until as white as possible. Gradually beat in half the sifted icing sugar, milk, then remaining icing sugar.

Fairies

fresh violet lemonade

—

butterfly fairy bread

—

cheesy chicken strips

—

fairy wings cake

Ages 3-6

Put on your wings and play at the bottom of the garden.

fresh violet lemonade

preparation time 5 minutes (plus freezing time)
serves 12

12 fresh violets
1.25 litre bottle chilled lemonade

1 Remove stems from violets; place one violet, facing up, into a 12-hole ice cube tray.
2 Carefully pour water over each violet to fill ice-cube tray; push violets down so they are submerged. Freeze until solid.
3 Just before serving, divide lemonade among 12 glasses; add ice cubes.
nutritional count per serving 0g total fat (0g saturated fat); 192kJ (46 cal); 11.3g carbohydrate; 0g protein; 0g fibre

butterfly fairy bread

preparation time 15 minutes
makes 36

12 large slices white bread
60g soft butter
6 pink candy sticks, halved lengthways
½ cup hundreds and thousands

1 Spread butter on one side of each bread slice. Using a 6cm butterfly cutter, cut out three butterflies from each slice.
2 Cut each candy stick into 2cm lengths; place one piece of musk stick in centre of each butterfly.
3 Sprinkle hundreds and thousands into small shallow dish; gently press each butterfly, buttered-side down, into hundreds and thousands. Place on serving plate.
nutritional count per butterfly 1.6g total fat (0.9g saturated fat); 188kJ (45 cal); 6.7g carbohydrate; 0.7g protein; 0.2g fibre

cheesy chicken strips

preparation time 15 minutes
cooking time 25 minutes
serves 12

1kg small chicken tenderloins, halved lengthways
½ cup (75g) plain flour
2 eggs
¼ cup (60ml) milk
1½ cups (240g) cornflake crumbs
½ cup (40g) finely grated parmesan cheese
cooking-oil spray

1 Preheat oven to 200°C /180°C fan-assisted.
2 Coat chicken in flour; shake away excess. Dip chicken in combined egg and milk; coat in combined crumbs and cheese.
3 Place chicken, in single layer, on wire rack over oven tray; spray with oil. Cook about 25 minutes or until cooked through.
4 Serve chicken strips with tomato ketcup.
nutritional count per serving 7.3g total fat (2.6g saturated fat); 1024kJ (245 cal); 21.6g carbohydrate; 22.4g protein; 0.8g fibre

fairy wings cake

preparation time 1 hour 10 minutes (plus standing time)
cooking time 20 minutes
makes 54 cupcakes

Buy the birthday girl a doll she'll love then choose the colour for the wings to match the doll.

470g packet sponge cake mix
pink food colouring
¼ cup (80g) apricot jam, warmed, sieved
35cm x 45cm prepared cake board

DECORATIONS
½ cup (80g) icing sugar
300g ready-made white icing
28cm doll
60g jar silver cachous
6 blue ready-made icing flowers
6 pink ready-made icing flowers

1 Preheat oven to 180°C/160°C fan-assisted. Line 12-hole (2-tablespoon/40ml) deep flat-based patty tin with standard silver paper cases. Line four 12-hole mini (1-tablespoon/20ml) muffin tins with mini silver paper cases.
2 Make cake according to directions on packet. Drop 2 level tablespoons of the mixture into each standard paper case; drop 2 level teaspoons of the mixture into each mini paper case. Bake large cakes about 20 minutes; bake small cakes about 15 minutes. Stand cakes in pans 5 minutes; turn, top-side up, onto wire rack to cool.
3 Brush tops of all cakes with jam. On a surface dusted with sifted icing sugar, knead the ready-made icing until smooth. Tint two-thirds of the icing pale pink; tint remaining icing dark pink.
4 Roll dark pink icing until 3mm thick. Using a 4.5cm fluted cutter, cut 10 rounds from the icing; position rounds on large cakes. Roll pale pink icing until 3mm thick. Using a 3cm fluted cutter, cut 44 rounds from icing; position rounds on small cakes.
5 Position doll on prepared board. Using picture as a guide, position cakes around doll for wings; secure with a little butter cream. Gently push cachous onto pale pink cakes. Brush the backs of the ready-made icing flowers with a little water, then position on dark pink cakes.
TIP You'll have about 1 cup of the cake mixture left over, enough for about six more little cakes

Jungle Beat

jungle slush

–

king of the jungle cupcakes

–

bacon-wrapped chicken patties

–

swamp cake

Ages 4-8

Watch your little Tarzan or Jane go wild with delight.

jungle slush

preparation time 30 minutes
serves 12

12 kiwi fruit (1kg)
3½ cups ice cubes
3 cups (750ml) chilled kiwi mix fruit juice

1 Peel kiwi fruit, quarter lengthways; remove core and as many black seeds as possible.
2 Just before serving, blend kiwifruit, ice cubes and juice, in batches, until almost smooth. Pour slush into large jug to serve.
nutritional count per serving 0.1g total fat (0g saturated fat); 272kJ (65 cal); 13.6g carbohydrate; 1g protein; 2.3g fibre

king of the jungle cupcakes

preparation time 40 minutes
cooking time 20 minutes
makes 12

340g packet sponge cake mix
1 quantity buttercream (see page 322)
caramel food colouring

DECORATIONS
5 x 50g Crunchie bars
1 licorice bootlace
24 dark chocolate chips

1 Preheat oven to 180°C/160°C fan-assisted. Line 12-hole (⅓-cup/80ml) muffin tin with paper cases.
2 Make cake according to directions on packet; divide mixture evenly among cases. Bake about 20 minutes. Stand cakes 5 minutes before turning, top-side up, onto wire rack to cool.
3 Tint butter cream with caramel colouring. Spread cakes with butter cream.
4 Cut Crunchie bars into thin shards. Cut licorice bootlace into 12 small triangles for nose; cut remaining licorice into strips to make whiskers and mouth.
5 Position licorice on cakes to make face; use chocolate chips for eyes. Use crumble bar shards to make lions' manes.
nutritional count per serving 21.3g total fat (12g saturated fat); 1806kJ (432 cal); 56.2g carbohydrate; 3.4g protein; 0.6g fibre

bacon-wrapped chicken patties

preparation time 45 minutes (plus freezing time)
cooking time 15 minutes
makes 24

400g minced chicken
1 tablespoon finely chopped chives
2 tablespoons finely chopped fresh flat-leaf parsley
1 trimmed celery stick (100g), chopped finely
1 clove garlic, crushed
1 teaspoon finely grated lemon rind
2 tablespoons packaged breadcrumbs
¼ cup (20g) finely grated parmesan cheese
¼ cup (75g) mayonnaise
3 thin rindless rashers bacon (90g)

1 Combine chicken, herbs, celery, garlic, rind, breadcrumbs, cheese and mayonnaise in medium bowl. Shape rounded tablespoons of mixture into patties; place on baking-parchment-lined tray. Freeze 30 minutes.
2 Meanwhile, cut each bacon rasher in half crossways then cut each half into four lengthways strips. Wrap a strip of bacon around each patty; secure with toothpicks.
3 Cook patties in heated oiled large frying pan until browned all over and cooked through. Remove toothpicks before serving.
nutritional count per serving 3.2g total fat (0.9g saturated fat); 213kJ (51 cal); 1.1g carbohydrate; 4.4g protein; 0.2g fibre

swamp cake

preparation time 1 hour (plus refrigeration and standing time)
cooking time 1 hour 20 minutes
serves 12

3 x 340g packets sponge cake mix
85g packet purple jelly crystals
85g packet green jelly crystals
1 quantity buttercream (see page 322)
180g white eating chocolate, melted
green and brown food colourings

DECORATIONS
fresh violet leaves
assorted toy swamp animals
green jelly snakes
milk chocolate-covered sultanas
red and orange boiled sweets
30g Flake bar, halved
150g white eating chocolate, melted
25 fresh camellia leaves, approximately

1 Preheat oven to 180°C/160°C fan-assisted. Grease and line deep 26cm x 36cm baking dish.

2 Make cakes according to directions on packets, pour into dish; bake about 1 hour. Stand cake 20 minutes before turning onto wire rack to cool.

3 Make jellies, separately, according to directions on packets; pour enough of the purple jelly into the green jelly until it becomes a 'swampy' green colour. Refrigerate until set.

4 Using serrated knife, level top of cake. Turn cake cut-side down. Cut free-form shape of swamp from outside edge of cake, as pictured.

5 Position cake, cut-side down, on platter. Mark a rough outline on cake for swamp water; hollow out area, making it about 2cm deep.

6 Tint buttercream green.

7 Make chocolate leaves by tinting melted white chocolate pale green using the green colouring. Brush chocolate onto back of clean, dry camellia leaves. When leaves have set (best at room temperature), carefully peel leaves away from the chocolate.

8 Cover top and sides of cake with buttercream up to the swamp-water line. Using whisk, break up jelly; spoon into swamp hollow. Position violet leaves on jelly and animals and snakes on and around cake.

9 Make campfire by using sultanas and crushed boiled sweets. Position Flake for logs near campfire. Make a 'no swimming' sign; secure to wooden skewer or lolly stick, position on cake. Decorate side of cake with chocolate leaves.

Disco

iced chocolate latte

—

mini pizzas with 3 toppings

—

microphone ice-creams

—

disco cake

Ages 8-10

Boogie on down for the hottest party in town.

iced chocolate latte

preparation time 15 minutes
serves 12

255g bottle Monster Crackin' chocolate dessert topping
300ml whipping cream
3 litres (12 cups) chilled milk
1 cup (250 ml) chocolate dessert topping
2 litres chocolate and vanilla swirl ice-cream
2 x 30g Flake bars, crumbled

1 Drizzle Monster Crackin' topping down the inside of 12 chilled glasses. Stand about 5 minutes or until set.
2 Meanwhile, beat cream in small bowl with electric mixer until soft peaks form.
3 Combine milk and topping in large jug; pour chocolate milk into glasses.
4 Just before serving, top each glass with a scoop of ice-cream then a dollop of cream; sprinkle with crumbled Flakes. Serve with a long spoon and a drinking straw.
nutritional count per serving 37.6g total fat (24.2g saturated fat); 2583kJ (618 cal); 56.3g carbohydrate; 13.8g protein; 0g fibre

mini pizzas with 3 toppings

preparation time 20 minutes
cooking time 20 minutes
makes 12

Each of the toppings makes enough for four pizza bases.

1 cup (280) tomato paste
12 x 225g mini pizza bases

HAM AND PINEAPPLE
1½ cups (150g) pizza cheese
150g sliced ham, chopped coarsely
1 cup (180g) drained canned pineapple pieces

VEGETARIAN
1½ cups (150g) pizza cheese
½ cup (120g) coarsely chopped char-grilled pepper
50g button mushrooms, sliced thinly
¼ cup (30g) pitted black olives, sliced thinly
⅓ cup (50g) drained semi-dried tomatoes,
   chopped coarsely

CHICKEN, BROCCOLI AND SWEET CHILLI
1 cup (85g) small broccoli florets
1½ cups (150g) pizza cheese
2 cups (320g) shredded cooked chicken
¼ cup (60ml) sweet chilli sauce

1 Preheat oven to 200°C/180°C fan-assisted.
2 Spread 1 tablespoon of the tomato paste over each pizza base. Place bases on oven trays; sprinkle with toppings, as instructed, below. Bake about 20 minutes or until browned.
HAM AND PINEAPPLE
Sprinkle 1 cup of the cheese over four bases. Top with ham, pineapple then remaining cheese.
nutritional count per pizza 18.2g total fat (6.9g saturated fat); 3557kJ (851 cal); 126g carbohydrate; 39.1g protein; 10g fibre
VEGETARIAN
Sprinkle 1 cup of the pizza cheese over four bases. Top with pepper, mushrooms, olives and tomato then remaining pizza cheese.
nutritional count per pizza 20g total fat (6.7g saturated fat); 3582kJ (857 cal); 128g carbohydrate; 34g protein; 11.4g fibre
CHICKEN, BROCCOLI AND SWEET CHILLI
Drop broccoli into small saucepan of boiling water; return to a boil, drain. Sprinkle 1 cup of the cheese over four bases. Top with chicken and remaining cheese. Serve sprinkled with broccoli and sauce.
nutritional count per pizza 29.5g total fat (10.1g saturated fat); 4147kJ (992 cal); 125g carbohydrate; 50.3g protein; 10.8g fibre

microphone ice-creams

preparation time 20 minutes (plus freezing time)
makes 12

45cm licorice bootlace
12 square-based ice-cream cones
2 litres vanilla ice-cream
255g bottle Monster Crackin' chocolate dessert topping
edible silver glitter

1 Cut licorice bootlace into three 15cm lengths, cut each length into 4 strips.
2 Using skewer, make a small hole near the base of each cone (not through the bottom, otherwise the cones won't stand up). Push end of licorice strip into each hole for microphone lead.
3 Push some ice-cream firmly into cones to hold licorice in place. Fill cones with ice-cream until level with tops of cones.
4 Using ice-cream scoop, top cones with ice-cream domes. Place cones on tray; freeze about 10 minutes or until firm.
5 Pour Monster Crackin' topping into small bowl; dip ice-cream into chocolate, sprinkle with glitter. Return cones to freezer until required.
nutritional count per microphone 17g total fat (10.6g saturated fat); 1195kJ (286 cal); 28.6g carbohydrate; 4.7g protein; 0.1g fibre

disco cake

preparation time 45 minutes
cooking time 1 hour
serves 12

3 x 340g packets sponge cake mix
30cm x 46cm cake board
2 quantities buttercream (see page 322)
pink food colouring

DECORATIONS
red, yellow, orange and green fruit rings
red, orange, green, purple and yellow 'fruit salad'
   soft jellies
red, orange, yellow, green and purple jelly beans
yellow, red, orange, purple and green mixed sweets
purple, yellow, red, orange and green Smarties
2cm silver disco ball
edible silver glitter
4 x 30cm silver pipe cleaners (tinsel sticks)

1 Preheat oven to 180°C/160°C fan-assisted. Grease and line deep 26cm x 36cm baking dish.
2 Make cakes according to directions on packets, pour into dish; bake about 1 hour. Stand cake 20 minutes before turning, top-side up, onto wire rack to cool.
3 Using serrated knife, level top of cake. Place cake on prepared board, cut-side down.
4 Tint buttercream with colouring; spread all over cake.
5 Sort sweets into five small bowls according to colour. Mark out the letters of 'DISCO' with a skewer.
6 Using one colour for each letter, arrange sweets, overlapping, pressing to secure to cake. Position disco ball above the 'i'. Sprinkle edible glitter all over top of cake. Position pipe cleaners around base of cake.

Attach party invitations to a mini disco ball, and decorate the table with glitter and brightly coloured plates and cups. Play karaoke, limbo, or for that professional touch, hire a DJ.

Teen Dream

mixed berry punch

—

vegetable rice paper rolls

—

mascarpone and ham
pizza bites

—

cheeseburgers

—

watermelon and
strawberry ice-block

—

cookies and cream cheesecake

Ages 13-18

Alfresco fun.

mixed berry punch

preparation time 15 minutes (plus refrigeration time)
serves 8

1 teabag
1 cup (250ml) boiling water
120g raspberries
150g blueberries
125g strawberries, halved
¼ cup loosely packed fresh mint leaves
750ml chilled non-alcoholic apple cider
2½ cups (625ml) chilled lemonade

1 Place teabag in mug, cover with the boiling water;
stand 10 minutes. Squeeze teabag over mug, discard
teabag; cool tea 10 minutes.
2 Using fork, crush raspberries in punch bowl; add
blueberries, strawberries, mint and tea. Stir to combine,
cover; refrigerate 1 hour. Stir cider and lemonade into punch
just before serving; sprinkle with extra mint leaves, if desired.
nutritional count per serving 0.1g total fat (0g saturated fat);
393kJ (94 cal); 21.6g carbohydrate; 0.6g protein; 1.5g fibre

vegetable rice paper rolls

preparation time 30 minutes
makes 24

1 large carrot (180g), grated coarsely
2 trimmed celery sticks (200g), chopped finely
150g wombok (chinese cabbage), shredded finely
2 teaspoons fish sauce
2 teaspoons brown sugar
1 tablespoon lemon juice
24 x 17cm-square rice paper sheets
24 fresh mint leaves
sweet chilli sauce, to serve

1 Combine carrot, celery, wombok, sauce, sugar and juice in medium bowl.
2 Place 1 sheet of rice paper in medium bowl of warm water until just softened; lift sheet carefully from water, place on tea-towel-covered board.
3 Place 1 level tablespoon of vegetable mixture across edge of sheet; top with mint leaf. Roll to enclose filling, folding in ends. Repeat with remaining rice paper sheets, vegetable mixture and mint leaves.
4 Serve with sweet chilli sauce.
nutritional count per roll 0.2g total fat (0g saturated fat); 92kJ (22 cal); 3.9g carbohydrate; 0.8g protein; 0.7g fibre

mascarpone and ham pizza bites

preparation time 20 minutes
cooking time 10 minutes
makes 24

335g (30cm) ready-made pizza base
2 tablespoons tomato paste
100g wafer-thin ham
2 tablespoons mascarpone cheese
2 teaspoons finely chopped fresh chives

1 Preheat oven to 220°C/200°C fan-assisted.
2 Using 4.5cm-round cutter, cut rounds from pizza base.
3 Place rounds on oven trays. Divide paste evenly over rounds; top with ham, cheese and chives.
4 Bake pizzas about 5 minutes or until heated through.
nutritional count per pizza 1.5g total fat (0.7g saturated fat); 226kJ (54 cal); 7.6g carbohydrate; 2.2g protein; 0.6g fibre

cheeseburgers

preparation time 20 minutes (plus refrigeration time)
cooking time 20 minutes
makes 24

200g minced beef
2 spring onions, chopped finely
2 tablespoons barbecue sauce
¾ cup (75g) packaged breadcrumbs
1 egg
1 clove garlic, crushed
6 hamburger buns
2 tablespoons tomato sauce
1 tablespoon american mustard
4 slices packaged cheddar cheese
1 large dill pickle (50g), sliced thinly

1 Using one hand, combine beef, onion, barbecue sauce, breadcrumbs, egg and garlic in medium bowl. Using hands, shape beef mixture into 24 patties. Place on tray, cover; refrigerate 10 minutes.
2 Heat large oiled non-stick frying pan; cook patties, in batches, until browned both sides and cooked as desired. Cover patties to keep hot.
3 Meanwhile, preheat grill.
4 Slice buns in half horizontally. Using 4cm-round cutter, cut four rounds from each bun half; place on oven trays. Toast buns, cut-side up, under hot grill until browned lightly.
5 Combine tomato sauce and mustard in small bowl; divide mixture evenly among bun bases. Cut each slice of cheese into six rectangles. Top each bun base with pickle slice, hot patty, cheese then bun top.
nutritional count per burger 2.6g total fat (1.1g saturated fat); 364kJ (87 cal); 10.9g carbohydrate; 4.5g protein; 0.7g fibre

watermelon and strawberry ice-block

preparation time 10 minutes (plus freezing time)
cooking time 5 minutes (plus cooling time)
serves 4

⅓ cup (80ml) water
2 tablespoons sugar
250g piece watermelon, peeled, deseeded,
  chopped coarsely
80g strawberries, chopped coarsely
2 teaspoons lemon juice

1 Stir the water and sugar in small saucepan over low heat until sugar dissolves. Bring to the boil; boil, uncovered about 2 minutes or until mixture thickens slightly. Transfer syrup to small bowl; refrigerate until cold.
2 Blend or process cold syrup, watermelon, strawberries and juice until smooth. Pour mixture into four ⅓-cup (80ml) ice-block moulds. Freeze overnight until firm.
nutritional count per serving 0.2g total fat (0g saturated fat); 238kJ (57 cal); 12.7g carbohydrate; 0.5g protein; 0.8g fibre

Ice-blocks make the perfect ending to a teenager's summer party. Make more than you need – they're bound to come back for seconds.

cookies and cream cheesecake

preparation time 20 minutes (plus refrigeration time)
cooking time 5 minutes
serves 12

250g plain chocolate biscuits
150g butter, melted
2 teaspoons gelatine
¼ cup (60ml) water
1½ cups (360g) packaged cream cheese, softened
300ml whipping cream
1 teaspoon vanilla extract
½ cup (110g) caster sugar
180g white eating chocolate, melted
150g cream-filled chocolate biscuits, quartered
50g dark eating chocolate, melted

1 Line base of 23cm springform tin with baking parchment.
2 Blend or process plain chocolate biscuits until mixture resembles fine breadcrumbs. Add butter; process until just combined. Using hand, press biscuit mixture evenly over base and 3cm up side of prepared tin, cover; refrigerate 20 minutes.
3 Sprinkle gelatine over the water in small heatproof jug; stand jug in small saucepan of simmering water. Stir until gelatine dissolves; cool 5 minutes.
4 Beat cheese, cream, extract and sugar in medium bowl with electric mixer until smooth. Stir in gelatine mixture and white chocolate; fold in quartered biscuits. Pour cheesecake mixture over biscuit mixture in tin, cover; refrigerate about 3 hours or until set. Drizzle with dark chocolate to serve.
per serving 41.9g total fat (26.7g saturated fat); 2362kJ (565 cal); 42.8g carbohydrate; 6.8g protein; 0.8g fibre
TIP Place the dark chocolate in a small plastic bag with the corner snipped off to help you drizzle the chocolate evenly over the cheesecake.

You are invited to a

Big
Party

Increase quantities according to the party's size...

New Year's Eve

classic cosmopolitan
—
steak with salsa verde
on mini toasts
—
oak leaf and mixed herb salad
with dijon vinaigrette
—
paella with aïoli
—
whole fish in a salt crust
with gremolata
—
decadent chocolate roulade

Bring in the new year with a fire-cracker of a menu.

classic cosmopolitan

preparation time 5 minutes
serves 8

4 cup ice cubes
⅔ cups (160ml) vodka
½ cup (125ml) Cointreau
1 cup (250ml) cranberry juice
¼ cup (60ml) lime juice

1 Combine a quarter of the ice cubes, vodka, Cointreau, and juices in cocktail shaker; shake vigorously. Strain into chilled 230ml martini glass.
2 Repeat with remaining ingredients to make eight cosmopolitans. Garnish with 2cm strip orange rind, if desired.
nutritional count per serving 0.1g total fat (0.1g saturated fat); 539kJ (129 cal); 12g carbohydrate; 0.1g protein; 0g fibre

steak with salsa verde on mini toasts

preparation time 20 minutes
cooking time 10 minutes
makes 36

200g piece beef fillet steak
½ cup finely chopped fresh flat-leaf parsley
¼ cup finely chopped fresh basil
1 tablespoon drained baby capers, rinsed
1 clove garlic, crushed
1 tablespoon lemon juice
1 tablespoon olive oil
1 packet mini toasts (80g)
2 tablespoons dijon mustard

1 Cook steak on heated oiled grill plate (or grill or barbecue) until cooked as desired. Cover steak; stand 10 minutes, slice thinly.
2 Meanwhile, combine herbs, capers, garlic, juice and oil in medium bowl, add steak; toss gently to coat in mixture.
3 Place mini toasts on serving platter; divide mustard and steak among mini toasts.
nutritional count per piece 1.0g total fat (0.2g saturated fat); 92kJ (22 cal); 1.7g carbohydrate; 1.5g protein; 0.2g fibre

oak leaf and mixed herb salad with dijon vinaigrette

preparation time 10 minutes
serves 8

2 green oak leaf lettuces, leaves separated
¼ cup coarsely chopped fresh chives
1 cup firmly packed fresh flat-leaf parsley leaves
½ cup firmly packed fresh chervil leaves

DIJON VINAIGRETTE
¼ cup (60ml) olive oil
¼ cup (60ml) white wine vinegar
1 tablespoon dijon mustard
2 teaspoons white sugar

1 Place ingredients for dijon vinaigrette in screw-top jar; shake well.
2 Place lettuce and herbs in medium bowl with dressing; toss gently to combine.
nutritional count per serving 7g total fat (1g saturated fat); 318kJ (76 cal); 1.8g carbohydrate; 0.9g protein; 1.5g fibre

paella with aïoli

preparation time 20 minutes
cooking time 40 minutes
serves 8

large pinch saffron threads
¼ cup (60ml) boiling water
700g uncooked medium king prawns
700g large black mussels
1 tablespoon olive oil
600g chicken thigh fillets, chopped coarsely
300g chorizo sausage, sliced thinly
1 large red onion (300g), chopped finely
2 medium red pepper (400g), chopped finely
2 cloves garlic, crushed
1 teaspoon smoked paprika
400g can whole peeled tomatoes, drained,
  chopped coarsely
1½ cups (300g) calasparra rice (or medium grain rice)
3 cups (750ml) chicken stock
½ cup (60g) frozen peas
1 tablespoon finely chopped fresh flat-leaf parsley

AIOLI
2 egg yolks
4 cloves garlic, quartered
1 teaspoon sea salt
¾ cup (180ml) olive oil
1 tablespoon lemon juice
1 tablespoon boiling water

1 Make aïoli.
2 Place saffron and water in small bowl. Stand 15 minutes.
3 Shell and de-vein prawns, leaving tails intact. Scrub mussels, remove beards.
4 Heat oil in 30cm (top measurement) paella pan, add chicken, cook until browned all over; remove from pan. Add chorizo to same pan, cook until browned on both sides; drain on absorbent paper.
5 Add onion, red pepper, garlic and paprika to same pan; cook, stirring, until soft. Stir in tomatoes. Add rice and stir to coat in mixture.
6 Return chicken and chorizo to pan with stock and saffron mixture; stir only until combined. Don't stir again. Bring to the boil, then simmer, uncovered, about 15 minutes or until rice is almost tender.
7 Sprinkle peas over the rice; place prawns and mussels evenly over surface of paella. Cover pan with large sheets of foil; simmer, covered, for 5-10 minutes or until prawns are just cooked through and mussels have opened (discard any that do not).
8 Sprinkle with parsley, serve with aïoli.
AIOLI
Blend or process the egg yolks, garlic and sea salt until smooth. With the motor operating, gradually add the oil; process until thick. Stir in juice and water. Cover surface with plastic wrap.
nutritional count per serving 42.4g total fat (9.8g saturated fat); 2926kJ (700 cal); 39.7g carbohydrate; 39.2g protein; 3.5g fibre

whole fish in a salt crust with gremolata

preparation time 10 minutes
cooking time 35 minutes
serves 8

2 x 1kg whole snapper, cleaned, scales left on
3kg coarse cooking salt, approximately

GREMOLATA
½ cup finely chopped fresh flat-leaf parsley
2 cloves garlic, crushed
1 tablespoon finely grated lemon rind
2 tablespoons extra virgin olive oil

1 Preheat oven to 240°C/220°C fan-assisted.
2 Combine ingredients for gremolata in small bowl.
3 Wash fish, pat dry inside and out. Fill cavities of fish with half the gremolata.
4 Divide half the salt between two ovenproof trays large enough to hold fish (ovenproof metal oval platters are ideal). Place fish on salt.
5 Place remaining salt in large sieve or colander and run quickly under cold water until salt is damp. Press salt firmly over fish to completely cover fish.
6 Bake fish 35 minutes. Remove from oven; stand 5 minutes. Using a hammer or meat mallet and old knife, break open the crust then lift away with the scales and skin.
7 Serve fish with remaining gremolata.
nutritional count per serving 6.1g total fat (1.2g saturated fat); 560kJ (134 cal); 0.1g carbohydrate; 19.4g protein; 0.4g fibre
TIP We used snapper for this dish, but any suitable whole white fish can be used.

The fish is not scaled because a rough surface helps the salt adhere better. And, when the salt crust is removed, the skin will stick to it leaving the moist flesh behind. While the amount of salt used sounds a lot, this is not a salty dish.

decadent chocolate roulade

preparation time 15 minutes (plus refrigeration time)
cooking time 20 minutes (plus cooling time)
serves 8

1 tablespoon caster sugar
200g dark eating chocolate, chopped
¼ cup (60ml) hot water
1 teaspoon dry instant coffee
4 eggs, separated
½ cup (110g) caster sugar, extra
300ml whipping cream
120g raspberries

1 Preheat oven to 180°C/160°C fan-assisted. Grease 25cm x 30cm swiss roll tin; line base with baking parchment, extending paper 5cm over two long sides of pan. Place a piece of baking parchment, cut the same size as swiss roll tin, on bench; sprinkle evenly with caster sugar.
2 Combine chocolate, the hot water and coffee in medium heatproof bowl. Stir over medium saucepan of simmering water until smooth; remove from heat.
3 Beat egg yolks and extra sugar in small bowl with an electric mixer until thick and creamy. Fold egg mixture into warm chocolate mixture.
4 Beat egg whites in small clean bowl with electric mixer until soft peaks form. Gently fold egg whites into chocolate mixture, in two batches. Spread mixture into tin.
5 Bake cake about 15 minutes.
6 Turn cake onto sugared paper, peeling baking parchment away; use serrated knife to cut away crisp edges from all sides. Cover cake with tea towel; cool.
7 Beat cream in small bowl with electric mixer until firm peaks form. Spread cake evenly with cream; sprinkle evenly with raspberries. Roll cake, from long side, by lifting parchment and using it to guide the roll into log shape. Cover roll; refrigerate 30 minutes before serving.
nutritional count per serving 31.5g total fat (18.8g saturated fat); 2023kJ (484 cal); 45.4g carbohydrate; 7.5g protein; 1.8g fibre

Winter Feast

pork, chicken and
black-eyed bean cassoulet
—
osso buco with semi-dried
tomatoes and olives
—
soft polenta
—
beans with lemon
chilli breadcrumbs
—
classic trifle

Enjoy the great indoors with a slow-cooked banquet.

pork, chicken and black-eyed bean cassoulet

preparation time 20 minutes (plus standing time)
cooking time 2 hours 45 minutes
serves 6

1 cup (200g) black-eyed beans
1 tablespoon olive oil
500g boned pork belly, rind removed, sliced thinly
8 chicken drumsticks (640g)
4 thin pork sausages (320g)
1 trimmed celery stalk (100g), sliced thinly
1 medium brown onion (150g), chopped coarsely
1 small leek (200g), sliced thinly
1 teaspoon fresh thyme leaves
½ cup (125ml) dry white wine
400g can diced tomatoes
2 cups (500ml) chicken stock
3 cups (210g) stale breadcrumbs
½ cup finely chopped fresh flat-leaf parsley
50g butter, melted

1 Place beans in medium bowl, cover with cold water; stand 3 hours or overnight, drain. Rinse beans under cold water; drain.
2 Preheat oven to 180°C/160°C fan-assisted.
3 Heat oil in large flameproof casserole dish; cook pork, chicken and sausages, in batches, until browned all over.
4 Cook celery, onion, leek and thyme in same dish, stirring, until onion softens. Add wine; cook, stirring, 5 minutes. Return pork, chicken and sausages to dish with undrained tomatoes, stock and beans; cook, covered, in oven 40 minutes.
5 Sprinkle cassoulet with combined breadcrumbs, parsley and butter. Cook, uncovered, in oven further 40 minutes or until meat is tender and top is lightly browned.
nutritional count per serving 48.5g total fat (18.2g saturated fat); 3474kJ (831 cal); 43.6g carbohydrate; 47g protein; 10.6g fibre

osso buco with semi-dried tomatoes and olives

preparation time 30 minutes
cooking time 2 hours 35 minutes
serves 6

12 pieces veal osso buco (3kg)
¼ cup (35g) plain flour
¼ cup (60ml) olive oil
40g butter
1 medium brown onion (150g), chopped coarsely
2 cloves garlic, chopped finely
3 trimmed celery stalks (300g), chopped coarsely
2 large carrots (360g), chopped coarsely
4 medium tomatoes (600g), chopped coarsely
2 tablespoons tomato paste
1 cup (250ml) dry white wine
1 cup (250ml) beef stock
400g can crushed tomatoes
4 sprigs fresh lemon thyme
½ cup (75g) drained semi-dried tomatoes
¼ cup (60ml) lemon juice
1 tablespoon finely grated lemon rind
½ cup (75g) pitted kalamata olives

GREMOLATA
1 tablespoon finely grated lemon rind
⅓ cup finely chopped fresh flat-leaf parsley
2 cloves garlic, chopped finely

1 Coat veal in flour; shake off excess. Heat oil in large deep saucepan; cook veal, in batches, until browned all over.
2 Melt butter in same pan; cook onion, garlic, celery and carrot, stirring, until vegetables just soften. Stir in fresh tomato, paste, wine, stock, undrained tomatoes and thyme. Return veal to pan, fitting pieces upright and tightly together in single layer; bring to the boil. Reduce heat; simmer, covered, 1¾ hours. Stir in semi-dried tomatoes; simmer, uncovered, about 30 minutes or until veal is tender.
3 Meanwhile, combine ingredients for gremolata in small bowl.
4 Remove veal from pan; cover to keep warm.
5 Bring sauce to the boil; boil, uncovered, about 10 minutes or until sauce thickens slightly. Stir in juice, rind and olives. Serve veal with gremolata.
nutritional count per serving 21.4g total fat (6.6g saturated fat); 2859kJ (684 cal); 22.3g carbohydrate; 89g protein; 8.1g fibre

soft polenta

preparation time 5 minutes
cooking time 12 minutes
serves 6

3 cups (750ml) water
2 cups (500ml) vegetable stock
2 cups (340g) polenta
1 cup (250ml) milk
¼ cup (25g) finely grated parmesan cheese

1 Bring the water and stock to the boil in large saucepan. Gradually add polenta to liquid, stirring constantly. Reduce heat; simmer, stirring, about 10 minutes or until it thickens.
2 Add milk and cheese; stir until cheese melts.
nutritional count per serving 4.2g total fat (2.1g saturated fat); 1016kJ (243 cal); 41.7g carbohydrate; 8.2g protein; 1.6g fibre

beans with lemon chilli breadcrumbs

preparation time 10 minutes
cooking time 20 minutes
serves 6

150g green beans, trimmed
150g yellow beans, trimmed
300g frozen broad beans
2 tablespoons olive oil
2 tablespoons lemon juice

LEMON CHILLI BREADCRUMBS
25g butter
1 tablespoon finely grated lemon rind
1/3 cup (25g) stale breadcrumbs
¼ teaspoon chilli powder

1 Make lemon chilli breadcrumbs.
2 Boil, steam or microwave green, yellow and broad beans, separately, until tender; drain. Peel away grey outer shells from broad beans.
3 Place all beans in medium bowl with oil and juice; toss gently to combine. Sprinkle with breadcrumbs.
LEMON CHILLI BREADCRUMBS
Melt butter in small frying pan; cook remaining ingredients over low heat, stirring, until crumbs are browned.
nutritional count per serving 10g total fat (3.2g saturated fat); 577kJ (138 cal); 5.2g carbohydrate; 4.9g protein; 4.4g fibre

classic trifle

preparation time 30 minutes (plus refrigeration time)
cooking time 10 minutes
serves 6

85g packet raspberry jelly crystals
200g sponge cake, cut into 3cm pieces
2 tablespoons sweet sherry
¼ cup (30g) custard powder
¼ cup (55g) caster sugar
½ teaspoon vanilla extract
1½ cups (375ml) milk
825g can sliced peaches, drained
300ml whipping cream
2 tablespoons flaked almonds, roasted

1 Make jelly according to directions on packet; pour into shallow container. Refrigerate 20 minutes or until jelly is almost set.
2 Arrange cake in 3-litre (12-cup) bowl; sprinkle with sherry.
3 Blend custard powder, sugar and extract with a little of the milk in small saucepan; stir in remaining milk. Stir over heat until mixture boils and thickens. Cover surface with cling film; cool.
4 Pour jelly over cake; refrigerate 15 minutes.
5 Top jelly layer with peaches. Stir a third of the cream into custard; pour over peaches.
6 Whip remaining cream; spread over custard, sprinkle with nuts. Refrigerate 3 hours or overnight.
nutritional count per serving 25.9g total fat (14.5g saturated fat); 2123kJ (508 cal); 57.4g carbohydrate; 8.7g protein; 2g fibre

Greek

dolmades

—

mezethes

—

pastitsio

—

meatballs with tomato and
green olive sauce

—

greek shortbread

Make a toast to Dionysus – god of wine and merriment.

dolmades

preparation time 40 minutes
cooking time 1 hour 5 minutes
makes about 32

½ cup (125ml) extra virgin olive oil
400g spring onions, chopped
½ cup (80g) pine nuts
2 cloves garlic, crushed
1¼ cups (250g) white medium-grain rice
½ cup finely chopped fresh flat-leaf parsley
⅓ cup finely chopped fresh dill
½ cup (80g) sultanas
¼ cup (60ml) lemon juice
200g packet vine leaves in brine
1 (140g) lemon, sliced thinly
3 cups (750ml) water

1 Heat half the oil in large frying pan; cook onion, pine nuts and garlic, stirring, until onion is softened and pine nuts are browned lightly. Add rice; cook, stirring, for 1 minute. Add herbs, sultanas, juice and remaining oil; remove from heat.
2 Rinse vine leaves under cold water; drain well and pat dry. Line base of a large heavy-based saucepan with about 10 of the damaged vine leaves. Place another leaf, vein-side-up, on a board. Cut off stem if it's attached. Place 1 level tablespoon of rice mixture in the centre of the leaf, above the point where the stem was. Fold in two sides; roll tightly to enclose filling. Repeat with remaining leaves and rice mixture.
3 Place rolls, in single layer, on leaves in the pan; pack in tightly so they cannot unroll during cooking. Cover dolmades with lemon slices, then remaining vine leaves. Place a large heatproof plate on top of dolmades so they can't move during cooking. Add the water to the saucepan; bring to the boil. Reduce heat; simmer gently, covered, for about 1 hour or until rice is cooked.
4 Serve dolmades at room temperature.
nutritional count per serving 5.4g total fat (0.6g saturated fat); 376kJ (90 cal); 8.7g carbohydrate; 1.3g protein; 0.9g fibre

mezethes

preparation time 1 hour (plus refrigeration time)
cooking time 30 minutes
serves 12

roasted pepper with fried walnuts

2 medium red peppers (400g)
2 tablespoons extra virgin olive oil
⅓ cup (35g) whole walnuts

1 Halve peppers; discard seeds and membranes. Roast under grill or in very hot oven, skin-side up, until skin blisters and blackens. Cover pepper pieces with plastic or paper for 5 minutes; peel away skin, then slice pepper flesh thickly.
2 Combine oil and walnuts in small saucepan; stir gently over low heat until warm and walnuts are crisp. Serve pepper slices drizzled with warmed walnuts and oil.
nutritional count per serving 5.1g total fat (0.6g saturated fat); 226kJ (54 cal); 1.2g carbohydrate; 0.9g protein; 0.5g fibre

tzatziki

250g plain greek yogurt
½ cucumber (130g), deseeded, chopped finely
1 tablespoon finely chopped fresh mint
1 clove garlic, crushed
½ teaspoon sea salt flakes

1 Place yogurt in muslin-lined sieve over bowl. Cover; refrigerate for 3 hours or until thick.
2 Combine drained yogurt with cucumber, mint, garlic and salt in small bowl.
3 Serve tzatziki with toasted pitta bread and olives, if desired.
nutritional count per tablespoon 1g total fat (0.6g saturated fat); 75kJ (18 cal); 1.4g carbohydrate; 0.8g protein; 0.1g fibre

baked chilli and oregano feta

2 x 200g pieces greek feta cheese
2 teaspoons extra virgin olive oil
¼ teaspoon chilli flakes
½ teaspoon dried oregano

1 Preheat oven to 200°C/ 180°C fan-assisted.
2 Place both pieces of cheese on separate squares of foil large enough to enclose the cheese. Drizzle cheese with oil; sprinkle with chilli and oregano. Enclose foil to form a parcel.
3 Bake cheese 10 minutes or until heated through.
nutritional count per serving 8.5g total fat (5.2g saturated fat); 418kJ (100 cal); 0.1g carbohydrate; 5.9g protein; 0g fibre

fried calamari

800g small whole calamari (squid)
olive oil, for deep-frying
½ cup (75g) plain flour
2 teaspoons sea salt flakes

1 Gently separate the body and tentacles of the calamari by pulling on the tentacles. Cut the head from the tentacles just below the eyes and discard the head. Trim the long tentacle from each calamari. Remove the clear quill from inside the body. Peel the side flaps from the body with salted fingers, then peel away the dark skin (the salt gives more grip). Cut the body into 2cm rings. Wash the calamari well and pat dry with absorbent paper.
2 Heat oil in large saucepan. Toss calamari in combined flour and salt; shake away the excess. Deep-fry calamari, in batches, until just browned and tender; drain on absorbent paper.
3 Serve calamari with lemon wedges, if desired.
nutritional count per serving 1.9g total fat (0.3g saturated fat); 238kJ (57 cal); 4.5g carbohydrate; 5.5g protein; 0.2g fibre

Clockwise from back: Tzatziki; Fried calamari;
Baked chilli and oregano feta; Roasted pepper with fried walnuts

pastitsio

preparation time 30 minutes (plus standing time)
cooking time 1 hour 45 minutes (plus cooling time)
serves 12

250g macaroni
2 eggs, beaten lightly
¾ cup (60g) grated parmesan cheese
2 tablespoons stale breadcrumbs

MEAT SAUCE
2 tablespoons olive oil
2 medium brown onions (300g), chopped finely
750g minced beef
400g can tomatoes
⅓ cup (95g) tomato paste
½ cup (125ml) beef stock
¼ cup (60ml) dry white wine
½ teaspoon ground cinnamon
1 egg, beaten lightly

TOPPING
90g butter
½ cup (75g) plain flour
3½ cups (875ml) milk
1 cup (80g) grated parmesan cheese
2 egg yolks

1 Preheat oven to 180°C/160°C fan-assisted. Grease shallow 2.5-litre (10 cup) ovenproof dish.
2 Make meat sauce and topping.
3 Cook pasta in large saucepan of boiling water, uncovered, until just tender; drain. Combine hot pasta, egg and cheese in bowl; mix well. Press pasta over base of dish.
4 Top pasta evenly with meat sauce; pour over topping, smooth surface then sprinkle with breadcrumbs. Bake about 1 hour or until lightly browned. Stand 10 minutes before serving.
MEAT SAUCE
Heat oil in large saucepan, add onion and beef; cook, stirring, until beef is well browned. Stir in undrained crushed tomatoes, paste, stock, wine and cinnamon; simmer, uncovered, until thick. Cool; stir in egg.
TOPPING
Melt butter in medium saucepan, add flour; stir over heat until bubbling. Remove from heat; gradually stir in milk. Stir over heat until sauce boils and thickens; stir in cheese, cool slightly. Stir in egg yolks.
nutritional count per serving 20.8g total fat (10.9g saturated fat); 1718kJ (411 cal); 27.2g carbohydrate; 27g protein; 1.9g fibre

meatballs with tomato and green olive sauce

preparation time 40 minutes (plus standing time)
cooking time 20 minutes
makes about 48

4 slices white bread (160g), crusts removed
⅓ cup (80ml) water
250g minced lamb
100g minced pork
2 spring onions (50g), chopped finely
1 egg, beaten lightly
1 teaspoon grated lemon rind
1 teaspoon ground cumin
½ teaspoon dried oregano
1 cup (150g) plain flour
vegetable oil, for shallow-frying

TOMATO AND GREEN OLIVE SAUCE
3 medium tomatoes (450g), chopped
½ cup (50g) pitted green olives, chopped
1 tablespoon extra virgin olive oil

1 Combine bread and water in medium bowl; stand 5 minutes. Using hands, squeeze excess water from bread.
2 Place minces, bread, onion, egg, rind, cumin and oregano in large bowl; mix well. Cover; refrigerate 1 hour.
3 Combine ingredients for tomato and green olive sauce in small bowl.
4 With damp hands, roll mince mixture into 48 balls, about 2 teaspoons each. Roll balls in flour seasoned with salt and pepper; shake away excess flour.
5 Heat oil in large frying pan, cook meatballs, in batches, for about 8 minutes, shaking pan frequently, or until browned and cooked through. Drain on absorbent paper.
6 Serve meatballs with tomato and green olive sauce.
nutritional count per meatball 2.6g total fat (0.5g saturated fat); 209kJ (50 cal); 4.2g carbohydrate; 2.4g protein; 0.4g fibre

greek shortbread

preparation time 30 minutes
cooking time 20 minutes
makes about 32

250g unsalted butter, chopped
1 teaspoon vanilla extract
½ cup (80g) icing sugar, sifted
1 egg yolk
1 tablespoon brandy
½ cup (70g) finely chopped toasted flaked almonds
2 cups (300g) plain flour
½ cup (75g) self-raising flour
icing sugar, to coat, extra

1 Beat butter, vanilla and sugar in small bowl with electric mixer until light and fluffy. Beat in egg yolk and brandy. Transfer mixture to large bowl; stir in almonds and combined sifted flours.
2 Preheat oven to 160°C/140°C fan-assisted.
3 Take a level tablespoon of dough and roll between palms into sausage shape, tapering at ends; bend into a crescent. Repeat with remaining dough. Place on greased oven trays, 3cm apart.
4 Bake shortbread about 15 minutes or until browned lightly. Cool on trays 5 minutes.
5 Sift a thick layer of the extra icing sugar onto large sheet of greaseproof paper. Place shortbreads on icing sugar, dust tops heavily with icing sugar. Cool.
nutritional count per shortbread 7.9g total fat (4.4g saturated fat); 523kJ (125 cal); 11g carbohydrate; 1.8g protein; 0.6g fibre

Mexican

corn and bean stew with tortillas

—

chicken enchiladas

—

chilli con carne with
corn dumplings

—

grilled corn and courgette salsa

—

crème catalana

Turn up the heat with this much-loved party food.

corn and bean stew with tortillas

preparation time 15 minutes
cooking time 15 minutes
serves 8

2 teaspoons olive oil
1 medium green pepper (200g), sliced thinly
1 medium brown onion (150g), sliced thinly
1 cup (165g) fresh corn kernels
3 medium tomatoes (450g), chopped coarsely
420g can kidney beans, rinsed, drained
1 fresh small red thai chilli, chopped finely
8 corn tortillas, warmed

GUACAMOLE
1 medium avocado (250g)
1 medium tomato (150g), seeded, chopped finely
½ small red onion (50g), chopped finely
1 tablespoon lime juice
1 tablespoon coarsely chopped fresh coriander

1 Heat half the oil in large frying pan; cook pepper, stirring, until just tender. Remove from pan.
2 Heat remaining oil in same pan; cook onion and corn, stirring, until onion softens. Add tomato, beans and chilli; simmer, uncovered, 10 minutes.
3 Stir pepper into tomato mixture; serve with warm tortillas and guacamole.
nutritional count per serving 9.9g total fat (1.4g saturated fat); 1935kJ (463 cal); 70.3g carbohydrate; 16.6g protein; 11.5g fibre
GUACAMOLE
Mash avocado roughly in medium bowl; stir in remaining ingredients until combined.
nutritional count per serving 7.9g total fat (1.7g saturated fat); 339kJ (81 cal); 1.0g carbohydrate; 1.0g protein; 0.8g fibre

chicken enchiladas

preparation time 50 minutes (plus standing time)
cooking time 35 minutes
serves 8

3 chipotle chillies
1 cup (250ml) boiling water
400g chicken breast fillets
1 tablespoon vegetable oil
1 large red onion (300g), chopped finely
2 cloves garlic, crushed
1 teaspoon ground cumin
1 tablespoon tomato paste
2 x 425g cans crushed tomatoes
1 tablespoon finely chopped fresh oregano
⅔ cup (160g) soured cream
1½ cups (240g) coarsely grated cheddar cheese
8 large flour tortillas

1 Cover chillies with the water in small heatproof bowl; stand 20 minutes. Remove stems from chillies; discard stems. Blend or process chillies with soaking liquid until smooth.
2 Meanwhile, place chicken in medium saucepan of boiling water; return to the boil. Reduce heat; simmer, covered, about 10 minutes or until chicken is cooked through. Remove chicken from poaching liquid; cool 10 minutes. Discard poaching liquid; shred chicken finely.
3 Preheat oven to 180°C/160°C fan-assisted. Oil a shallow rectangular 3-litre (12-cup) ovenproof dish.
4 Heat oil in large frying pan; cook onion, stirring, until soft. Reserve half of the onion in small bowl.
5 Add garlic and cumin to remaining onion in pan; cook, stirring, until fragrant. Add chilli mixture, paste, undrained tomatoes and oregano; bring to the boil. Reduce heat; simmer, uncovered, 1 minute. Remove sauce from heat.
6 Meanwhile, combine shredded chicken, reserved onion, half of the soured cream and one-third of the cheese in medium bowl.
7 Warm tortillas according to instructions on packet. Dip tortillas, one at a time, in tomato sauce in pan; place on board. Place ¼ cup of the chicken mixture along edge of each tortilla; roll enchiladas to enclose filling.
8 Spread ½ cup tomato sauce into dish. Place enchiladas, seam-side down, in dish. Pour remaining tomato sauce over enchiladas; sprinkle with remaining cheese. Cook, uncovered, about 15 minutes or until cheese melts and enchiladas are heated through. Sprinkle with coriander leaves, if desired. Serve with remaining soured cream.
nutritional count per serving 24g total fat (11.7g saturated fat); 1956kJ (468 cal); 36.5g carbohydrate; 24.7g protein; 3.8g fibre

chilli con carne with corn dumplings

preparation time 25 minutes
cooking time 2 hours 45 minutes
serves 8

2 tablespoons olive oil
1.5kg braising steak, cut into 4cm cubes
2 medium brown onions (300g), chopped
2 cloves garlic, crushed
1 large green pepper (350g), chopped
2 teaspoons sweet paprika
2 teaspoons ground cumin
2 teaspoons chilli powder
2 x 400g cans whole peeled tomatoes
2 tablespoons tomato paste
1 cup (250ml) beef stock
400g can red kidney beans, rinsed, drained
CORN DUMPLINGS
½ cup (75g) self-raising flour
½ cup (85g) polenta
50g butter, chopped
1 egg, beaten lightly
¼ cup (30g) coarsely grated cheddar cheese
¼ cup chopped fresh coriander
130g can corn kernels, drained
1 tablespoon milk, approximately

1 Heat half the oil in large flameproof casserole dish. Cook steak, in batches, until browned all over. Remove from pan.
2 Heat remaining oil in same pan; cook onion, garlic and pepper, stirring, until vegetables soften. Add spices; cook, stirring until fragrant.
3 Return steak to pan with undrained tomatoes, paste and stock; bring to the boil. Reduce heat; simmer, covered, 2½ hours or until tender.
4 Shred a quarter of the steak coarsely with two forks. Return to pan with beans. If sauce is too liquid, simmer, uncovered, until reduced.
5 Make corn dumplings.
6 Drop level tablespoons of corn dumpling mixture, about 2cm apart, on top of the steak mixture. Simmer, covered, about 20 minutes or until dumplings are cooked through.
CORN DUMPLINGS
Place flour and polenta in medium bowl; rub in butter. Stir in egg, cheese, coriander, corn and enough milk to make a soft, sticky dough.
nutritional count per serving 21.1g total fat (8.8g saturated fat); 2086kJ (499 cal); 27.8g carbohydrate; 46.6g protein; 5.6g fibre

grilled corn and courgette salsa

preparation time 20 minutes
cooking time 10 minutes
makes 7 cups

2 corn cobs (800g), trimmed
100g baby courgettes, halved lengthways
2 large avocados (640g), chopped coarsely
200g cherry tomatoes, halved
1 medium red onion (170g), sliced thickly
¼ cup coarsely chopped fresh coriander
1 tablespoon sweet chilli sauce
⅓ cup (80ml) lime juice
2 fresh small red thai chillies, sliced thinly

1 Cook corn and courgettes on heated oiled grill plate (or grill or barbecue) until tender and browned lightly. Using sharp knife, remove kernels from cobs.
2 Combine corn and courgettes in large bowl with avocado, tomato, onion and coriander. Add remaining ingredients; toss gently to combine.
nutritional count per tablespoon 1.3g total fat (0.3g saturated fat); 84kJ (20 cal); 1.4g carbohydrate; 0.5g protein; 0.5g fibre

crème catalana

preparation time 15 minutes
cooking time 10 minutes (plus refrigeration time)
serves 8

8 egg yolks
1 cup (220g) caster sugar
1.125 litres (4½ cups) milk
2 teaspoons finely grated lemon rind
1 cinnamon stick
½ cup (75g) cornflour
⅓ cup (75g) caster sugar, extra

1 Beat yolks and sugar in large bowl with balloon whisk until creamy.
2 Stir 1 litre (4 cups) of the milk, rind and cinnamon in large saucepan over medium heat until mixture just comes to the boil. Remove immediately from heat.
3 Strain milk into large heatproof jug; pour milk into egg mixture, whisking constantly. Stir remaining milk and cornflour in small jug until smooth; add to egg mixture.
4 Return mixture to pan; stir constantly over heat until mixture boils and thickens.
5 Pour mixture into 26cm heatproof pie dish; cover, refrigerate 4 hours or overnight.
6 Just before serving, sprinkle with extra sugar. Grill until sugar is caramelised.
nutritional count per serving 11.2g total fat (5.4g saturated fat); 1437kJ (316 cal); 52.3g carbohydrate; 7.9g protein; 0g fibre

Have the margaritas and the Mexican beer chilled and ready to go to get your guests in the mood. Decorate the house with plenty of colour and maybe even a piñata.

You are invited to a

Christmas Feast

Deck the halls and celebrate with family...

Traditional

prawns with avocado cream
and baby cos leaves

–

turkey with lemon parsley stuffing

–

perfect roast potatoes

–

blood orange marmalade
glazed ham

–

maple-glazed sweet potato
and red onions

–

peas and beans with hazelnuts

–

boiled christmas pudding

A traditional Christmas meal is a beautiful thing.

prawns with avocado cream and baby cos leaves

preparation time 15 minutes
serves 8

2 baby cos lettuces, leaves separated
2 cucumbers (520g), sliced lengthways into ribbons
2kg cooked medium prawns, peeled and de-veined
¼ cup loosely packed fresh chervil leaves

AVOCADO CREAM
1 large avocado (320g)
pinch salt
½ clove garlic, crushed
1 tablespoon lemon juice
⅔ cup (160ml) whipping cream

1 Make avocado cream.
2 Arrange lettuce leaves, cucumber, prawns and chervil on serving plates.
3 Serve with avocado cream and lemon wedges, if desired.
AVOCADO CREAM
Blend ingredients until smooth.
nutritional count per serving 14.7g total fat (6.4g saturated fat); 1083kJ (259 cal); 3.0g carbohydrate; 25.6g protein; 2.2g fibre

turkey with lemon parsley stuffing

preparation time 40 minutes
cooking time 3 hours 20 minutes (plus standing time)
serves 8

4.5kg turkey
50g butter, melted
1 cup (250ml) water

LEMON PARSLEY STUFFING
125g butter
2 trimmed celery sticks (200g), chopped finely
8 spring onions, chopped finely
2 cloves garlic, crushed
6 cups (420g) fresh white breadcrumbs
1 cup coarsely chopped fresh flat-leaf parsley
1 tablespoon finely grated lemon rind
1 egg, beaten lightly

GRAVY
¼ cup (35g) plain flour
3 cups (750ml) chicken stock
1 tablespoon redcurrant jelly
2 teaspoons finely chopped fresh mint

1 Make lemon parsley stuffing.
2 Preheat oven to 180°C/160°C fan-assisted.
3 Discard neck from turkey. Rinse turkey under cold water; pat dry inside and out with absorbent paper. Fill neck cavity loosely with seasoning; secure skin over opening with toothpicks. Fill large cavity loosely with stuffing; reserve remaining stuffing. Tie legs together with kitchen string; tuck wings under.
4 Place turkey on oiled wire rack in large flameproof baking dish. Brush turkey all over with half the butter. Pour the water into the dish. Cover dish tightly with greased foil; roast for 2 hours. Uncover turkey; brush with remaining butter. Roast a further 1 hour or until browned all over and cooked through, brushing with pan juices every 20 minutes. Remove turkey from dish, cover turkey; stand 20 minutes while preparing gravy and finishing vegetables.
5 Increase oven temperature to 240°C/220°C fan-assisted. Oil 12-hole mini (1-tablespoon/20ml) muffin tin.
6 Place 1 tablespoon of reserved stuffing in each muffin tin hole. Bake about 10 minutes or until browned and crisp.
7 Meanwhile, make gravy.
8 Serve turkey with stuffing muffins and gravy.
LEMON PARSLEY STUFFING
Melt butter in large frying pan; cook celery, stirring, until soft. Add onion and garlic; cook, stirring, until fragrant. Combine onion mixture with remaining ingredients in large bowl.
GRAVY
Pour turkey pan juices from baking dish into medium jug, reserve 2 tablespoons of fat from the top; discard remaining fat on surface of juices. Heat fat in same baking dish, add flour; cook, stirring, until well browned. Gradually stir in reserved pan juices and stock; bring to the boil. Simmer, stirring, until gravy thickens slightly. Stir in jelly and mint; strain.
nutritional count per serving 56.0g total fat (23.0g saturated fat); 4017kJ (961 cal); 43.0g carbohydrate; 70.0g protein; 3.7g fibre

perfect roast potatoes

preparation time 10 minutes (plus cooling time)
cooking time 55 minutes
serves 8

2.5kg desirée potatoes, peeled, halved horizontally
⅓ cup (80ml) olive oil

1 Preheat oven to 220°C/200°C fan-assisted. Oil oven tray.
2 Boil, steam or microwave potatoes 5 minutes; drain. Pat dry with absorbent paper; cool 10 minutes.
3 Gently rake rounded sides of potatoes with tines of fork; place potatoes in single layer, cut-side down, on tray. Brush with oil; roast, uncovered, about 50 minutes or until browned and crisp.
nutritional count per serving 9.4g total fat (1.3g saturated fat); 1078kJ (258 cal); 34.8g carbohydrate; 6.4g protein; 4.3g fibre

blood orange marmalade glazed ham

preparation time 20 minutes
cooking time 1 hour 30 minutes
serves 8

7kg cooked leg of ham
whole cloves, to decorate
BLOOD ORANGE MARMALADE GLAZE
350g jar blood orange marmalade
¼ cup (55g) brown sugar
¼ cup (60ml) orange juice

1 Preheat oven to 180°C/160°C fan-assisted.
2 Cut through rind about 10cm from shank end of leg in decorative pattern; run thumb around edge of rind just under skin to remove rind. Start pulling rind from shank end to widest edge of ham; discard rind.
3 Using sharp knife, make shallow cuts in one direction diagonally across fat at 3cm intervals, then shallow-cut in opposite direction, forming diamonds. Do not cut through top fat or fat will spread apart during cooking.
4 Make blood orange marmalade glaze.
5 Line a large baking dish with overlapping sheets of baking parchment. Place ham on wire rack in baking dish; brush with marmalade glaze. Cover shank end with foil.
6 Bake ham 40 minutes; decorate ham with cloves. Bake a further 30 minutes or until browned all over, brushing occasionally with the glaze during cooking.
BLOOD ORANGE MARMALADE GLAZE
Stir ingredients in small saucepan over low heat until sugar is dissolved.
nutritional count per serving 49.2g total fat (16.8g saturated fat); 4393kJ (1053 cal); 35.9g carbohydrate; 116g protein; 0.4g fibre

"In my experience, clever food is not appreciated at Christmas. It makes the little ones cry and the old ones nervous."
Jane Grigson, British cookery writer

maple-glazed sweet potato and red onions

preparation time 15 minutes
cooking time 40 minutes
serves 8

1.5kg white sweet potatoes
2 tablespoons lemon juice
4 medium red onions (680g), peeled, quartered
2 tablespoons extra virgin olive oil
2 tablespoons maple syrup
1 teaspoon sea salt flakes

1 Preheat oven to 180°C/160°C fan-assisted. Line shallow oven tray with baking parchment.
2 Peel sweet potatoes; place in bowl of cold water with juice to prevent browning. Cut potatoes into thick slices, return to water. Drain potato; pat dry with absorbent paper.
3 Place potato and onion on tray; drizzle olive oil over vegetables. Drizzle sweet potato only with maple syrup. Sprinkle with salt.
4 Roast vegetables with turkey about 40 minutes or until tender and browned.
nutritional count per serving 4.8g total fat (0.6g saturated fat); 895kJ (214 cal); 36.8g carbohydrate; 3.5g protein; 4.3g fibre

peas and beans with hazelnuts

preparation time 15 minutes
cooking time 12 minutes
serves 8

1½ cups (240g) peas
300g baby beans, trimmed
300g sugar snap peas, trimmed
30g butter
⅓ cup (35g) roasted hazelnuts, chopped coarsely
1 clove garlic, crushed

1 Boil, steam or microwave peas and beans until almost tender; add sugar snap peas. Cook a further 30 seconds or until just tender; drain well.
2 Melt butter in large frying pan; cook nuts until browned. Remove nuts from pan with slotted spoon. Add garlic and vegetables to pan; toss until combined.
3 Serve vegetables topped with nuts.
nutritional count per serving 6.1g total fat (2.1g saturated fat); 431kJ (103 cal); 5.9g carbohydrate; 4.4g protein; 4.1g fibre

boiled christmas pudding

preparation time 30 minutes (plus standing time)
cooking time 6 hours (plus cooling time)
serves 8

You need a 60cm square of unbleached calico for the pudding cloth. If calico has not been used before, soak in cold water overnight; next day, boil it for 20 minutes then rinse in cold water.

1½ cups (250g) raisins
1½ cups (240g) sultanas
1 cup (150g) currants
¾ cup (120g) mixed peel
1 teaspoon finely grated lemon rind
2 tablespoons lemon juice
2 tablespoons brandy
250g butter, softened
2 cups (440g) firmly packed brown sugar
5 eggs
1¼ cups (185g) plain flour
½ teaspoon ground nutmeg
½ teaspoon mixed spice
4 cups (280g) stale breadcrumbs

1 Combine fruit, rind, juice and brandy in large bowl; mix well. Cover tightly with plastic wrap; store in a cool, dark place overnight or up to a week, stirring every day.

2 Beat butter and sugar in large bowl with electric mixer only until combined. Beat in eggs, one at a time, beat only until combined between each addition. Add butter mixture to fruit mixture then sifted dry ingredients and breadcrumbs; mix well.

3 Fill extra-large pan three-quarters full of hot water, cover; bring to the boil. Have ready 2.5m of kitchen string and an extra ½ cup of plain flour. Wearing thick rubber gloves, dip pudding cloth in boiling water; boil 1 minute then remove, carefully squeeze excess water from cloth. Working quickly, spread hot cloth on worktop, rub flour into centre of cloth to cover an area about 40cm in diameter, leaving flour a little thicker in centre of cloth where 'skin' on the pudding needs to be thickest.

4 Place pudding mixture in centre of cloth. Gather cloth evenly around mixture, avoiding any deep pleats; then pat into round shape. Tie cloth tightly with string as close to mixture as possible. Pull ends of cloth tightly to ensure pudding is as round and firm as possible. Knot two pairs of corners together to make pudding easier to remove.

5 Lower pudding into boiling water; tie free ends of string to handles of boiler to suspend pudding. Cover with tight-fitting lid, boil for 6 hours, replenishing water as necessary to maintain level.

6 Untie pudding from handles; place wooden spoon through knotted calico loops to lift pudding from water. Do not put pudding on bench; suspend from spoon by placing over rungs of upturned stool or wedging handle in drawer. Pudding must be suspended freely. Twist ends of cloth around string to avoid them touching pudding. If pudding has been cooked correctly, cloth will dry in patches within a few minutes; hang 10 minutes.

7 Place pudding on board; cut string, carefully peel back cloth. Turn pudding onto a plate then carefully peel cloth away completely; cool. Stand at least 20 minutes or until skin darkens and pudding becomes firm.

nutritional count per serving 31.0g total fat (18.3g saturated fat); 4184kJ (1001 cal); 159.5g carbohydrate; 13.9g protein; 6.6g fibre

TIPS Pudding can be stored, covered well, in refrigerator for up to 2 months.

To reheat: Remove from refrigerator 12 hours before reheating. Remove cling film; tie dry unfloured cloth around pudding. Boil 2 hours, following instructions in step 5. Hang hot pudding 10 minutes. Remove cloth; stand at least 20 minutes or until skin darkens before serving.

To reheat in microwave oven: Reheat up to four single serves at once. Cover with plastic wrap; microwave on HIGH (100%) up to 1 minute per serve. To reheat whole pudding, cover with cling film; microwave on MEDIUM (55%) about 15 minutes or until hot.

Contemporary

coffee liqueur eggnog

—

jerusalem artichoke soup
with caramelised onion
and artichoke crisps

—

pork loin with spinach and
pancetta stuffing

—

mustard and honey-glazed
roasted sweet potatoes

—

fruit mince swirl pies

Modern cuisine with a traditional heritage.

coffee liqueur eggnog

preparation time 10 minutes (plus refrigeration time)
makes 1½ litres (6 cups)

4 eggs, separated
⅓ cup (75g) caster sugar
2 cups (500ml) hot milk
⅔ cup (160ml) Kahlua
½ cup (125ml) double cream

1 Place egg yolks, sugar and milk in large heatproof bowl over a saucepan of simmering water (don't allow water to touch the bottom of the bowl). Whisk about 15 minutes or until mixture lightly coats back of a metal spoon. Remove from heat, stir in liqueur, cover; refrigerate 1 hour.
2 Beat cream in small bowl until soft peaks form; fold into liqueur mixture.
3 Beat egg whites in small bowl with electric mixer until soft peaks form; gently fold into liqueur mixture, in two batches.
nutritional count per cup 20.2g total fat (11.9g saturated fat); 1396kJ (334 cal); 23.1g carbohydrate; 8.5g protein; 0g fibre

jerusalem artichoke soup with caramelised onion and artichoke crisps

preparation time 40 minutes (plus cooling time)
cooking time 40 minutes
serves 6

1 tablespoon lemon juice
1.25 litres (5 cups) water
12 medium jerusalem artichokes (720g)
1 tablespoon olive oil
1 large brown onion (200g), chopped coarsely
4 cloves garlic, crushed
2 large potatoes (600g), chopped coarsely
1.25 litre (5 cups) chicken stock

ARTICHOKE CRISPS
6 medium jerusalem artichokes (300g),
  unpeeled, sliced thinly
1 tablespoon olive oil
½ teaspoon salt
¼ teaspoon ground black pepper

CARAMELISED ONION
25g butter
2 large brown onions (400g), sliced thinly
2 teaspoons brown sugar
1 tablespoon balsamic vinegar

1 Combine juice and the water in large bowl. Peel and coarsely chop artichokes; place in acidulated water.
2 Heat oil in large saucepan; cook onion and garlic, stirring, until onion softens. Add drained artichoke, potato and stock; bring to the boil. Reduce heat; simmer, covered, about 20 minutes or until potato is tender. Cool 15 minutes.
3 Meanwhile, make artichoke crisps. Make caramelised onion.
4 Blend or process soup, in batches, until smooth. Reheat soup in same pan.
5 Serve bowls of soup topped with onion then crisps.
ARTICHOKE CRISPS
Preheat oven to 200°C/180°C fan-assisted. Combine ingredients in medium bowl; place artichoke, in single layer, on wire rack set over baking dish. Roast, uncovered, about 20 minutes or until crisp.
CARAMELISED ONION
Melt butter in medium saucepan; cook onion over medium heat, stirring, about 10 minutes or until soft. Add sugar and vinegar; cook, stirring, about 10 minutes or until caramelised.
nutritional count per serving 10.2g total fat (3.2g saturated fat); 886kJ (212 cal); 19.8g carbohydrate; 6.9g protein; 6.8g fibre

pork loin with spinach and pancetta stuffing

preparation time 30 minutes
cooking time 1 hour 30 minutes
serves 6

3 slices white bread (90g)
2 tablespoons olive oil
1 clove garlic, crushed
1 medium brown onion (150g), chopped coarsely
4 slices pancetta (60g), chopped coarsely
80g baby spinach leaves
¼ cup (35g) roasted macadamias, chopped coarsely
½ cup (125ml) chicken stock
1.5kg boned pork loin
PLUM AND RED WINE SAUCE
1½ cups (480g) plum jam
2 tablespoons dry red wine
⅔ cup (160ml) chicken stock

1 Preheat oven to 200°C/180°C fan-assisted.
2 Discard bread crusts; cut bread into 1cm cubes. Heat half of the oil in large frying pan; cook bread, stirring, until browned and crisp. Drain croûtons on absorbent paper.
3 Heat remaining oil in same pan; cook garlic, onion and pancetta until onion browns lightly. Stir in spinach; remove from heat. Gently stir in croûtons, nuts and stock.
4 Place pork on board, fat-side down; slice through thickest part of pork horizontally, without cutting through other side. Open out pork to form one large piece; press stuffing mixture against loin along width of pork. Roll pork to enclose stuffing, securing with kitchen string at 2cm intervals.
5 Place rolled pork on rack in large shallow baking dish. Roast about 1¼ hours or until cooked through.
6 Meanwhile, make plum and red wine sauce.
7 Serve sliced pork with sauce.
PLUM AND RED WINE SAUCE
Bring ingredients to the boil in small saucepan. Reduce heat; simmer, uncovered, about 10 minutes or until sauce thickens slightly.
nutritional count per serving 32.5g total fat (8.9g saturated fat); 3248kJ (777 cal); 60.4g carbohydrate; 58.1g protein; 2.3g fibre

mustard and honey-glazed roasted sweet potatoes

preparation time 10 minutes
cooking time 1 hour
serves 6

2kg sweet potatoes, unpeeled
⅓ cup (120g) honey
¼ cup (70g) wholegrain mustard
2 tablespoons coarsely chopped fresh rosemary

1 Preheat oven to 220°C/200°C fan-assisted.
2 Halve sweet potatoes lengthways; cut each half into 2cm wedges.
3 Combine remaining ingredients in large bowl, add sweet potatoes; toss sweet potato to coat in mixture. Divide sweet potato mixture between two large shallow baking dishes.
4 Roast sweet potato about 1 hour or until tender and slightly caramelised.
nutritional count per serving 0.6g total fat (0.0g saturated fat); 1141kJ (273 cal); 57.0g carbohydrate; 6.1g protein; 5.6g fibre

fruit mince swirl pies

preparation time 1 hour
cooking time 15 minutes
makes 24

475g jar mincemeat
½ cup (125g) finely chopped glacé peaches
⅓ cup (45g) finely chopped roasted slivered almonds
¼ cup (30g) ground almonds
½ teaspoon brandy essence
4 sheets ready-rolled butter puff pastry
2 tablespoons icing sugar
icing sugar, extra
1 egg, beaten lightly
1 tablespoon milk

1 Preheat oven to 220°C/200°C fan-assisted. Grease oven trays.
2 Combine mincemeat, peaches, chopped nuts, ground almonds and essence in medium bowl.
3 Sprinkle one pastry sheet with half the measured icing sugar. Place another sheet of pastry on top, press down firmly. Roll pastry tightly, then mark log into 24 pieces, about 1cm each. Cut about 6 pieces at a time.
4 Lay pieces, cut-side up, on board dusted with extra sifted icing sugar. Roll each piece into an 8cm round.
5 Spoon 1 tablespoon of mincemeat mixture onto centre of each round. Brush edges with combined egg and milk. Top with remaining rounds; press edges to seal. Cut each pie with a fluted 7cm round cutter to neaten; place on trays. Repeat with remaining pastry sheets and icing sugar.
6 Brush tops of pies lightly with remaining egg and milk mixture. Bake about 15 minutes or until well browned. Cool on wire racks.
nutritional count per pie 8.9g total fat (3.8g saturated fat); 807kJ (193 cal); 24.7g carbohydrate; 2.8g protein; 1.3g fibre

These are like mince pies but with a twist – or a swirl. They're made from ready-rolled puff pastry instead of the more traditional shortcrust.

Glossary

ALL-BRAN a low-fat, high-fibre breakfast cereal based on wheat bran.

ALLSPICE also called pimento or jamaican pepper.

ALMONDS

blanched brown skins removed.

caramelised toffee-coated almonds.

ground also called almond meal; nuts are powdered to a coarse flour texture.

slivered small pieces cut lengthways.

ARTICHOKES

hearts tender centre of the globe artichoke; can be harvested from the plant after the prickly choke is removed. Cooked hearts can be bought from delicatessens or canned in brine.

jerusalem neither from Jerusalem nor an artichoke; crunchy brown-skinned tuber tastes a bit like a water chestnut and belongs to the sunflower family. Eaten raw in salads or cooked like potatoes.

AUBERGINE also called eggplant; range in size from tiny to very large and in colour from pale green to deep purple. Also available char-grilled, in oil, in jars.

BAKING POWDER a raising agent consisting mainly of two parts cream of tartar to one part bicarbonate of soda.

BASIL, THAI also called horapa; differs from holy basil and sweet basil in look and taste – smaller leaves and purplish stems, and a slight aniseed taste. Is an identifying flavour of Thai food.

BEANS

black-eyed also called black-eyed peas or cowpea; the dried seed of a variant of the snake or yard-long bean. Not too dissimilar to white beans in flavour.

broad also called fava, windsor and horse beans; available dried, fresh, canned and frozen. Fresh should be peeled twice (discarding both the outer long green pod and the beige-green tough inner shell); the frozen beans have had their pods removed but the beige shell still needs removal.

cannellini small white bean similar in flavour and look to other *phaseolus vulgaris* varieties (navy, haricot or great northern). Available dried or canned.

kidney medium-size red bean, slightly floury in texture yet sweet in flavour; sold dried or canned, it's found in bean mixes and is the bean used in chile con carne.

white a generic term we use for canned or dried cannellini, haricot, navy or great northern beans; all of the same family.

beansprouts also called bean shoots; tender new growths of assorted beans and seeds germinated for consumption as sprouts. Mung bean, soybean and alfalfa sprouts are the most common.

BEEF

braising steak inexpensive cut from the neck and shoulder area; good minced and slow-cooked.

tenderloin eye-fillet; fine texture, most expensive and extremely tender.

minced also known as ground beef.

new-york cut boneless striploin steak.

rump steak boneless tender cut taken from the upper part of the round (hindquarter).

skirt steak lean, flavourful coarse-grained cut from the inner thigh. Needs slow-cooking; good for stews or casseroles.

t-bone sirloin steak with bone in and fillet eye attached; good barbecued or grilled.

BEETROOT also called red beets.

BELGIAN endive also called witlof; related to and confused with chicory. A versatile vegetable, it tastes as good cooked as it does eaten raw. Grown in darkness like white asparagus to prevent it becoming green; looks somewhat like a tightly furled, cream to very light-green cigar. The leaves can be removed and used to hold a canapé filling; the whole vegetable can be opened up, stuffed then baked or casseroled; and the leaves can be tossed in a salad with other vegetables.

BETEL LEAVES grown and consumed in India and throughout South-East Asia; used raw as a wrap, cooked as a vegetable. Available at most Asian food stores and some greengrocers.

BICARBONATE OF SODA also called baking soda.

BLOOD ORANGE a virtually seedless citrus fruit with blood-red-streaked rind and flesh; sweet, non-acidic, salmon-coloured pulp and juice wtih slight strawberry or raspberry overtones. The rind is not as bitter as an ordinary orange.

BREADCRUMBS

fresh bread, usually white, processed into crumbs; good for stuffings and as a thickening agent.

packaged prepared fine-textured but crunchy white breadcrumbs; good for coating or crumbing foods to be fried.

stale crumbs made by grating, blending or processing 1 or 2-day-old bread.

BRIOCHE French in origin; a rich, yeast-leavened, cake-like bread made with butter and eggs. Available from cake or specialty bread shops.

BROCCOLI, TENDERSTEM also known as broccolini; a cross between broccoli and Chinese kale; long asparagus-like stems with a long loose floret, both completely edible. Resembles broccoli in look but is milder and sweeter in taste.

BULGAR WHEAT also called burghul; hulled steamed wheat kernels, once dried, are crushed into various sized grains.

BUTTER we use salted butter in this book unless stated otherwise.

BUTTERMILK originally the term given to the slightly sour liquid left after butter was churned from cream, today it is commercially made similarly to yogurt. Sold alongside fresh milk products in supermarkets. Despite the implication of its name, buttermilk is low in fat.

CAPERBERRIES olive-sized fruit formed after the buds of the caper bush have flowered; usually sold pickled in a vinegar brine with stalks intact.

CAPERS the grey-green buds of a warm climate (usually Mediterranean) shrub, sold either dried and salted or pickled in a vinegar brine; tiny young ones, called baby capers, are also available both in brine or dried in salt.

CARAWAY SEEDS small, half-moon-shaped dried seed of the parsley family; adds a sharp anise flavour.

CARDAMOM a spice native to India; can be purchased in pod, seed or ground form. Has a distinctive aromatic, sweetly rich flavour.

CASHEWS plump, kidney-shaped, golden-brown nuts with a sweet, buttery flavour; contains about 48 per cent fat so should be stored in the refrigerator to avoid becoming rancid. We use roasted unsalted cashews.

CAYENNE PEPPER a thin-fleshed, long, extremely hot, dried red chilli, usually bought ground.

CHAR SIU SAUCE also called Chinese barbecue sauce; a paste-like ingredient dark-red-brown in colour with a sharp sweet and spicy flavour. Made with fermented soybeans, honey and spices.

CHEESE

bocconcini from the diminutive of 'boccone', meaning mouthful in Italian; walnut-sized, baby mozzarella, a delicate, semi-soft, white cheese traditionally made from buffalo milk. Sold fresh, it spoils rapidly; refrigerate in brine for 1 or 2 days at the most.

brie soft-ripened cows'-milk cheese with a delicate, creamy texture and a rich, sweet taste. Best served at room temperature, brie should have a bloomy white rind and creamy, voluptuous centre which becomes runny with ripening.

feta a Greek crumbly textured goats'- or sheeps'-milk cheese with a sharp, salty taste. Ripened and stored in salted whey.

fontina a smooth, firm Italian cows'-milk cheese with a creamy, nutty taste and red or brown rind; ideal for melting or grilling.

goats' made from goats' milk, has an earthy, strong taste. Available in soft, firm and crumbly textures, various shapes and sizes, and also rolled in ash or herbs.

gruyère a hard-rind Swiss cheese with small holes and a nutty, slightly salty flavour; popular for soufflés.

haloumi a Greek Cypriot cheese with a semi-firm, spongy texture and very salty yet sweet flavour. Ripened and stored in salted whey; it's best grilled or fried, and holds its shape when heated. Eat while warm as it becomes tough and rubbery on cooling.

mascarpone an Italian fresh cultured-cream product made in much the same way as yogurt. Whiteish to creamy yellow in colour, with a buttery-rich, luscious texture. Soft, creamy and spreadable.

mozzarella soft, spun-curd cheese from southern Italy and traditionally made from water-buffalo milk. Now generally made from cows' milk, it is the most popular pizza cheese due to its low melting point and elasticity when heated.

parmesan also called parmigiano; a hard, grainy cows'-milk cheese originating in Parma, Italy. The curd for this cheese is salted in brine for a month before being aged for up to 2 years, preferably in humid conditions. Reggiano is the best and made only in Emilia-Romagna, Italy.

pizza cheese a commercial blend of varying proportions of processed grated mozzarella, cheddar and parmesan.

provolone a mild stretched-curd cheese similar to mozzarella when young, becoming hard, spicy and grainy the longer it's aged. Golden yellow in colour, with a smooth waxy rind; a good all-purpose cheese.

ricotta a soft, sweet, moist, white cows'-milk cheese with a low fat content and a slightly grainy texture. The name roughly translates as 'cooked again' and refers to ricotta's manufacture from a whey that is a by-product of other cheese making.

CHERVIL mildly fennel-flavoured member of the parsley family with curly dark-green leaves. Available fresh and dried but is best fresh; its delicate flavour diminishes the longer it is cooked.

CHICKEN

tenderloin thin strip of meat lying just under the breast; good for stir-frying.

thigh skin and bone intact.

thigh cutlet thigh with skin and centre bone intact; sometimes found skinned with bone intact.

thigh fillet thigh with skin and centre bone removed.

CHICKPEAS also called garbanzos, hummus or channa; an irregularly round, sandy-coloured legume. Firm textured even after cooking, with a floury mouth-feel and robust nutty flavour; available canned or dried (the latter need several hours soaking in cold water before use).

CHILLI

jalapeño pronounced hah-lah-pain-yo. Fairly hot, medium-sized, plump, dark green chilli; available pickled, sold bottled or canned, and fresh, from greengrocers.

powder made from dried ground thai chillies; can be used instead of fresh chillies in the proportion of ½ teaspoon chilli powder to 1 medium chopped fresh red chilli.

red thai also called 'scuds'; tiny, very hot and bright red in colour.

CHINESE BARBECUED DUCK

dipped into and brushed during roasting with a sticky sweet coating made from soy sauce, sherry, ginger, five-spice, star anise and hoisin sauce. Available from Asian food shops and delicatessens.

CHINESE COOKING WINE also

called hao hsing or chinese rice wine; made from fermented rice, wheat, sugar and salt with a 13.5 per cent alcohol content. Inexpensive and found in Asian food shops; replace with mirin or sherry.

CHIVES related to the onion and leek; has a subtle onion flavour. Used more for flavour than as an ingredient; chopped finely, they're good in sauces, dressings, omelettes or as a garnish. Chinese (or garlic) chives have rougher, flatter leaves.

CHOCOLATE

dark eating also called semi-sweet or luxury chocolate; made of a high percentage of cocoa liquor and cocoa butter, and little added sugar. We use dark eating chocolate unless stated otherwise.

milk most popular eating chocolate, mild and very sweet; similar in make-up to dark with the difference being the addition of milk solids.

white contains no cocoa solids but derives its sweet flavour from cocoa butter. Very sensitive to heat.

CHOCOLATE HAZELNUT SPREAD

also called Nutella; made of cocoa powder, hazelnuts, sugar and milk.

CHORIZO Spanish sausage made of coarsely ground pork and highly seasoned with garlic and chilli.

CINNAMON available in pieces (sticks or quills) and ground; is the dried inner bark of the shoots of the Sri Lankan native cinnamon tree. Much of what is sold as the real thing is in fact cassia, Chinese cinnamon, from the bark of the cassia tree. Less expensive to process than true cinnamon, it is often blended with Sri Lankan cinnamon to produce the type of 'cinnamon' most commonly found in supermarkets.

CLOVES dried flower buds of a tropical tree; can be used whole or ground. Has a strong scent and taste; use sparingly.

COCOA POWDER also known as unsweetened cocoa.

COCONUT

cream obtained commercially from the first pressing of the coconut flesh alone, without the addition of water. Available in cans and cartons at most supermarkets.

desiccated concentrated, dried, unsweetened and finely shredded coconut flesh.

flaked dried flaked coconut flesh.

milk not the liquid found inside the fruit (coconut water), but the diluted liquid from the second pressing of the white flesh of a mature coconut. Available in cans and cartons at most supermarkets.

shredded unsweetened thin strips of dried coconut flesh.

COINTREAU citrus-flavoured liqueur.

CORIANDER also called cilantro or chinese parsley; bright-green-leafed herb with a pungent aroma and taste. Like other leafy herbs, its characteristics diminish with cooking so add just before serving for maximum impact. Stems and roots are also used: wash well before chopping. Coriander seeds are dried and sold whole or ground – neither form tastes remotely like the fresh leaf.

CORNFLOUR also called cornstarch.

CORNICHONS French for gherkin, a very small variety of cucumber.

COS LETTUCE also called romaine lettuce; traditional lettuce used in caesar salad.

COURGETTE also known as zucchini; small, pale- or dark-green, yellow or white vegetable belonging to the squash family. Harvested when young, its edible flowers can be stuffed with a mild cheese or other similarly delicate ingredients then deep-fried or oven-baked to make a delicious appetiser.

COUSCOUS a fine, grain-like cereal product made from semolina. A semolina flour and water dough is sieved then dehydrated to produce minuscule even-sized pellets. Rehydrate by steaming or adding warm liquid; it swells to three or four times its original size.

CREAM OF TARTAR the acid ingredient in baking powder.

CREME FRAICHE a mature, naturally fermented cream (minimum fat content 35 per cent) with a velvety texture and slightly tangy, nutty flavour. This French soured cream can boil without curdling.

CUMIN also called zeera or comino; resembling caraway in size, cumin is the dried seed of a plant related to the parsley family. It has a spicy, almost curry-like flavour. Available dried as seeds or ground. Black cumin seeds are smaller than standard cumin, and dark brown rather than true black; they are mistakenly confused with kalonji.

CURLY ENDIVE also called frisée; a prickly-looking, curly-leafed green vegetable with an edible white heart.

Fairly bitter in flavour (like chicory), it is used mainly in salads.

CURRANTS dried tiny, almost black raisins so-named from the grape type native to Corinth, Greece; most often used in jams, jellies and sauces. These are not the same as fresh currants, which are the fruit of a plant in the gooseberry family.

CUSTARD POWDER instant mixture used to make pouring custard; similar to North American instant pudding mixes.

DAIKON also called white radish; this long, white horseradish has a wonderful, sweet flavour. The flesh is white but the skin can be either white or black; buy those that are firm and unwrinkled from Asian food shops.

DATES fruit of the date palm tree, eaten fresh or dried, on their own or in dishes. Oval and plump, thin-skinned, with a honey-sweet flavour and sticky texture.

DILL also called dill weed; used fresh or dried, in seed form or ground, has an anise/celery sweetness. Distinctive feathery, frond-like fresh leaves are grassier and more subtle than the dried version or the seeds.

DRIED CRANBERRIES dried sweetened cranberries.

DRIED SHRIMP also known as goong hang, salted sun-dried prawns ranging in size. They are sold packaged, shelled as a rule, in all Asian grocery stores.

EDIBLE GLITTER is available from some craft shops, cake decorating suppliers and gourmet food stores.

EGGS if recipes in this book call for raw or barely cooked eggs, exercise caution if there is a salmonella problem in your area, particularly in food eaten by children and pregnant women.

FENNEL also called finocchio or anise; a crunchy green vegetable slightly resembling celery that's eaten raw in salads, fried as an accompaniment, or used as an ingredient. Also the name given to the dried seeds of the plant which have a stronger licorice flavour.

FISH SAUCE called naam pla if Thai-made, nuoc naam if Vietnamese; the two are almost identical. Made from pulverised salted fermented fish (most often anchovies); has a pungent smell and strong taste. It varies in degrees of intensity, so use according to taste.

FIVE-SPICE POWDER although the ingredients vary from country to country, it is usually a fragrant mixture of ground cinnamon, cloves, star anise, sichuan pepper and fennel seeds. Available from most supermarkets or Asian food shops.

FLOUR
buckwheat a herb in the same plant family as rhubarb; not a cereal so it is gluten-free. Available as flour, granules or groats (whole roasted kernels).
plain also called all-purpose.
self-raising all-purpose flour with added baking powder and salt; make at home in the proportion of 1 cup sifted plain flour to 2 teaspoons baking powder.

GALANGAL also called ka or lengkaus if fresh and laos if dried and powdered; a root, similar to ginger in its use. It has a hot-sour ginger-citrusy flavour.

GARAM MASALA literally meaning blended spices in northern India; based on varying proportions of cardamom, cinnamon, cloves, coriander, fennel and cumin, roasted and ground together.

GELATINE we used dried (powdered) gelatine in this book; is also available in sheet form (leaf gelatine). The two types are interchangable but leaf gelatine gives a much clearer mixture.

GHEE clarified butter; with the milk solids removed, this fat has a high smoking point so can be heated to a high temperature without burning.

GINGER
fresh also called green or root ginger; the thick gnarled root of a tropical plant. Store, peeled, covered with dry sherry in a jar and refrigerated, or frozen in an airtight container.
ground also called powdered ginger; cannot be substituted for fresh ginger.
pickled pink or red coloured; available, packaged, from Asian food shops. Pickled paper-thin shavings of ginger in a mixture of vinegar, sugar and natural colouring; used in Japanese cooking.
stem fresh ginger root preserved in sugar syrup; crystallised ginger (sweetened with cane sugar) can be substituted if rinsed with warm water and dried before using.

GLACE FRUIT such as apricots, pears, peaches and pineapple cooked in a heavy sugar syrup then dried.

GLUCOSE SYRUP also called liquid glucose, made from wheat starch. Available at health-food stores and supermarkets.

GOLDEN SYRUP a by-product of refined sugarcane; pure maple syrup or honey can be substituted.

HARISSA a North African paste made from dried red chillies, garlic, olive oil and caraway seeds; can be used as a rub for meat, an ingredient or a condiment. Available from Middle Eastern food shops and some supermarkets.

HAZELNUTS also called filberts; plump, grape-sized, rich, sweet nut with a brown skin (which can be removed by rubbing heated nuts together vigorously in a tea-towel). For ground hazelnuts, they are ground to a coarse flour texture for use in baking or as a thickening agent.

HOISIN SAUCE a thick, sweet and spicy Chinese barbecue sauce made from salted fermented soybeans, onions and garlic. Available from Asian food shops and supermarkets.

HORSERADISH CREAM is a commercially prepared creamy paste made of grated horseradish, vinegar, oil and sugar.

HUNDREDS AND THOUSANDS also known as 100's & 1000's.

INDIRECT METHOD (BARBECUE) this is used in a covered barbecue. With gas, the food is placed in a preheated covered barbecue. The burners directly under the food are turned off while the side burners remain on. With a charcoal barbecue, metal bars hold two stacks of coals against the barbecue's sides leaving the centre of the barbecue rack empty. A disposable aluminium baking dish can be placed here for fat drips, if desired.

KAFFIR LIME LEAVES also called bai magrood and looks like two glossy dark green leaves joined end to end, forming a rounded hourglass shape. Used fresh or dried in many South-East Asian dishes, they are used like bay leaves or curry leaves, especially in Thai cooking. Sold fresh, dried or frozen, the dried leaves are less potent so double the number if using them as a substitute for fresh; a strip of fresh lime peel may be substituted for each kaffir lime leaf.

KAHLUA coffee-flavoured liqueur.

KECAP MANIS a dark, thick sweet soy sauce used in most South-East Asian cuisines. Depending on the manufacturer, the sauces's sweetness is derived from the addition of either molasses or palm sugar.

LAMB

eye fillet also called eye of loin; the larger fillet from a row of loin chops or cutlets. Tender, best cooked rapidly: barbecued or pan-fried.

cutlet small, tender rib chop; also sold french-trimmed with all the fat and gristle at the narrow end of the bone removed.

fillets fine texture, most expensive and extremely tender.

shank forequarter leg; sometimes sold as drumsticks or frenched shanks if the gristle and narrow end of the bone are discarded and remaining meat trimmed.

shoulder large, tasty piece having much connective tissue so is best pot-roasted or braised. Makes the best mince.

LEMONGRASS also called takrai, scrai or serah. A tall, clumping, lemon-smelling and tasting, sharp-edged aromatic tropical grass; the white lower part of the stem is used, finely chopped, in much of the cooking of South-East Asia. Can be found, fresh, dried, powdered and frozen, in supermarkets and greengrocers as well as Asian food shops.

LENTILS (red, brown, yellow) dried pulses often identified by and named after their colour. Lentils have high food value.

french green are a local cousin to the famous (and very expensive) French lentils du puy; green-blue, tiny lentils with a nutty, earthy flavour and a hardy nature that allows them to be rapidly cooked without disintegrating.

LYCHEE a small fruit from China with a hard shell and sweet, juicy flesh. The white flesh has a gelatinous texture and musky, perfumed taste. Discard the rough skin and seed before using in salads or as a dessert fruit. Also available canned in a sugar syrup.

MAPLE SYRUP distilled from the sap of sugar maple trees found only in Canada and about ten states in the USA. Maple-flavoured syrup or pancake syrup is not an adequate substitute for the real thing.

MARSALA a fortified Italian wine produced in the Sicilian city of Marsala; recognisable by its intense amber colour and complex aroma. Used in cooking.

MAYONNAISE we use whole-egg mayonnaise; a commercial mayonnaise of high quality made with whole eggs.

MERGUEZ SAUSAGES small, spicy sausages believed to have originated in Tunisia; traditionally made with lamb meat and is easily recognised because of its chilli-red colour. Available from butchers, delicatessens and specialty sausage stores.

MILK we use full-cream homogenised milk unless otherwise specified.

MINCEMEAT also called fruit mince. A mixture of dried fruits such as raisins, sultanas and candied peel, nuts, spices, apple, brandy or rum. Is used as a filling for cakes, puddings and mince pies.

MIRIN a Japanese champagne-coloured cooking wine, made of glutinous rice and alcohol. It is used expressly for cooking and should not be confused with sake. A seasoned sweet mirin is also available.

MISO fermented soybean paste. There are many types, each with its own aroma, flavour, colour and texture; it can be kept, airtight, for up to a year in the fridge. Generally, the darker the miso, the saltier the taste and denser the texture. Buy in tubs or plastic packs.

MIXED DRIED FRUIT a combination of sultanas, raisins, currants, mixed peel and cherries.

MIXED PEEL candied citrus peel.

MIXED SPICE a mixture generally containing caraway, allspice, coriander, cumin, nutmeg and ginger; cinnamon and other spices can be added.

MIZUNA Japanese in origin; the frizzy green salad leaves have a delicate mustard flavour.

MUSHROOMS

button small, cultivated white mushroom with a mild flavour. When a recipe in this book calls for an unspecified type of mushroom, use button.

chestnut light to dark brown mushrooms with full-bodied flavour.

shiitake *fresh* also known as Chinese black. Although cultivated, they have the earthiness and taste of wild mushrooms. Large and meaty, they can be used as a substitute for meat in some Asian vegetarian dishes.
dried also called donko or dried Chinese mushrooms; have a unique meaty flavour. Rehydrate before use.

MUSTARD

american-style bright yellow in colour, a sweet mustard containing mustard seeds, sugar, salt, spices and garlic.

dijon also called french. Pale brown, creamy, distinctively flavoured, yet mild.

wholegrain also known as seeded. A French-style coarse-grain mustard made from crushed mustard seeds and dijon-style french mustard.

NOODLES

rice stick also called sen lek, ho fun or kway teow; available in different widths – soak in hot water to soften before use.

singapore pre-cooked wheat noodles best described as a thinner version of hokkien; sold, packaged, in the refrigerated section of supermarkets.

udon available fresh and dried, these broad, white, wheat Japanese noodles are similar to the ones in home-made chicken noodle soup.

vermicelli also called sen mee, mei fun or bee hoon. Used in spring rolls and cold salads; similar to bean threads, only longer and made with rice flour instead of mung bean starch. Soak dried noodles in hot water until softened, boil briefly then rinse with hot water. They can also be deep-fried until crunchy.

NUTMEG a strong and pungent spice ground from the dried nut of an evergreen Indonesian tree. Usually found ground but the flavour is more intense from a whole nut, available from spice shops, so it's best to grate your own.

OIL

cooking-spray we use a cholesterol-free cooking spray made from canola oil.

groundnut pressed from ground peanuts; the most commonly used oil in Asian cooking due to its capacity to handle high heat without burning.

olive made from ripened olives. Extra virgin and virgin are the first and second press, respectively, of the olives and are therefore considered the best; 'extra light' or 'light' refers to taste not fat levels.

sesame made from roasted, crushed, white sesame seeds; used as a flavouring more so than for cooking.

vegetable any number of oils sourced from plant rather than animal fats.

ONIONS

red also called spanish, red spanish or bermuda onion; a sweet-flavoured, large, purple-red onion.

purple shallots also called Asian shallots; related to the onion but grow in bulbs of multiple cloves like garlic. Thin-layered and intensely flavoured.

shallots also called french shallots, golden shallots or eschalots. Small and elongated, with a brown-skin, they grow in tight clusters similar to garlic.

spring also called scallion or (incorrectly) shallot; an immature onion picked before the bulb has formed, having a long, bright-green edible stalk.

ORANGE-FLAVOURED LIQUEUR brandy-based liqueur such as Grand Marnier or Cointreau.

ORANGE FLOWER WATER concentrated flavouring made from orange blossoms.

OYSTER SAUCE this thick, richly flavoured brown sauce is made from oysters and their brine, cooked with salt and soy sauce, and thickened with starches. Use as a condiment.

PAK CHOY also called bok choy, pak choi, chinese white cabbage or chinese chard, has a fresh, mild mustard taste. Use both stems and leaves, stir-fried or braised. *Baby pak choy*, is much smaller and more tender than pak choy. Its mildly acrid, distinctively appealing taste has made it one of the most commonly used Asian greens.

PANCETTA an Italian unsmoked bacon, pork belly cured in salt and spices then rolled into a sausage shape and dried for several weeks.

PAPRIKA ground dried sweet red capsicum (bell pepper); there are many grades and types available.

PEPPER also called capsicum or bell pepper. Discard seeds and membrane before use.

PECANS native to the US; pecans are golden brown, buttery and rich. Walnuts are a good substitute.

PINE NUTS also called pignoli; not a nut but a small, cream-coloured kernel from pine cones. They are best roasted before use to bring out the flavour.

PISTACHIOS green, delicately flavoured nuts inside hard off-white shells. Available salted or unsalted in their shells; also available shelled.

MILK we use full-cream homogenised milk unless otherwise spcified.

powder instant powdered milk made from whole cow milk with liquid removed and emulsifiers added.

PITTA BREAD also known as lebanese bread; wheat-flour pocket bread sold in large, flat pieces that separate into two thin rounds. Also available in small thick pieces called pocket pitta.

POLENTA also called cornmeal; a flour-like cereal made of dried corn (maize). Also the name of the dish made from it.

PORK

american-style spare ribs well-trimmed mid-loin ribs.

belly fatty cut sold in rashers or in a piece, with or without rind or bone.

fillet skinless, boneless eye-fillet cut from the loin.

shoulder joint sold with bone in or out.

POTATOES

desiree oval, smooth and pink-skinned, waxy yellow flesh; good in salads, boiled and roasted.

salad small, oval, nutty flavour; great baked and in salads.

red salad long and oval, red skin with shallow eyes, waxy yellow flesh; good in salads, boiled and roasted.

PRESERVED TURNIP also called hua chai po or cu cai muoi, or dried radish because of its similarity to daikon. Sold packaged whole or sliced, it is very salty; must be rinsed and dried before use.

PROSCIUTTO a kind of unsmoked Italian ham; salted, air-cured and aged, it is usually eaten uncooked.

PUFF PASTRY SHEETS packaged sheets of frozen ready-rolled puff pastry, available from supermarkets.

PUMPERNICKEL bread a dark, dense sourdough of German origin, made with a high proportion of rye flour and meal to wheat flour, frequently with added molasses for colour and flavour.

RADICCHIO Italian in origin; a member of the chicory family. The dark burgundy leaves and strong, bitter flavour can be cooked or eaten raw in salads.

REDCURRANT JELLY a preserve made from redcurrants used as a glaze for desserts and meats or in sauces.

RICE

arborio small, round grain rice able to absorb a large amount of liquid; the high level of starch makes it especially suitable for risottos, giving the dish its classic creaminess.

calrose a medium-grain rice that is extremely versatile; can be substituted for short- or long-grain rices if needed.

jasmine a long-grain perfumed white rice; it clings together after cooking.

koshihikari small, round-grain white rice. Substitute white short-grain rice and cook by the absorption method.

RISONI small rice-shape pasta; very similar to another small pasta, orzo.

ROCKET also called arugula, rugula and rucola; peppery green leaf eaten raw in salads or used in cooking. Baby rocket leaves are smaller and less peppery.

SAMBAL OELEK also ulek or olek; Indonesian in origin, this is a salty paste made from ground chillies and vinegar.

SASHIMI a Japanese method of slicing raw fish. When purchasing fish for sashimi, make sure it has a firm texture and a pleasant (but not 'fishy') sea-smell.

SEAFOOD

crayfish freshwater crustaceans resembling small lobsters, to which they are related. Substitute with king prawns or scampi.

lobster (rock lobster) also called cray, spiny lobster, eastern, southern or western lobster.

mussels should only be bought from a reliable fish market: they must be tightly closed when bought, indicating they are alive. Before cooking, scrub shells with a strong brush and remove beards; do not eat any that are unopened after cooking. Varieties include black and green-lip.

prawns also called shrimp. Varieties include, king and tiger. Can be bought uncooked or cooked, with or without shells. Dublin Bay prawns are actually a member of the lobster family. Also known as 'langoustine' in French, the shelled meat of the tail is known as 'scampi'.

scallops a bivalve mollusc with fluted shell valve; we use scallops that have the coral (roe) attached.

squid also called calamari; a type of mollusc. Buy squid hoods to make preparation and cooking faster.

vongole (clams) we use a small ridge-shelled variety of this bivalve mollusc.

white fish means non-oily fish. This category includes bream, flathead, ling, whiting and snapper.

SEMOLINA coarsely ground flour from durum wheat; the flour used in making gnocchi, pasta and couscous.

SHRIMP PASTE also called kapi, trasi and blanchan; a strong-scented, very firm preserved paste made of salted dried shrimp. Before use, chop or slice thinly, wrap in foil and roast.

SWISS CHARD also called silver beet and incorrectly, spinach; has fleshy stalks and large leaves, both of which can be prepared as for spinach.

SOY SAUCE also called sieu; made from fermented soybeans. Variations include dark, light and Japanese, found in supermarkets and Asian food stores. We use Japanese unless stated otherwise.

SPINACH also called english spinach and incorrectly, silver beet. Baby spinach leaves are best eaten raw in salads; the larger leaves should be added last to dishes and cooked until barely wilted.

STAR ANISE a dried star-shaped pod whose seeds have an astringent aniseed flavour; used to flavour stocks.

SUGAR

brown an extremely soft, fine granulated sugar retaining molasses for its characteristic colour and flavour.

caster also called superfine or finely granulated table sugar. The fine crystals dissolve easily so it is perfect for cakes, meringues and desserts.

icing also called confectioners' sugar or powdered sugar; contains a small amount (about 3 per cent) of cornflour.

palm also called nam tan pip, jaggery, jawa or gula melaka; made from the sap of the sugar palm tree. Light brown to black in colour and usually sold in rock-hard cakes; substitute with brown sugar.

SUMAC a purple-red, astringent ground spice from berries of a wild Mediterranean shrub; adds a tart, lemony flavour. Can be found in Middle Eastern food stores.

SWEET POTATO an orange-fleshed sweet potato often confused with yam; good baked, boiled, mashed or fried similarly to potatoes.

TABASCO SAUCE brand-name of an extremely fiery sauce made from vinegar, hot red peppers and salt.

TAHINI sesame seed paste available from Middle Eastern food stores.

TAMARI similar to, but thicker, than japanese soy; very dark in colour with a distinctively mellow flavour.

TAMARIND the tamarind tree produces clusters of hairy brown pods, each of which is filled with seeds and a viscous pulp, that are dried and pressed into the blocks of tamarind found in Asian food shops. Gives a sweet-sour, slightly astringent taste to marinades, pastes, sauces and dressings.

TOFU also called soybean curd or bean curd; an off-white, custard-like product made from the "milk" of crushed soybeans. Comes fresh as soft or firm, and processed as fried or pressed dried sheets. Fresh tofu can be refrigerated in water (changed daily) for up to 4 days.

TOMATO

cherry also called tiny tim or tom thumb tomatoes; small and round.

paste triple-concentrated tomato puree used to flavour soups, stews, sauces and casseroles.

plum also called egg or roma, these are smallish, oval-shaped tomatoes much used in Italian cooking or salads.

semi-dried partially dried tomato pieces in olive oil; softer and juicier than sun-dried, these are not a preserve thus do not keep as long as sun-dried.

TURMERIC also called kamin; a rhizome related to ginger and galangal. Grate or pound to release its aroma and pungent flavour and imparts a golden colour. Fresh turmeric can be substituted with the commonly found dried powder.

VANILLA

extract obtained from vanilla beans infused in water; a non-alcoholic version of essence.

pod dried, long, thin pod from a tropical golden orchid; minuscule black seeds inside the pod are used to impart a luscious vanilla flavour.

VINE LEAVES used as wrappers. Found, fresh, in specialist greengrocers from early spring; also found in cryovac-packages containing about 60 leaves in brine (rinse well and dry before using)

from Middle Eastern food shops and some delicatessens.

VINEGAR

balsamic originally from Modena, Italy, there are now many balsamic vinegars on the market ranging in pungency and quality depending on how, and for how long, they have been aged. Quality can be determined up to a point by price; use the most expensive sparingly.

brown made from fermented malt and beech shavings.

cider made from fermented apples.

raspberry made from fresh raspberries steeped in a white wine vinegar.

rice a colourless vinegar made from fermented rice and flavoured with sugar and salt. Also called seasoned rice vinegar; sherry can be substituted.

WALNUTS as well as being a good source of fibre and healthy oils, nuts contain a range of vitamins, minerals and other beneficial plant components called phytochemicals. Each type of nut has a special make-up and walnuts contain the beneficial omega-3 fatty acids, which is terrific news for people who dislike the taste of fish.

WASABI PASTE an Asian horseradish used to make the pungent, green-coloured sauce traditionally served with Japanese raw fish dishes; sold in powdered or paste form.

WATERCRESS one of the cress family, a large group of peppery greens used raw in salads, dips and

sandwiches, or cooked in soups. Highly perishable, so it must be used as soon as possible after purchase.

WOMBOK also called chinese cabbage, peking or napa cabbage; elongated in shape with pale green, crinkly leaves. Can be shredded or chopped and eaten raw or braised, steamed or stir-fried.

WORCESTERSHIRE SAUCE thin, dark-brown spicy sauce developed by the British when in India; used as a seasoning and as a condiment.

WRAPPERS

spring roll also called egg roll wrappers; available fresh or frozen in various sizes. A wheat-based pastry, are used for gow gee and samosas as well as spring rolls.

wonton also called wonton skins; made of flour, eggs and water, they come in varying thicknesses. Sold packaged in large amounts in the refrigerated section of Asian grocery stores; use gow gee, egg or spring roll wrappers instead.

YEAST (dried and fresh), a raising agent used in dough making. Granular (7g sachets) and fresh compressed (20g blocks) yeast can almost always be substituted one for the other when yeast is called for.yogurt we use plain full-cream yogurt unless stated otherwise.

Index

Conversion chart

MEASURES

The cup and spoon measurements used in this book are metric: one measuring cup holds approximately 250ml; one metric tablespoon holds 20ml; one metric teaspoon holds 5ml. All cup and spoon measurements are level. The most accurate way of measuring dry ingredients is to weigh them. When measuring liquids, use a clear glass or plastic jug with metric markings.
We use large eggs with an average weight of 60g.

WARNING

This book contains recipes for dishes made with raw or lightly cooked eggs. These should be avoided by vulnerable people such as pregnant and nursing mothers, invalids, the elderly, babies and young children.

DRY MEASURES

METRIC	IMPERIAL
15g	½oz
30g	1oz
60g	2oz
90g	3oz
125g	4oz (¼lb)
155g	5oz
185g	6oz
220g	7oz
250g	8oz (½lb)
280g	9oz
315g	10oz
345g	11oz
375g	12oz (¾lb)
410g	13oz
440g	14oz
470g	15oz
500g	16oz (1lb)
750g	24oz (1½lb)
1kg	32oz (2lb)

LIQUID MEASURES

METRIC	IMPERIAL
30ml	1 fluid oz
60ml	2 fluid oz
100ml	3 fluid oz
125ml	4 fluid oz
150ml	5 fluid oz (¼ pint/1 gill)
190ml	6 fluid oz
250ml	8 fluid oz
300ml	10 fluid oz (½ pint)
500ml	16 fluid oz
600ml	20 fluid oz (1 pint)
1000ml (1 litre)	1¾ pints

LENGTH MEASURES

METRIC	IMPERIAL
3mm	⅛in
6mm	¼in
1cm	½in
2cm	¾in
2.5cm	1in
5cm	2in
6cm	2½in
8cm	3in
10cm	4in
13cm	5in
15cm	6in
18cm	7in
20cm	8in
23cm	9in
25cm	10in
28cm	11in
30cm	12in (1ft)

OVEN TEMPERATURES

These oven temperatures are only a guide for conventional ovens. For fan-assisted ovens, check the manufacturer's manual.

	°C (CELSIUS)	°F (FAHRENHEIT)	GAS MARK
Very low	120	250	½
Low	150	275-300	1-2
Moderately low	160	325	3
Moderate	180	350-375	4-5
Moderately hot	200	400	6
Hot	220	425-450	7-8
Very hot	240	475	9